atic followers
W9-AMS-523
Peter to quit as Dr Who
DOCTOR WHO
WHO GOES THERE?
Who do you think you are, scaring my innocent child?
He just hates to be nice
By PHILIP PHILLIPS
The new Dr. Who (and the BBC) are raising eyebrows
JON PERTWEE, TV hero and real-life danger man, is the person forcing Dr. Who to grow up.
is the
w-Who
Screwdriver in galactic adventures
Dr Who is too terrifying for Europe
Dr Who's lad is dead unlucky
EXTERMINATE THEM!
By CHRIS KENWORTHY
'Tougher' Dr. Who is chosen
Dr Who actor to quit series
Daleks herald attack on new season
ROBIN STRINGER
Time traveller clocks up 20 years
By David Hewson, Arts Correspondent
DR WHO PRESUM

DOCTOR WHO
THE KEY TO TIME
A Year-by-Year Record

This book is published by arrangement
with the British Broadcasting Corporation

W.H. ALLEN · LONDON
1984

Typeset by Phoenix Photosetting, Chatham
Printed and bound in Great Britain by
Mackays of Chatham Ltd, Kent
for the Publishers W.H. Allen & Co. PLC
44 Hill Street, London W1X 8LB

ISBN 0 491 03283 8

Design by Deborah Hart and Mike Brett

'Although time-travel is only a speculative concept, *Doctor Who* brings to it a fantastic reality. Conjecture or pure fantasy, the series touches the imagination and the dreamer inside us all. The Doctor is a positive extreme: a blatant non-conforming individualist with solid principles, a brilliant mind, a sparkling sense of humour, a childlike curiosity and a machine bigger inside than out that can take him anywhere he wants or put him somewhere he'd probably want to explore anyway.'
Starlog
June 1979
Mark Bentham

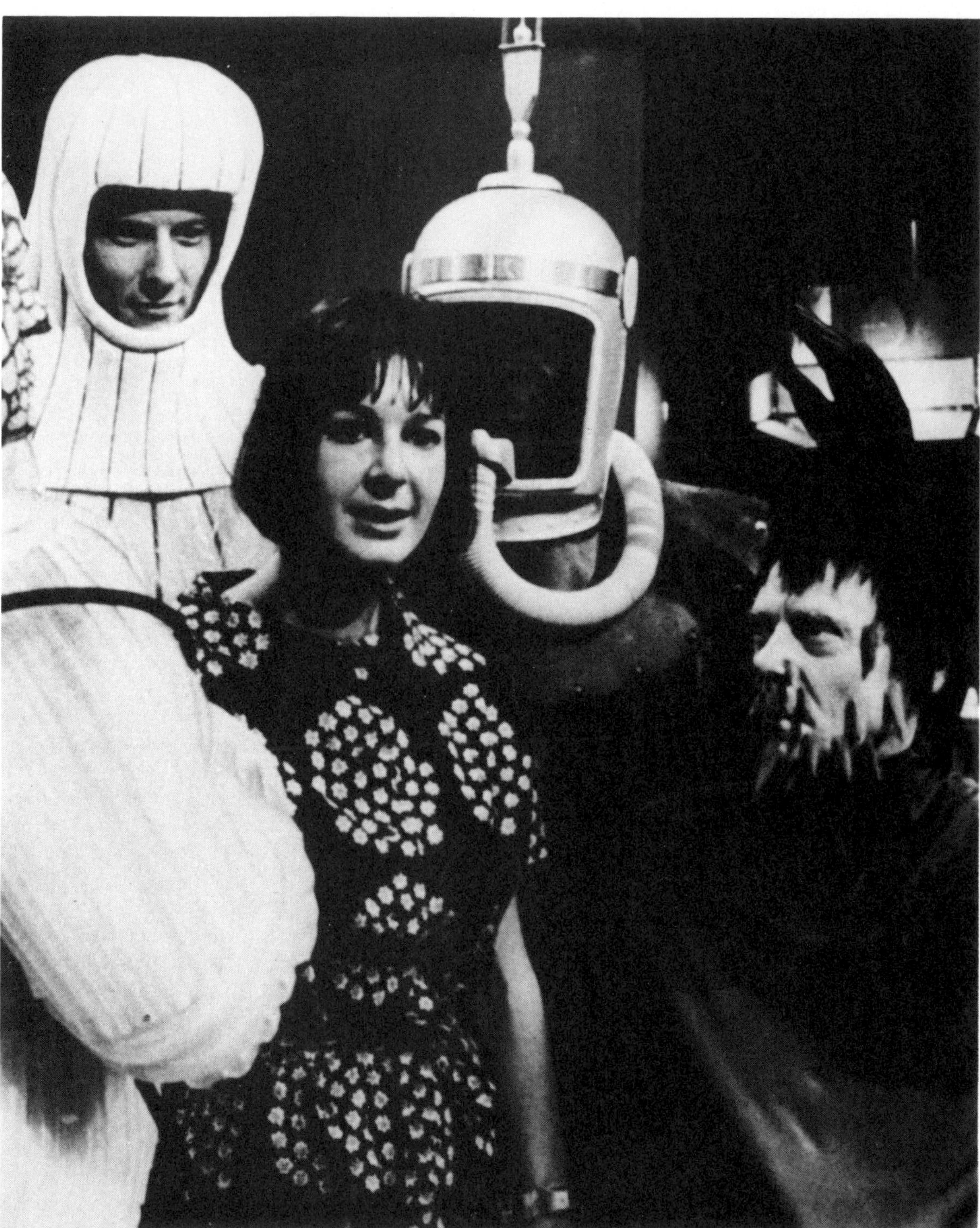

For
Verity Lambert
who first turned the key

With especial thanks to
John Nathan-Turner,
producer of *Doctor Who*,
and
Jeremy Bentham
for technical advice

GEMMA HAINING

500 YEAR DIARY

By Way of a Prologue...

In the first episode of 'The Power of the Daleks' in 1966, the Doctor (then in his Patrick Troughton regeneration) rummaged around among his things in the TARDIS and produced before the surprised eyes of his companions, Ben and Polly, a small, leather-bound book fastened with a clasp, on the front of which were printed the words *500 Year Diary*. It was a record of some of the more interesting moments in his journeys, he indicated. It was a key to his times.

The revelation that the Doctor kept a note of his adventures excited me all those years ago and has nagged away at my consciousness ever since. So much so, that when I was invited to write a sequel to my book, *Doctor Who: A Celebration*, which marked twenty years of the show, the diary sprang almost immediately to mind. There was my inspiration. I would compile my own version, detailing the important events in the series, now that it has – to use that once common expression heard when a person reached twenty-one – 'come of age'. It would be my key to those remarkable times.

While it has obviously been impossible to include everything that has happened to *Doctor Who* and those associated with it during such a long period of time (and bearing in mind what I have already covered in *A Celebration*), there are certainly no important landmarks missing, no historic moments overlooked, no major technical details omitted. Indeed, here are the events that shaped the fabulously successful programme and the people who made them possible, almost all captured in contemporary detail or the words of the protagonists themselves.

I dare to say all, as the Doctor himself might do, though I could be wrong. But I have the assurance gained from being granted unrestricted access to the *Doctor Who* Production Office files, and having had extensive contact with many of those involved in making, or acting in, the programme. That, plus exhaustive research of television, film and newspaper files, and the help of some long-standing and very well-informed fans, does make me confident that this Key to the Doctor's life and times (such as are so far known to us) does the phenomenon that the series most assuredly is, full justice. I hope that when we have travelled together from the past to today, you will agree.

Peter Haining

1963

April 23

A man with a 'dramatic' mission and a dream for a revolutionary new kind of television series joins the BBC. He is Canadian-born Sydney Newman, formerly with ABC TV (now Thames Television), who has been recruited to shake up BBC drama programmes to compete with the popularist shows of its commercial rival. As the Head of Drama, the vastly experienced Newman has a free hand, and one of the projects he decides to initiate is an idea he had conceived while at ABC but had been unable to get off the ground. The former Managing Director of ABC, Howard Thomas, recalls how what is to become one of the great success stories in television went 'over to the other side'. 'Back in the early Sixties we were considering a children's programme called *Doctor Who,*' he says. 'But we came to the conclusion that the Authority would never allow us to broadcast it. When Sydney Newman joined the BBC he took *Doctor Who* with him.'

At the BBC, Sydney Newman's idea takes shape in the form of a page of notes which he discusses with the Head of Serials, Donald Wilson. Newman recalls: 'I wanted to bridge the gap on a Saturday between the afternoon's sports coverage, which attracted a huge adult audience, and *Juke Box Jury,* which had a very large teenage following. *Doctor Who* was never intended to be simply a children's programme, but something that would appeal to people who were in a rather childlike frame of mind.' Of his actual concept, he says: 'My original idea was to have an irascible, absent-minded, unpredictable old man, running away from his own planet in a time-machine which looked like a police box on the outside but was in fact a large space station inside, and which he didn't really know how to operate, so he was always ending up in the wrong place and time. We called him Doctor Who because no one knew who he was, where he came from, what he was running away from, and where he was headed.'

July 22

BBC staff writer David Whitaker is the first person recruited by Sydney Newman as script editor for his embryo team to create *Doctor Who.* With the concept for the new series outlined in a memo, Whitaker is asked to commission a pilot script. He gives the job to Australian-born Anthony Coburn, a versatile writer with a particular interest in science and history. David Whitaker later recalls his brief: 'Sydney Newman wanted to use the format to combine the latest ideas about space-travel with a way of educating viewers about the past. If stories went into the future or onto other planets we also had to stick to what was known or generally accepted to be true.'

August 29

With the concept now fast becoming the written word, Sydney Newman looks for a producer for *Doctor Who.* From the BBC ranks he picks Mervyn Pinfield for his profound knowledge of production techniques to be associate producer, but to head up the operation he brings over from ABC Television a former production assistant on *Armchair Theatre,* Verity Lambert. Verity, British-born but American-trained (with David Susskind), and an enormously energetic young woman, finds herself with an established format, but quickly determines to put her own stamp on the project. A few months later she is to state: 'I have strong views on the level of intelligence we should be aiming at. *Doctor Who* goes out at a time when there is a large child audience, but it is intended more as a story for the whole family. And anyway, children today are very sophisticated and I won't allow scripts which seem to talk down to them.'

Anthony Coburn's script for the first *Doctor Who* story, 'An Unearthly Child', portrays the Doctor as rather malign and makes a fundamental change in the intended status of the girl Susan who is to travel with him. Verity Lambert explains: 'Susan was his original travelling

NICK HARRIS

companion to mix knowledge with naivety, but it was Anthony who cast her as the Doctor's grand-daughter. I know it is very much a part of the programme nowadays, but at the beginning he thought there was something not quite proper about an old man travelling around the galaxy with a young girl for a companion.'

September 27

Sydney Newman's long-cherished idea takes a giant step nearer fulfilment with the filming of a pilot episode to check the viability of the proposed series. In the interim, Verity Lambert has found her first Doctor Who in the form of character-actor William Hartnell, fifty-five, a man best known for his roles as tough soldiers or hard-bitten policemen. Her conviction that he is the right man comes from viewing his most recent picture, *This Sporting Life,* in which he plays an ageing rugby-football talent scout. As Susan, the Doctor's grand-daughter, she picks Carole Anne Ford, and for the two school teachers, Ian and Barbara, who are to represent the link with the viewer, William Russell and Jacqueline Hill.

It takes just one day and a budget of £2,000 to make the pilot at Lime Grove Studios, and Verity Lambert is full of praise for the contributions of David Whitaker, the director Warris Hussein, and particularly Mervyn Pinfield. 'Mervyn was appointed to be our technical adviser because neither David nor I were scientists. Our brief was to 'use television' and make use of all its resources to achieve a scientific look. It was Mervyn who created the famous opening credits by having a camera film its own feedback to make the image "bleed" into a pattern formation. Today that's known as a "signal howlaround".'

The haunting signature tune for *Doctor Who* is also created in a unique way. Sound expert Dick Mills explains: 'It was composed by Ron Grainer but there are, in fact, no musicians playing contemporary instruments on it. It was all done by cutting separate notes from pre-recordings of different sound sources and mixing them together. We used to tune the sounds, then copy them at different speeds to give us the notes we required. All the notes for the melody and bass lines were then played together until we got the signature tune.' Mills also reveals that the sound of the TARDIS is created by Brian Hodgson from the sounds of the bass strings of an old piano taped and re-recorded at different speeds.

October 4

The pilot for *Doctor Who* is screened for Sydney Newman and Donald Wilson – but both have immediate reservations. There are several flaws in the actual production, and the two men are agreed that the character of the Doctor must be 'softened'. Because Anthony Coburn is not available to amend his script, David Whitaker brings in a BBC staff writer, C. E. Webber, to revise certain scenes and change some of the dialogue. Satisfied that these changes will make *Doctor Who* a workable series, Newman and Wilson approve the almost unparalleled action of remounting the production for 'another go'. As Verity Lambert is later to recall of this time, 'We were all very nervous because we were doing things that had rarely been done before, and certainly not by the BBC.'

TIM PIERACCINI

October 18

Once again the episode 'An Unearthly Child' is recorded in Studio D at Lime Grove, taking just forty-five minutes from the moment director Waris Hussein cues the rolling of the title credits to the last notes of the theme music. Direction of this episode, which is destined to be the version finally shown on television, is very much as though it is a live theatre show – scene following scene in their natural order – and this is to lead to later rumours that the first *Doctor Who* stories went out 'live'.

Two inserts are pre-filmed for the episode: the title effects (later re-used in full for the flight-through-time sequence); and the scene of the caveman's shadow falling over the ground before the TARDIS on the Neolithic landscape. (This later scene had been shot at the BBC's Ealing film studios as the set was too large to be mounted in Lime Grove.) The inserts are played onto a screen being 'seen' by one of the electronic cameras transferring the image onto 2-inch master video-tape. This is done for two reasons. Firstly, most

shows both at the BBC and ITV are still done as live productions even though there is a crude but effective system in existence to record them. Used to this style of performance, most actors and actresses then prefer the medium to out-of-sequence filming as it enables them to follow the mood of the plot more easily. Second, and more logistically, so difficult is it to edit 2-inch master tape on these machines (all editing has to be done by hand, using scissors and sticky tape) that the less edits, stop/starts occurring in an episode the better. 'An Unearthly Child' is recorded with just one post-production edit – the interface as the two teachers step through the police-box doors and are instantly inside the vast arena of the TARDIS.

Sydney Newman and Donald Wilson are satisfied with this new version and the go-ahead for a 52-episode season is given. Although producing the first *Doctor Who* story has proved demanding in the extreme, Verity Lambert and her team press on with making the series as the first transmission date is set . . .

November 23

The tragedy of President Kennedy's assassination the previous day overshadows the transmission of the first episode of *Doctor Who* – and such is the overload of news that it goes out ten minutes later than the scheduled time of 5.15 p.m. The *Radio Times* announces the new serial: 'Doctor Who? That is just the point. Nobody knows precisely who he is, this mysterious exile from another world and a distant future whose adventures begin today. But this much is known: he has a ship in which he can travel through

space and time – although owing to a defect in its instruments he can never be sure where and when his "landings" may take place . . .'

Verity Lambert and her team have little chance to think about the reaction to their creation, however, for they are well into producing the second *Doctor Who* story. (As a matter of record, the general assumption that 'An Unearthly Child' was being recorded when news of President Kennedy's death was received on Friday, 22 November, is incorrect: it was actually the second episode of 'The Daleks' which was before the Lime Grove cameras.)

November 25

Doctor Who receives its first newspaper review by Michael Gowers in the *Daily Mail* – and it is a good one. 'It goes without saying', Gowers writes, 'that circumstances were hardly favourable for the launching of the BBC's space satellite, *Doctor Who* on Saturday afternoon. But the machine which carries this mysterious old man, his inordinately precious grand-daughter, and her unfortunate science and history teachers, will apparently be circumnavigating our screens for the next fifty-two weeks at least, as well as the infinities of heavens and of time. William Hartnell, gazing from under locks of flowing white hair, and the appealing Carole Ann Ford, represent the Unknown Them, William Russell and Jacqueline Hill the ignorant, sceptical Us, and their craft is cunningly disguised as a police callbox. The penultimate shot of this, nevertheless, after a three-point touchdown in a Neolithic landscape, must have delighted the hearts of the *Telegoons* who followed.'

November 30

The BBC takes the unusual – virtually unique – decision to re-screen the first episode of 'An Unearthly Child' at 4.50 p.m. for the benefit of those who may have missed it the previous Saturday – and to ensure its impact. Stewart Lane of the *Daily Worker* catches this re-showing and enthuses to his readers the next day: 'I for one intend following closely the new BBC serial, *Doctor Who.* The opening sequence, with an old police-box in a junkyard turning out to be a space-and-time ship, ended up with a very satisfying "cliffhanger" – a deserted-looking planet with an eerie weirdie wandering around.'

December 14

End of the fourth episode of 'An Unearthly Child' and the completion of the Doctor's very first adventure. Despite all the tension of getting the programme to the screen, two members of the team remember funny moments from its production. Douglas Camfield, production assistant to Waris Hussein who is himself later to become a director on the series, recalls a humorous moment while filming episode two. 'We were trying to get the feel of the Stone Age, with groups of primitives. Skin-clad, grubby people, huddling in caves. But one of the extras, a girl, refused to appear without her false eyelashes! We had to fire her in the end, which made the tribe one female short!'

Carole Ann Ford also recalls this part of the story. 'I nearly got eaten alive,' she says,' but not by monsters. A lot of tropical plants had been brought into the studio for the set and they were full of insects. I had to be fumigated after filming!'

December 21

Four days before Christmas, in the opening episode of the second *Doctor Who* story, 'The Daleks', viewers get their first partial glimpse of a character destined to become as familiar as Father Christmas himself. Creator of the Daleks, Terry Nation, a furniture salesman, turned comedian, turned scriptwriter, who had been somewhat reluctantly recruited for the series by David Whitaker, is sceptical about the success of either the Daleks or the programme itself. 'I didn't have any confidence in it,' he confesses later. 'I read the brochure at the briefing and said, "There's no way this show can ever succeed." And I don't think it could have done if it had followed the planned route of going into historical situations and being reasonably educational.' Nation says that Sydney Newman wanted to scrap his seven-episode story when he first saw it. 'It

MARTIN F. PROCTOR

was only the determination of Verity Lambert that got them on,' he says. 'Or maybe it was the fact that the BBC *had* to go on. They'd had them built and they'd spent so much money that they had to go on. Nobody had faith in them, including myself.'

Sydney Newman confirms this opinion. 'I had specifically said at the start that I didn't want any bug-eyed monsters, so when Verity came up with the Daleks I bawled her out. She protested that they weren't bug-eyed monsters; they were human brains whose bodies had atrophied, and therefore they needed those metal shells! Although it was absolutely not what I had wanted, I must admit that it was the Daleks which really established the programme as a great success.'

Verity Lambert, too, has recalled this crucial moment for the fledgling series. 'The crisis came when Donald Wilson saw the scripts for the first Dalek serial. Having spent so much time defending *Doctor Who* because he believed in it, he saw the Daleks just as bug-eyed monsters, which went against what he felt should be the theme of the science-fiction stories. There was a strong disagreement between us which went as far as Donald telling us not to do the show. What saved it in the end was purely the fact that we had nothing to replace it in the time allotted. It was the Daleks or nothing. What was nice, though, was Donald coming to me afterwards and saying, "You obviously understand this programme better than I do. I'll leave it to you!"'

December 28

The Daleks appear in full and a legend begins. *Doctor Who* earns audience ratings of eight million, up to this date the largest total for its time-slot in BBC history. The sceptics are dumbfounded, including Terry Nation, who reveals he wrote the seven episodes of the story in just *seven days* because of other commitments. 'After the Daleks appeared,' he said, 'I started to get mail. It wasn't just a couple of letters; it was thousands. They were coming in by the sackload. So I twigged I had something going for me here. And of course the BBC twigged it as well and they knew they had to change the direction that *Doctor Who* was intended to go. So a lot of the stuff they had prepared was put aside and they went much more into the SF area. And I think that actually established the ultimate pattern of where it was going.'

Terry Nation says he got the idea for the Daleks from watching the long gliding skirts of the Georgian State Dancers, 'but I didn't want them to be men dressed up.' He also knew he made a mistake by initially giving them hands which became too cumbersome *and* by killing them off at the end of the serial. But he was in no doubt about the *character* of the Daleks. 'They represent government, officialdom, that unhearing, unthinking, blanked-out face of authority that will destroy you because it *wants* to destroy you.'

Designer Raymond Cusick, who turned Terry Nation's idea into a reality, recalls that he was allocated £700 to build six Daleks. 'But because of the high cost I could only run to four,' he says. 'All the others that you see on the screen are photographic copies of those four blown-up and mounted on cardboard.' Cusick also confirms that a long-standing tradition that a glass Dalek was seen in this serial is totally without foundation – the idea for one proved to be just too expensive to build.

CAS ADAMSON

SIMON LEWIS

1964

February 6

Less than a week after their defeat at the hands of the Doctor, the Daleks are resurrected to find a much more appreciative audience awaiting them in Essex. The *Doctor Who* Production Office, faced with sackfuls of mail bemoaning the killing off of the Daleks, decides to bow to public pressure, and donates two of them to the Dr Barnardo's Village for Orphaned Children near Ilford. Accompanied by a reporter, the two Daleks make the journey from Shepherd's Bush to Ilford on an open-sided lorry, attracting crowds of children each time the vehicle stops at traffic lights.

For Verity Lambert, this week is to prove the tip of an iceberg that will eventually grow into a mountain of requests for the Daleks to be brought back. Although quoted in the *Daily Mail* article 'Daleks Dead But Won't Lie Down' as saying there are no plans to bring back the alien robots, the year-long production schedule for *Doctor Who* is still flexible enough to permit Verity the option of a sequel *if* a suitable script can be delivered. That would then leave only one headache – the expensive construction of new Daleks to replace those given to Dr Barnardo's!

February 8

Because of the huge success of the Daleks, Verity Lambert and David Whitaker revise the style of *Doctor Who,* and the third scheduled serial, 'The Hidden Planet' by Malcolm Hulke, is dropped because it no longer fits the format. Hulke, who is later to become one of the most popular contributors to the series, had been one of the first scriptwriters approached by Whitaker (Nigel Kneale of *Quatermass* fame was another), and turned in an imaginative story about a world on the opposite side of the sun to the Earth where everything is a mirror image of our own planet. Faced with this sudden gap, David Whitaker sits down at the typewriter himself and turns out a two-part story, 'The Edge of Destruction', in just a single day. Because of the time and cost constraints, he cleverly utilises just the interior of the TARDIS and the four regular members of the cast in his story.

February 22

The first episode of the lavish production of 'Marco Polo' is heralded by being featured on the front cover of *Radio Times* – the first of what has proved many such appearances. Scriptwriter John Lucarotti bases his story on Marco Polo's own diaries, *Description of the World,* and though the serial contains many special effects, everything is shot at the Lime Grove Studios. Animals are used in the programme for the first time, as is animation to show the travellers' progress, plus a narration spoken by Mark Eden (Marco Polo) as he makes entries in his diary. The lavish costumes and interchangeable sets designed by Barry Newbery also break new ground. By a strange quirk of fate, a character named Tegana is discussed, who provides the origin of the phrase 'checkmate' – an ability more than once observed in the fifth Doctor's air hostess turned companion, Tegan!

According to Heather Hartnell, 'Marco Polo' was one of her husband's favourite stories. 'In fact it was one of his ideas,' she says. 'At one time they were asking everybody for ideas and this was one of them.'

April 11

The media recognition of *Doctor Who* begins in earnest as the major national daily papers all carry photographically illustrated articles on the new story, 'The Keys of Marinus', written by Terry Nation, who offers viewers a new group of monsters in the Voords. However, not all the previews are quite in keeping with the seriousness aimed at by David Whitaker. One budding wit, writing in the *Daily Mail,* refers to the rubber suits worn by the Voord warriors as 'bouncing across the BBC TV screens tonight'. The article goes on to identify Peter Stenson, one of the Voords, as 'the actor with flappers on his feet and a triangle on his head', offering the advice that the best thing Carole Ann Ford can do when gripped by one of these creatures is – bite! Perhaps not surprisingly, the Voords fail to have the same impact on viewers as Terry Nation's Daleks.

Despite such over-zealous journalism, 'The Keys of Marinus' articles set a precedent for the future. With Dalekmania now well established, many feature writers eagerly scan the press releases put out by the BBC, looking for the next big-name monster scheduled for the programme. The story itself is notable for the TARDIS being seen materialising on the screen for the first time, and for the extensive use of models, including a miniature TARDIS, an island and four submarine craft. Soon inventive models are to become a striking feature of *Doctor Who.*

'The Keys of Marinus' is also unique in that the Doctor is absent from two whole episodes, 'The Screaming Jungle' and 'The Snows of Terror'. This is to allow William Hartnell to take a two-week holiday: a situation now quite unthinkable.

May 23

The Doctor nearly interferes crucially in Earth's history during John Lucarotti's second historical story, 'The Aztecs'. Lucarotti explains why this was his favourite show for the programme: 'The Aztec civilisation intrigued me. They were,

at the same time, a cultured yet savage people, who practised human sacrifice. Also, they didn't know about the wheel. So one became the key to the Doctor's escape – and he took it with him so as not to interfere with history.' It becomes a principle of *Doctor Who* that wherever the traveller lands in time he must never change the course of history.

The first episode earns recognition for the show as a whole in the trade publication *Television World,* and writer Bill Edmund also waxes lyrical over the principal baddie, Tlotoxl. 'John Ringham's villain also took my fancy,' he says. 'If we are to have a villain, let him be a villain right from the word go. This is the sort of character "The Temple of Evil" gave us – a man who glared, mouthed and hated from the moment he appeared. And he promised, in a grimacing close-up at the end, something special in the nasty line for Barbara . . .'

July 4

Jammed switchboards at the BBC from *Doctor Who* viewers are to become almost commonplace over the years – but on this occasion callers are not protesting at the show's content, but rather at the lack of it. For as a result of a marathon Singles Final on the Centre Court at Wimbledon, the producer of *Grandstand* wins extended coverage for his programme, and at 5.15 p.m. – with the tennis still going on – the announcement is made that the *Doctor Who* episode for the evening, part three of Peter Newman's 'The Sensorites', is to be postponed until the following week, thereby pushing the whole season back a week. Seven and a half million of the Doctor's fans are not amused . . .

August 8

The first season of *Doctor Who* closes with two more new innovations in the six-part French Revolution story 'The Reign of Terror' by Dennis Spooner. For the first time, location shooting takes place to show the Doctor strolling along cart-tracks and across meadows apparently towards Paris. And where previously all episodes have been shot at Lime Grove, director Henrick Hirsch goes to Television Centre for the fifth episode, 'A Bargain of Necessity'. After the Doctor is safely back in his TARDIS, the show goes off the air for seven weeks for its first break in transmission.

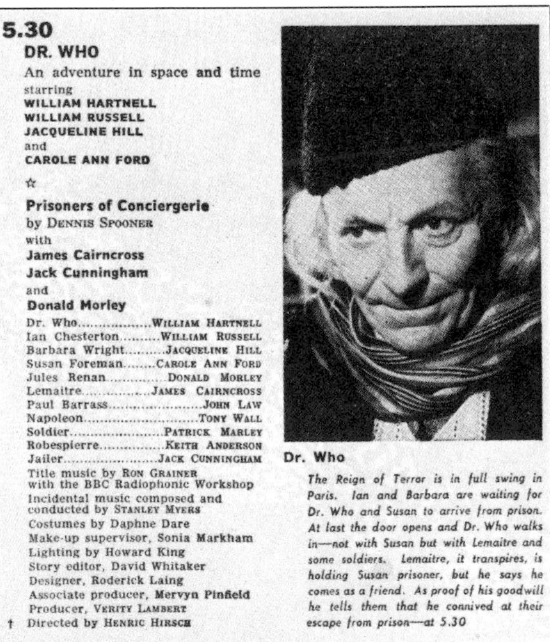

5.30
DR. WHO
An adventure in space and time
starring
WILLIAM HARTNELL
WILLIAM RUSSELL
JACQUELINE HILL
and
CAROLE ANN FORD

☆

Prisoners of Conciergerie
by Dennis Spooner
with
James Cairncross
Jack Cunningham
and
Donald Morley

Dr. Who....................William Hartnell
Ian Chesterton..........William Russell
Barbara Wright..........Jacqueline Hill
Susan Foreman........Carole Ann Ford
Jules Renan..............Donald Morley
Lemaitre..................James Cairncross
Paul Barrass........................John Law
Napoleon...........................Tony Wall
Soldier.......................Patrick Marley
Robespierre...............Keith Anderson
Jailer.......................Jack Cunningham
Title music by Ron Grainer
with the BBC Radiophonic Workshop
Incidental music composed and conducted by Stanley Myers
Costumes by Daphne Dare
Make-up supervisor, Sonia Markham
Lighting by Howard King
Story editor, David Whitaker
Designer, Roderick Laing
Associate producer, Mervyn Pinfield
Producer, Verity Lambert
† Directed by Henric Hirsch

Dr. Who

The Reign of Terror is in full swing in Paris. Ian and Barbara are waiting for Dr. Who and Susan to arrive from prison. At last the door opens and Dr. Who walks in—not with Susan but with Lemaitre and some soldiers. Lemaitre, it transpires, is holding Susan prisoner, but he says he comes as a friend. As proof of his goodwill he tells them that he connived at their escape from prison—at 5.30

Scriptwriter Dennis Spooner, who is destined shortly to take over from David Whitaker as script editor when Whitaker leaves the BBC to go to Australia, recalls how his entry into *Doctor Who* came about. 'It was Terry Nation who introduced me to David, and when I met him he said he was planning to do some historical stories and some science fiction – but as they had writers for the science fiction, did I fancy history? He gave me a list of about four possible subjects and I went away to the local library, did a bit of reading, and then phoned back and said I would like to do a story on the French Revolution. And that's how I came into *Doctor Who!*'

August 21

The *Daily Express* breaks the news first that the Daleks are to return in the second season of *Doctor Who.* Television reporter Martin Jackson writes: 'The Daleks, the tin robot monsters of BBC TV, are returning to the Saturday science-fiction serial, *Doctor Who* in November, after pleas by hundreds of young viewers.' This announcement is to herald an autumn of unprecedented Dalek promotion.

October 31

The first story of the second season is screened with viewers unaware that what was to be a four-part serial has been cut back to three by producer Verity Lambert. 'Planet of Giants' by Louis Marks was completed as a four-parter early in September, the last episode being titled 'The Urge to Live'. On seeing the finished story, however, Verity Lambert feels there is not enough drama in the last two episodes and orders that thirteen minutes from 'Crisis' (the original part three) be linked with twelve minutes of 'The Urge to Live' to complete the adventure.

November 14

The Doctor moves into a new medium and becomes the hero of a comic strip in *TV Comic*. Initially the BBC are reluctant to allow the adaptation, especially as *TV Comic* is strongly biased towards ITV programmes. But with a flood of requests

DAN SCHAEFER

pouring in about the Daleks, the comic-strip rights *are* granted to the publication and artist Neville Main begins what has proved to be an unbroken run of appearances for each of the Doctors in comic-strip form drawn by various artists. In the first strip, William Hartnell's Doctor is accompanied on his adventures by *two* children, his grandson John and grand-daughter Gillian, and he is also mistakenly called by the name 'Dr Who'. Neville Main, who was responsible for both the artwork and storyline, did however show a remarkable piece of foresight in a three-part story in 1965 called 'Moonshot' – for in it he indicated the Americans would land a two-man crew on the moon on 20 July 1970: just out by one year and one day!

November 21

In the week of its first anniversary, *Doctor Who* enters the list of Top Ten BBC programmes for the first time – and the expected return of the Doctor's most feared enemies inspires numerous newspaper headlines. The story, 'The Dalek Invasion of Earth', is written by Terry Nation and sees the first major use of OB (outside broadcast) filming, with location shooting taking place early on Sunday mornings in a number of central London spots usually bustling with people and traffic. The most important locations are the Embankment, Whitehall, Trafalgar Square, Hyde Park, the Albert Hall, and the bridges at Westminster and Hammersmith. A chase sequence is also shot at Ealing Studios. Because they are required to be more mobile, the Daleks are modified and given tyres to glide over rough terrain. In order to show one Dalek emerging from the river Thames, the operator, Robert Jewell, has to wear a complete skin-diver's outfit!

Following the filming of 'The Dalek Invasion of Earth', Verity Lambert completes the first fifty-two episodes of *Doctor Who* as sanctioned by Sydney Newman and Donald Wilson. Not surprisingly, the two executives agree to a continuation of the programme – their optimism for the future of the series underlined still further when these first fifty-two episodes are sold to television companies in Australia, New Zealand and Canada.

November 28

Because of only a fleeting glance of a Dalek at the end of the first episode of 'The Dalek Invasion of Earth' – a reprise of their very first appearance the previous year – there is enormous interest in the screening of the second episode. John Sandilands, the *Daily Mail*'s feature writer, takes the opportunity to write an extended piece on Dalekmania. 'Shortly after 5.40 this evening,' he says, 'a week of almost unbearable tension will come to an end. At that time the BBC TV adventure serial *Doctor Who* comes on the

air. And as ten million viewers can tell you, the dreaded Daleks are back and about to reveal their future plans. At the end of last week's episode, a single specimen of this radioactive race of what appear to be malevolent pepper-pots rose from the Thames and waved its antennae at the terror-stricken audience. Then the credit titles rolled. At once a howl of anguish went up all over Britain and the BBC switchboard was jammed with more than four hundred calls. Angry viewers protested that the Dalek's appearance was far too brief: that children who had waited months for another sign of the monsters were weeping and refusing to go to bed. And not only children, for *Doctor Who*'s massive audience includes millions of adults.'

The return of the Daleks is, of course, an enormous success and Dalek toys of all shapes and sizes appear in shops and stores in time for Christmas. There is even a record released entitled 'I'm Going to Spend My Christmas with a Dalek' by the Go-Joes, who sing in the first verse: 'I'm going to spend my Christmas with a Dalek, and hug him under the mistletoe. And if he's very nice, I'll feed him sugar and spice, and hang a Christmas stocking from his big red toe.'

December 26

The original companion of the Doctor, his grand-daughter, Susan, played by Carole Ann Ford, announces she is to leave the series: the first of what is to prove many comings and goings from *Doctor Who.* Later she says, 'The programme has never stopped being part of my life, and over the years I've continued to get loads of fan mail. It was a wonderful experience to be part of starting something that has become so enduring.' In her place is cast Maureen O'Brien, a former theatre floor-manager, who plays a castaway named Vicki from the planet Dido, and is first seen on screen on 2 January in another David Whitaker two-parter, 'The Rescue'.

It is still, though, the Daleks who dominate Christmas – the Christmas issue of the *Radio Times* carries the first colour photograph of one, and the presence of several of them at the *Daily Mail Boys' and Girls' Exhibition* attracts huge crowds. In the new year they even star in their own comic strip, 'The Daleks' in *TV-21*, written by David Whitaker. Aside from being featured in books, annuals, as battery toys and in construction kits, they are also mentioned on television shows as diverse as *Hugh and I, The Roy Castle Show* (he, of course, was later to star in the first Dalek feature film) and on *Crackerjack.*

Despite all this Dalekmania, Verity Lambert is quick to refute any suggestions that the Daleks might actually take over *Doctor Who.* And she adds: 'I feel in no way obligated to bring them back for a third time!'

CLIVE N. WILLIAMSON

1965

January 2

The opening shot of David Whitaker's 'The Rescue' shows a British rocket ship crashed on a barren rocky planet, its hull split in two, a radio dish turning ceaselessly in its search for a rescue ship. By coincidence it is the time-travellers who are the first to reach this world and, from their vantage point on a ledge above, the Doctor and Ian look down at the strewn wreckage of the space castaways. With the BBC's own Visual Effects Department unable to handle the requirements for *Doctor Who* in the early days, the show's designers farm out these needs to external freelance companies. Shawcraft, a firm of specialist engineers, are to produce many of the models for the Hartnell serials, including the wrecked Dido spaceship – a working prop on its own large table-stage with a battery-driven rotating radio aerial.

Integrating live actors with shots of model stages is to prove the forte of experienced BBC staff directors Richard Martin and Christopher Barry. Skilled in the facilities of television, Martin and Barry use a process called inlay to combine pictures. Basically, using specially cut-out masks, placed carefully over flat TV screens being seen by two cameras, the inlay operator can blank out one half of one picture and substitute into the blanked-out area half the picture from another screen. When perfectly matched up (so that no join is visible) a large-scale look can be given to a small production, enabling, as in the case of 'The Rescue', Ian and the Doctor, on a cliff set, to be seen looking down into a stage model valley below.

With this story, Dennis Spooner takes over for six months as script editor. He later comments: 'If we had any brief under Sydney Newman it was that the Doctor is an observer, a time-traveller, looking around; he did not initiate events. And I don't think if we had only done science fiction, *Doctor Who* would have caught on like it did.'

January 6

ALAN MORTON

That bastion of the business world, the *Financial Times*, chooses 'The Rescue' as the peg on which to examine what makes a television series a household word. TV critic T. C. Worsley writes: 'Since it is fun to be among the first spotters of such a winner, I overcame my allergy to science fiction to watch the new *Doctor Who* series, which replaces, temporarily I suspect, the Daleks. Will Mr Whitaker do it again with the half-animal automata from the planet Dido? I rather doubt it. Koquilion is, though, a memorable enough name to catch on.' In what is to prove a prophetic look at some future critical attitudes towards the show, he adds: 'Incidentally, if I believed, which I do not, in the baleful effects on children of tales of violence and horror, *Doctor Who* would be high on the danger list.'

What Mr Worsley does not know about Koquilion is that in order to avoid giving away an important development in the plot, the credits initially list the actor playing the villain as 'Sydney Wilson' – an amalgam of the series' creators. Only when Koquilion is revealed to be the spaceship pilot, Bennett, is the Australian actor Ray Barrett given his due acknowledgement. It is an appropriate moment for him to be making his debut . . .

January 15

Doctor Who begins on ABC TV in Australia with 'An Unearthly Child'. With episodes being shown on four nights a week, the backlog is eventually cleared and a number of repeats are shown. As a result of widespread protests about repeats in general, in 1981 no *Doctor Who* programmes were screened at all in Australia until a campaign by local fans saw the reinstatement of the practice the following year.

Although the series has continued to the present day, because of a rating system which is applied to all shows and the hours at which they may be broadcast, four stories are banned in Australia: 'The Daleks' Master Plan', 'Invasion of the Dinosaurs', 'The Brain of Morbius' and 'The Deadly Assassin'.

January 18

Doctor Who is declared to be the 'best children's programme of 1964' by the *Daily Telegraph*. TV critic L. Marsland Gander, reviewing the impact of the programme, believes much of its success can be attributed to the monsters who so delight young viewers, and he adds: 'The grip of *Doctor Who* is well illustrated by a boy of my acquaintance who positively refused to accompany his parents to Spain on holiday because he would miss some instalments!'

January 30

The over-running of the state funeral of Sir Winston Churchill causes the third episode of Dennis Spooner's historical story 'The Romans' to be screened later than scheduled. The story is different from earlier *Doctor Who* adventures in that it is peppered with moments of comedy. Verity Lambert explains: 'Dennis Spooner was known mostly for comedy and as our scripts started coming in I decided I wanted to experiment with putting some humour into *Doctor Who.* 'The Romans' perhaps didn't work very well, although I liked it enormously and I knew William Hartnell felt much more comfortable doing comedy

ANDREW MARTIN

than all the scientific stuff.' A more serious highlight of the story is the burning of Rome achieved by setting fire to a two-dimensional photographic cut-out model of the city.

This is the last production on which Mervyn Pinfield works, leaving the show after having seen it grow from concept to reality. Says Verity Lambert in tribute, 'David and I relied heavily on Mervyn to read through scripts to see if they could be done easily and within our budget, or to suggest ways of modifying things so that they could be done by photographic tricks. His contribution to *Doctor Who* was enormous and invaluable.'

February 7

'I'm the High Lama of the Planet – and although I portray a mixed-up old man I have discovered I can hypnotise children,' says William Hartnell in his first major interview about his role as the Doctor. Talking to Matt White of the *Sunday Mirror*, he goes on: 'Hypnosis goes with the fear of the unknown. I communicate fear to children because they don't know where I'm going to take them. This frightens them and is the attraction of the series. I'm hypnotised by *Doctor Who* myself. When I look at a script I find it unbelievable. So I allow myself to be hypnotised by it. Otherwise I would have nothing to do with it.'

Matt White reports that Hartnell delights in replying to people who ask who he is: 'Yes, that's right, Doctor Who!' He is also overwhelmed at the reception he has received playing a part which is such a startling contrast to his previous roles of crooks, policemen or flint-hearted sergeant-majors. But, White says, 'I soon discovered there is to be no fooling around with the character he has created and endeared to 15,000,000 children aged from six to sixty.'

William Hartnell himself adds, 'Everyone calls me Doctor Who and I feel like him. I get letters addressed to me as Mr Who and even Uncle Who. But I love being this eccentric old man. I love it when my grand-daughter, Judith, calls me "barmy old grand-dad". I can see this series going on for five years at least.'

February 15

In the immediate aftermath of the screening of the first episode of the very costly serial 'The Web Planet' by Bill Strutton, many scenes of which were shot at Ealing Studios, the programme receives its first really stinging attack from Peter Black of the *Daily Mail.* Despite the fact that the lavish production enabled the first of the six episodes to attract the highest ratings for any of William Hartnell's appearances as the Doctor (well over ten million), and a professional dancer, Roslyn de Winter, was hired to choreograph the almost balletic movements of the Menoptera, Black complains: 'The heroes are the dullest quartet in fiction, and so remarkably incompetent that it would take their combined intellectual resources to toast a slice of bread. The dialogue reminds you of a gathering of relations, where

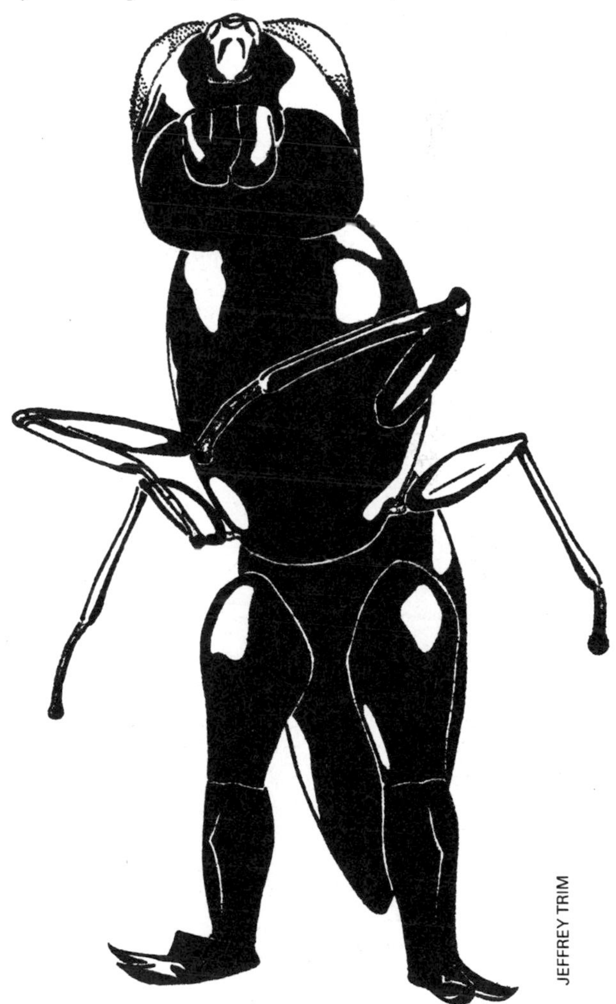
JEFFREY TRIM

nobody listens to what is being said. The serial proceeds on a level of solemn fatuity. Its success is a rum business.'

Mr Black continues by trying to explain this undeniable success. 'I can understand how it catches the imaginations of very young children, though I wish they had something better to feed on,' he says. 'As usual, television is cheating them. But whence comes its huge following of adults? I suppose the attraction is the ancient one of watching people who are dafter than yourself. And there is a weird fascination in the style of the production. It always suggests to me that some disaster occurred just before the off, and the thing is kept going only by breathtaking risks and desperate improvisation. When all the jokes about it are over, the weekend's children's serial shows a sharp and calamitous decline from older days. Nobody seems able to write for children any more.'

April 17

The extensive use of livestock in 'The Crusade' causes problems for the production staff of *Doctor Who.* Several zoos and private collections provide wildlife for David Whitaker's story of the Doctor's encounter with Richard the Lionheart – but it is the carcass of a dead cow that creates the worst trouble. Under the harsh studio lights, decomposition is accelerated and by the time the sequence is finished the stench is almost overpowering! For another episode, in

JOHN F. CRICHTON

which ants crawl all over Ian's arm which has been smeared in honey, a double has to be found when William Russell refuses to play the scene. Although the black ants are harmless, Russell cannot be persuaded, and a production assistant, Viktors Ritelis offers his arm instead. Because of the subject matter of 'The Crusade', it cannot be offered to Muslim countries and the marketing of the story is somewhat curtailed. As if all these problems are not galling enough for Verity Lambert and her team, the *New Statesman*'s critic John Holmstrom lambasts the show in much the same manner as Peter Black. 'I scarcely feel any warmth towards that established national tele-myth, *Doctor Who,'* he writes. 'Certainly the idea of a flying telephone box as a time-machine is pleasing, but where is the magnetism of the actual adventures in other ages or spheres? I can see only the wooden charmlessness of the adventurers, both as written and performed, the lamentably unchilling plastic monsters or (in the historical episodes) the pasteboard Romans, Saracens or French Revolutionaries. If this instructs a fraction as much as the far more amusing programme *Wonderworld* I'll eat my hot sweaty hat.'

May 22

The famous pop group the Beatles make a fleeting appearance in Terry Nation's six-episode serial 'The Chase'. The Liverpool quartet are seen by the Doctor through his space-time visualiser – although their segment is actually an edited version of the promotional film for their record 'Ticket to Ride'. Nation also introduces those famous fictional monsters, Frankenstein's creature and the vampire Count Dracula into his story, as well as offering a solution to that great sea-mystery, the *Marie Celeste.* Apparently, the reason the vessel was found deserted was because its crew were exterminated by the Daleks! Despite all these counter-attractions, it is still the Daleks who steal the honours, although Terry Nation even offers a completely new creation in the penultimate episode . . .

June 19

After a big press build-up and many weeks of waiting, the Mechonoid robots are introduced into *Doctor Who* in part five of 'The Chase.' With their geodesically designed casings, stuttery electronic voices and powerful flame-throwing guns the Mechonoids seize children's imaginations and, after their spectacular stand-off battle against the Daleks, an eager *Doctor Who* viewership hungers for more. But, despite numerous appearances in comics, annuals and even as toys, the Mechonoids' first appearance in *Doctor Who* was also their last. The problem, in days when studio space was at a premium, is their sheer size. Dennis Spooner explains: 'The Daleks were marvellous. They didn't take up any more room than William Hartnell in a cloak. At the time, we were working under very severe studio restrictions. Space-taking things killed it. The Mechonoids would have caught on if they'd been pushed a bit more; but they weren't pushed because no one could have stood the problems involved if they had caught on. They were just physically impossible to get in and out of the studio.'

The final episode also sees the departure

of Ian and Barbara, the last of the Doctor's original companions. William Russell and Jacqueline Hill tell the press, 'It's time to get the schoolroom association out of the series – but we've enjoyed it all tremendously.' A new companion is introduced in Peter Purves – playing Steven – who sees his role as that of 'a together, headstrong young man'.

June 25

The Doctor and the Daleks are transported from the television screen to the cinema with the opening in London of *Doctor Who and the Daleks*, made by Milton Subotsky and Max J. Rosenberg, directed by Gordon Flemyng, with Hammer Films' master of horror roles, Peter Cushing, as the Doctor. Roy Castle and Jennie Linden are cast as Ian and Barbara, and little Roberta Tovey as the Doctor's grand-daughter, Susan. Based on Terry Nation's original TV script for 'The Daleks', the story is extended to 83 minutes by Milton Subotsky aided by David Whitaker. Larger size Daleks are specially built for the film, which, of course is shot in Technicolor at Shepperton Studios. The total budget is a modest £200,000 with Terry Nation getting £500 for the use of his copyright. Audience reaction to the film is tremendous although critical reaction is mixed. Barry Norman of the *Daily Mail* thinks the picture has 'all the preposterous ingredients for success', and Alexander Walker of the *Evening Standard* declares that 'it even thrilled someone like me who doesn't give a damn who's Who.' Ewan Ross of the *Sunday Express* is in no doubt as to who the stars are: 'The Daleks, glowing, spitting death in all directions, grinding out their "destroy-the-Thals" lines like robots with laryngitis, are, as they ever were, one of the finest creations for children since Bambi.'

A dissenting voice – and one which contrasts strongly with the earlier attacks by Peter Black and John Holstrom – is that of *The Observer*'s distinguished critic Maurice Richardson, who writes: 'I've no wish to see that Dalek film. For me there can be only one *Doctor Who.* William Hartnell's rendering of the fusty, crusty, snuffy-trousered old succubus with that disconcerting air of equivocation which becomes extremely sinister at times, is superb. He rounds out the character beautifully. His begetters were absolutely right to give him that Edwardian ambiance, as if his clock had stopped before 1914. This helps to establish the timeless continuum of the traditional comic-cuts world of children's science fiction. It links *Who* with archetypes such as Professor Radium and wins him a huge extra age-group of fans, us pre-seniles who wouldn't want to know him if he looked streamlined and with-it, like the new-style American puppets.'

July 24

After the big-budget film, the last story of the second season of television programmes ends with the low-budget production of Dennis Spooner's 'The Time Meddler'. Despite the necessary cost-cutting, director Douglas Camfield produces a stylish four-parter with a dramatic fight between Saxons and Vikings all done in one long, continuous take which has to be painstakingly choreographed to avoid accidents. Aside from establishing the new companion, Steven, the story also introduces for the first time another Time

Lord apart from the Doctor – the Meddling Monk, played by veteran comedy-actor, Peter Butterworth.

During the seven-week break before *Doctor Who* returns to BBC screens, William Hartnell puts forward a possible new development for the series. 'I suggested that I might have a wicked son who looked exactly like me and had a TARDIS and also travelled in space and time,' he says later. 'It would have meant I would have had to play a dual role, but it opened up all sorts of possibilities. The BBC, though, found the idea unacceptable and so I let it drop. I still think *The Son of Doctor Who* could have worked and been exciting to children.'

September 4

A spectacular appearance by the Doctor at the Farnborough Air Show. Huge crowds gather for a much publicised 'appearance of Doctor Who' and midway through the events, a specially built TARDIS made of lightweight plastic suspended by a parachute drops into the arena from an aircraft. From this emerges William Hartnell in the complete Doctor's outfit and he is driven around the air base to a tremendous reception. Despite the fact that Hartnell is smuggled into the police box *after* it lands, many hundreds of children go home convinced they have seen the Doctor actually flying his TARDIS!

September 11

Although there is not even a hint of the Daleks in the opening story of the third season, 'Galaxy Four' by William Emms, it is they who are making the news before the final episode on 2 October. The popular magazine *Showtime,* in praising Sean Connery for his role as James Bond, observes: 'Your Bond has to be the best possible star, in order to hold his own amid all the gimmickery. Otherwise he suffers the fate of *Doctor Who* – forgotten in the wake of the Daleks.'

The observation is not, in fact, true, and indeed in America the Daleks have suffered two setbacks. The feature film *Doctor Who and the Daleks* has done badly at the box office (the television series has not, as yet, been shown in America, so both the Doctor and the Daleks are unknown to audiences), and a trip across the Atlantic by Terry Nation to launch his creations also comes to nothing. 'I went to the United States and

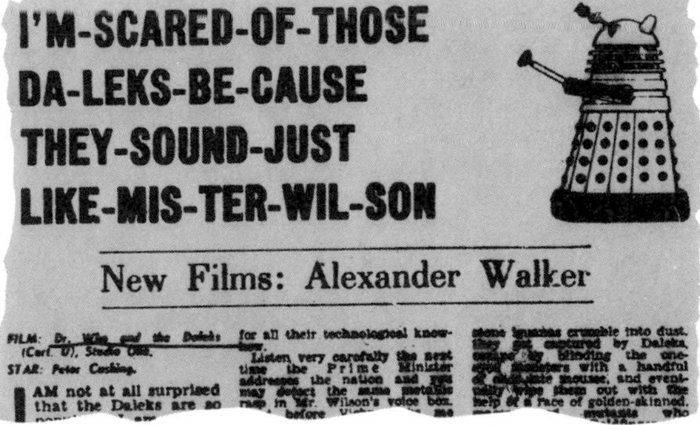
I'M-SCARED-OF-THOSE DA-LEKS-BE-CAUSE THEY-SOUND-JUST LIKE-MIS-TER-WIL-SON

New Films: Alexander Walker

I AM not at all surprised that the Daleks are so

said I wanted to make a series called "The Daleks",' he says later. 'I went there to hustle and got very close to doing it. There would have been no Doctor Who, of course, because I had no copyright in the character. But I could take the Daleks away and do it. Indeed, at one point the BBC were going to go with me on this series – but the whole thing sort of crumbled to dust, and I moved on to other things.' (Terry did have the compensation, however, of reportedly earning £50,000 from Dalek merchandising during 1965.)

October 9

The most curious of all *Doctor Who* stories is screened – a complete-in-one adventure, 'Mission to the Unknown', written by Terry Nation, in which neither the Doctor *nor* the companions appear! It is not, though, some fiendish plot by Nation to get rid of the Doctor, but rather a prelude to what will be (and still remains) the longest *Doctor Who* story ever, 'The Daleks' Master Plan', which is to bridge Christmas and the New Year in twelve episodes.

This prelude, which is known by the BBC title, 'Dalek Cut-away', has come about as a direct result of instructions from Sir Huw Weldon, Director General of the BBC, to Verity Lambert's team to produce a 'monster length' Dalek story, because – said later newspaper stories – his mother was a great fan of the Daleks! As well as this unprecedented move, the programme is granted an extra episode for the season, and Verity Lambert decides on using it as a trailer for the Dalek special. The only trouble is that the regular cast are on holiday during the only recording dates – the first week of August! The situation is resolved with the story of Dalek activity on the planet Kembel, where they are planning an invasion of Earth.

With this programme complete, Verity Lambert takes her leave of the programme, having brought Sydney Newman's bold concept to a huge, successful reality. 'As a programme it was very tiring to do,' she recalls later, 'but at the same time very stimulating due to the enormous freedom the format offers. There was always something fresh to see and the environment of the programme continually changed. It has never lost its ability to fascinate audiences and to frighten them a little as well.' Verity hands the show over to a veteran BBC staff man, John Wiles, who declares he wants to make the programme 'less childish'. And he adds: 'There are very exciting things going on now in space exploration and I want to push the show more towards adult science-fiction.'

October 16

'The Myth Makers' by Donald Cotton sees the departure of another companion, Vicki, and the arrival of Katarina played by Adrienne Hill, who is to lay down her life in the very next story to save the Doctor from the Daleks. Although the *Doctor Who* production team did not, in fact, build a full-size Trojan horse for this historical drama, as rumour has long suggested, the story is notable in that it is one of the few productions where the incidental music is provided by a full orchestra, the score composed and conducted by the well-known film musician Humphrey Searle.

November 13

The start of what is to prove the longest-ever *Doctor Who* story, Terry Nation's twelve-part 'The Daleks' Master Plan', still regarded as one of the classics of the entire series. The scope of the production throws enormous demands on costume and set design, as well as on director Douglas Camfield. John Wiles and his new script editor, Donald Tosh, have virtually to leave the making of the series to the established regulars.

An actor later to become a fixture in the series makes his debut. Nicholas Courtney appears as Space Security Agent Bret Vyon, who joins forces with the Doctor to thwart the Daleks. He suffers death at the hands of Sara Kingdom (Jean Marsh), a one-story companion, but unlike her he is to reappear later – as Brigadier Lethbridge-Stewart.

December 11

The 'Counter-Plot' episode of the epic 'The Daleks' Master Plan' is screened. A few days later producer John Wiles receives a phonecall from MGM's studios at Borehamwood, North London, where Stanley Kubrick's new film, *2001: A Space Odyssey,* is in production. Having watched some of the previous week's episodes, the Visual Effects team, headed by Wally Weevers and Douglas Trumbull, are intrigued by the *Doctor Who* crew's achievements both in the illusion of weightlessness – as seen with the death of Katarina in episode four – and in matter transportation, demonstrated when the Doctor, Sara and Steven are projected to the planet Mira. Giving credit to director Douglas Camfield, Wiles explains that the space-travel scenes were accomplished by techniques involving the use of special transparencies and video-effects generators, and that the weightless shots were done simply by aiming a camera vertically upwards at an actress suspended immediately above by a wire from the studio ceiling. Curiously enough, when *2001* is eventually released in 1967, permutations of those same techniques, pioneered by Camfield in *Doctor Who,* are clearly in evidence.

December 21

The curtain rises at Wyndham's Theatre, London, on the first performance of *Curse of the Daleks,* written by David Whitaker and Terry Nation, directed by Gillian Howell. Having cleaned up at the cinema box-office that summer, the Daleks are now set to conquer another horizon, the London theatre stage. Unlike the cinema film *Doctor Who and the Daleks,* for which special Dalek casings had been constructed, the Daleks featured here are the original BBC versions built by Shawcraft Models Ltd. For logistical reasons, though, none of the TV cast of *Doctor Who* are written into the play.

The plot concerns a star liner from Earth which crashes onto the Dalek planet of Skaro in the twenty-first century. The survivors eventually find the Dalek city and foolishly re-activate the Daleks, thought to be dead (presumably following the Doctor's first visit there in 1964). The Daleks there and then decide to invade the Earth using the repaired space liner. The Humans fight back valiantly but their efforts to destroy the Daleks are once more hampered by a traitor in their midst. Despite mixed press reactions, the show is still a hit with family audiences more used to conventional pantomime.

As with the films, joint credit for the stage play is given to David Whitaker and Terry Nation, though by far the greater bulk of the writing is Whitaker's. Ever since Nation's first script for 'The Dead Planet', Whitaker has had a fascination for the Daleks and collaborated greatly with Nation in devising the myth of 'The Dalek Chronicles' – cubes of technical data which both writers supposedly found and which purported to tell the history of the ancient race of Daleks. It was these 'Chronicles' which David Whitaker unfolded weekly in the children's comic *TV 21*, where he provided the majority of scripts for the one-page feature, drawn by such luminaries of the art field as Paul Jennings and Chris Achilleos.

CHRIS SENIOR

JIM McDADE

1966

February 5

Start of 'The Massacre' by John Lucarotti, which is the first *Doctor Who* story to be directed by a woman, Paddy Russell. The historical adventure also introduces a new companion, Dorothea 'Dodo' Chaplet (Jackie Lane) and a unique moment in the series when the Doctor is left quite alone for the first time in his (televised) travels.

Despite the success of its mammoth predecessor, Stewart Lane of the *Daily Worker* thinks the programme is on the decline. *'Doctor Who,* now in its "third successful year", is definitely showing signs of age,' he writes, 'and my spies have it that even the youngsters are getting tired of it. Today the programme moves to sixteenth-century Paris, with plotting between the Catholics and Huguenots, but I fear that the Daleks may return yet again. After all, the BBC has already granted sixty licences for the production of Dalek toys with more still being negotiated, and it gets 5 per cent of the wholesale price on each toy!' Mr Lane adds that he believes the new Australian science fiction series called *The Stranger* on BBC 1 is 'more interesting and has a peaceful theme'. Could the days of *Doctor Who* be numbered, he wonders . . .

March 5

More changes in the *Doctor Who* Production Office as 'The Ark' by husband-and-wife team Paul Erickson and Lesley Scott is screened. This is John Wiles's expensive-looking finale to the show after his brief six-month run as producer, and he says of it, 'This is a good indication of what Donald Tosh and I really wanted to do with the series. The other idea that he and I had was for a story called "The Face of God" with the TARDIS stopped in mid-air by this enormous face which claims to be that of God himself. Of course, towards the end it would be proven that all was not as it seemed – ironically, I think *Star Trek* did something very similar. Indeed they did a lot of ideas I would like to have done on *Doctor Who!'*

New script editor Gerry Davis makes his debut. Apart from notable work on *Doctor Who*, he is to form a most productive and imaginative writing partnership with Dr Kit Pedler of the Opthalmology Division of London's University College Hospital.

April 2

Innes Lloyd, an actor turned television presenter, takes over as producer with Brian Hayles's magical story, 'The Celestial Toymaker'. Although not enamoured of science fiction, Lloyd sees other challenges in his new job. 'It is a challenge to take over something that has been set up and is going so well,' he says, 'and every time you do a show your horizons have to be wider because you just cannot go down the same road that has been travelled before.'

'The Celestial Toymaker' shows just what Innes Lloyd has in mind. Gerry Davis is also extensively involved in working on the script, utilising part of a Fifties play which he had admired called *George and Margaret*, in which the central characters are never seen as themselves – much to the annoyance of the audience – but always as other characters in the play. The only

ANDREW J. WHITE

unhappy note about this story concerns the appearance of a fat boy named Cyril . . .

April 25

'Cyril, a bespectacled fat boy whom TV viewers thought looked like Billy Bunter's double has got the BBC into trouble.' So runs the opening line in a Daily Express piece commenting on the row following the appearance of Cyril the Schoolboy in 'The Celestial Toymaker.' The estate of Bunter author Frank Richards complain to the BBC after the character of Cyril appears in two episodes of *Doctor Who* clad in all too identifiable tight check trousers, blazer and bow tie. The BBC make their apology to Richards in the form of an announcement after the last episode saying that no similarity between Bunter and Cyril had been intended and that the only link between the two characters was their costumes. The problem had started after concerned viewers rang the BBC to explain that the 'real' Billy Bunter was nowhere near as cruel and unfeeling as Cyril had been towards the Doctor's two companions, Steven and Dodo.

April 26

After the stunning success of 'The Celestial Toymaker' comes 'The Gunfighters' by Donald Cotton, taking the Doctor to the Wild West, which is to prove a disaster and achieve the lowest-ever ratings for a *Doctor Who* serial: believed to be less than two million! Only the accurate sets of Tombstone and the O.K. Corral escape criticism – yet in an interview today, a week before the four-part story begins, William Hartnell claims the idea for a Western was his! In a seemingly appropriately headlined interview, 'Oh, the Agony of Being Doctor Who', Hartnell tells Jack Bell of the *Daily Mirror*, 'This idea of a Western story was my idea . . . children will always adore cowboys and Indians. And I'd like to see characters from children's books come into it.' Bell says that every Saturday Hartnell commands up to eleven and a half million BBC viewers. 'And nearly a quarter of the globe are also *Who* fans,' he adds. 'The Doctor's adventures in time and space are tops in Trinidad, "bonzer" in Australia, and a knock-out in Nigeria. Canadians, Maltese and Ghanaians all send him fan mail. And the BBC are now dubbing versions into Spanish, Arabic and Japanese!'

Hartnell talks about the pressures of playing the role. 'The BBC have flatteringly said that they'll keep it going as long as I'm willing to continue. But I want a change in conditions – more time off, more space between the stories. Still, you can never escape from the character – that's the agony of being Doctor Who . . . The character has given me a certain neurosis – and that's not easy for my wife to cope with. I get a little agitated and it makes me a little irritable with people. In fact, Doctor Who seems to be taking over!' He adds that this irritation can spill over into arguments with directors. 'Once or twice I've put my foot down with a new director and told him, "I know how to play Doctor Who and I don't want you to intrude on it or alter it."' Two changes are to result from the débâcle of 'The Gunfighters' – Innes Lloyd drops the policy of using historical stories in the series, and longer breaks between the seasons are agreed and scheduled.

May 28

Ian Stuart Black's 'The Savages' restores some of the lost prestige to *Doctor Who* with a story shot at one of the most dangerous locations ever used by the BBC, Oxshott Sandpit in Surrey. Unknown to anyone, the whole area is very marshy and a number of people have actually been drowned in the pits in previous years. Fortunately, filming is completed without mishap, although not long afterwards a young boy is lost in the sandpit and it has to be filled in. The story also marks the end of Steven's tour with the Doctor, and in a move rarely repeated since, the cast are actually allowed to smash up the set of the evil Senta's laboratory. The actors enjoyed the experience hugely, William Hartnell declaring afterwards, 'There is something very satisfying in destroying a place like that!'

The TARDIS – the key to all the Doctor's adventures

POLICE PUBLIC CALL BOX

Previous page: The journeying begins – the first Doctor, William Hartnell, at the TARDIS console. A rare colour still from the early black-and-white days of Doctor Who

Above: The charming side of the first Doctor as revealed in 'The Aztecs' (1964)

Left: Another rare colour photograph, from 'The Crusades' (1965)

Left: The irrepressible second Doctor, Patrick Troughton

Below: Patrick Troughton on location with a Yeti for 'The Abominable Snowmen' (1967)

Right: Emperor Dalek and Dalek minion from 'The Evil of the Daleks' (1967)

The third Doctor, Jon Pertwee, meets his two former selves, Patrick Troughton and William Hartnell, at a photocall for 'The Three Doctors' (1972)

June 25

The first return to modern times for the Doctor since his original appearance in 'An Unearthly Child'. In 'The War Machines', again by Ian Stuart Black, he confronts a super-computer called WOTAN and recruits two new companions, Polly (Anneke Wills) and Ben Jackson (Michael Craze). These two older companions help broaden the appeal of *Doctor Who* to teenagers as well as giving it a more trendy and less childish feel. The idea for the script is proposed by Dr Kit Pedler, now the show's uncredited technical adviser, who also designs the computer. To enhance the present-day feel of the story, BBC newsreader Kenneth Kendall is hired for episode four to announce the appearance of the War Machines in a news broadcast. As well as being the last story of the third season of *Doctor Who,* 'The War Machines' also sees the exit of Dodo. It has the dubious distinction, too, of being the only story to break with the long-established protocol by having the Doctor referred to as 'Doctor Who'.

July 22

During the eight weeks *Doctor Who* is off the air, the second feature film, *Daleks – Invasion Earth 2150 AD,* made by Rosenberg and Subotsky, opens in London. Once again Milton Subotsky is aided by David Whitaker on the script, which is based on Terry Nation's 'The Dalek Invasion of Earth' and Gordon Flemyng directs. (A provisional idea that this second film should be based on Nation's story 'The Keys of Marinus' is dropped when it is realised that it was the Daleks who had achieved success for the first movie.) Peter Cushing again plays the Doctor, with Roberta Tovey as Susan. Comedian Bernard Cribbins replaces Roy Castle as the bumbling Tom Campbell, and the Doctor gets a new niece in the form of Jill Curzon as Louise. Because of complaints from audiences that the Daleks have not been murderous enough, the larger budget of

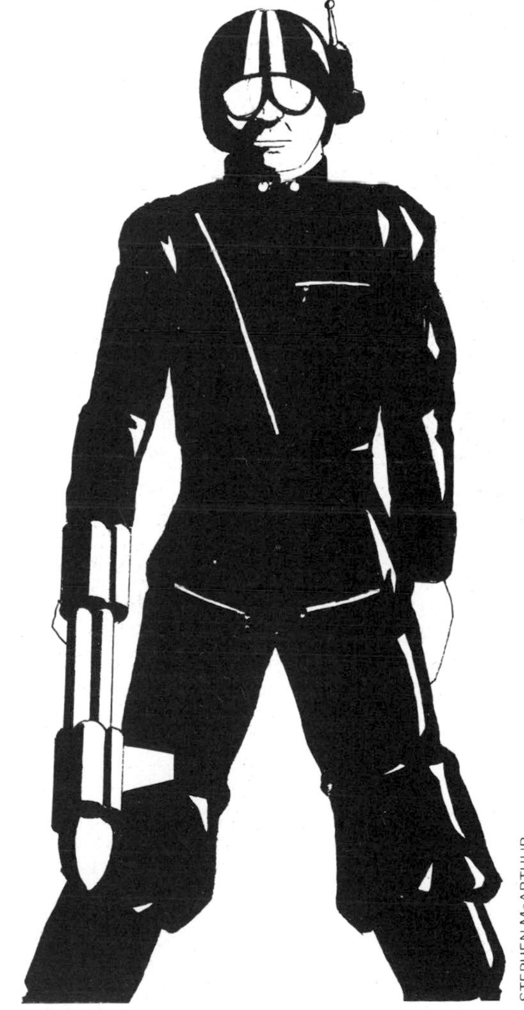
STEPHEN McARTHUR

the second picture is used for wholesale mayhem. Although Peter Cushing suffered illness while making the film, he remembers his two appearances as the Doctor as being among his favourite roles. 'It was no surprise to me to learn that the first film came into the top twenty box-office hits last year, despite the panning the critics gave us,' he says. 'It helps reconcile you to the oddities of show business. Why, there I was playing Winston Smith in *1984* on TV but when the film version was made the part was given to Edmond O'Brien. Now I'm playing the Doctor while Bill Hartnell is doing him on TV!' If Peter thought the first film had been 'panned', this one is in for an even rougher passage. *The Times* writes: 'The second cinematic excursion of the Daleks shows

little advance on the first. They are still trundling around issuing scrambled orders in humanoid speech, and Doctor Who, by judicious use of his time-machine, is still around to foil their dastardly schemes for world domination. The filming of all this is technically elementary – even the strings which hold up the flying saucer in which the Daleks land are clearly visible – and the cast, headed by the long-suffering, much ill-used Peter Cushing, seem able, unsurprisingly, to drum up no conviction whatever in anything they are called on to do. Grown-ups may enjoy it, but most children have more sense.' *The Financial Times*'s David Robinson agrees: 'I find the Daleks – cross little dustbins on wheels that they are – quite the most unattractive figures in science fiction. They really get no more than their desserts in *Daleks – Invasion Earth 2150 AD* which is a film of unusually low standards. The script is dim, the direction sloppy, the acting varying to execrable, and the editing loose enough to mislay whatever dramatic excitements there might otherwise have been.' Perhaps not surprisingly, after such a press, Milton Subotsky decides not to pick up his option for a third Dalek film – and has not done so to this day.

September 2

Before the fourth season of *Doctor Who* begins, the BBC announce the surprising news that William Hartnell is to leave the role of the Doctor and is to be replaced by the well-known character-actor Patrick Troughton. This now familiar change for the series is greeted with surprise and speculation as to whether such an unprecedented action with a central character can succeed. Although William Hartnell had not intended to leave the programme, his declining health has made it imperative, and a stand-in, Gordon Craig, has to double for him in a number of scenes shot for what is to be his last appearance in 'The Tenth Planet'. He actually records his final appearance on 8 October.

Patrick Troughton is filming *Viking Queen*

with Nicola Pagett when he is invited to play the Doctor. 'Well, I had always watched *Doctor Who* with the family ever since it started,' he says later. 'Everyone around just adored it. However, it had been going on about three years, and I didn't know how long the BBC were really thinking of keeping it. So, to be quite honest, I was very reluctant at first. To go and commit yourself to something out of the blue which you really didn't know would go on – I somehow had a feeling that the joke was over and that it had gone on too long.' But when Sydney Newman persists in his offer, Patrick finally capitulates. Newman also has the idea for Troughton playing the Doctor as a 'cosmic hobo'. 'He wanted him to be a sort of Chaplinesque character,' says Patrick, 'a sort of tramp, in contrast to Billy, and I suppose he must have known that I have a wicked glint in my eye for comedy and so we decided on that. It was much better than playing it tough.'

JULIAN VINCE

September 10

A special feel of authenticity is given to 'The Smugglers' the new season's first story by director Julia Smith, who has a wide knowledge of the Cornish coast where the story is set. Considerable location shooting is done between Land's End and the Lizard at a time when the weather should have been at its best – instead it is wet and windy, and the sea very rough, which gives several members of the cast seasickness during scenes on a fishing boat! Problems with transporting the TARDIS into a cave in Church Cove are only matched by the difficulty of avoiding contemporary artefacts at the rear of shots. A triumph of

SIMON MACKIE

MARGARET JONES

the story is the fight between revenue men and pirates, staged in the studios and completed in one take. This marks the debut of stuntman Terry Walsh, who over the years since has played more incidental characters in *Doctor Who* than any other actor or actress, including doubling for the Doctors in many stunt scenes. 'It's a great programme for me,' he says, 'because its so wide-ranging. You can get virtually everything and you never know what's coming next. I've been knocked down and blown up. I've been run down by a car and banged over an eighty-foot bank. I've had stair falls, cliff falls, car falls, falls from ladders, falls onto boxes, falls into water. And once I put my back out.' Terry particularly recalls his debut in 'The

Smugglers'. 'The Doctor was involved with pirates,' he says, 'and six of us had to stunt a fight between the pirates and the revenue men. The trouble was there weren't enough of us to go round, so as soon as one went down with a sword thrust, he'd crawl away behind a gravestone, put on a different wig and hat, and come storming back into the fight again!'

October 8

Start of 'The Tenth Planet', a landmark story in two respects: it is to feature the Doctor's regeneration from Hartnell into Troughton, and the arrival of some new monsters whose popularity is almost to equal that of the Daleks – the Cybermen: brain-children of technical adviser Dr Kit Pedler. The six original Cybermen created by costume designer Sandra Reid are very rudimentary compared to the later sophisticated models.

As the first of the four episodes is broadcast, William Hartnell and Patrick Troughton actually record the transformation scene, both men lying on the floor of the TARDIS set, in opera capes and scarves. (Strangely, despite their long careers, the two had never met before.) A camera is trained on each man's face, and an electronic effects generator is linked to the mixing console to enable the lines of the actors' faces to be 'speckled' and mixed one into the other. Patrick Troughton recalls the day vividly. 'Billy and I had to lie on the floor at either end of the set. With Edwina, the floor manager, keeping everyone cheerful, it took nearly all day to perfect the scene and transmogrify Billy into me. It was a really historic moment, I suppose.'

November 5

A night for fireworks in more ways than one. Before the astonished eyes of millions of *Doctor Who* viewers the new Doctor, Patrick Troughton, gets up off the TARDIS floor, throws back his cape revealing a crooked bow tie, baggy trousers and a shapeless coat, and proceeds to dance a little jig, accompanying himself with a

ROBERT SMITH

recorder. This radical recharacterisation of the Doctor has been the end result of much brainstorming by all those concerned with *Doctor Who*'s production, including the original creator, Sydney Newman. Weeks of wrangling have gone on trying to establish a personality for the new Doctor, whom Patrick Troughton has vowed he will not play as a clone of William Hartnell. These debates, including such outlandish ideas as blacking-up Troughton as a pirate captain, or giving him the silhouette of Gladstone, have come to nothing. In the end, and still in regard to Sydney Newman's suggestion that Troughton should play it as a 'cosmic hobo', script editor Gerry Davis delivers a *fait accompli* by presenting the new Doctor as a Chaplinesque figure, much to the approval of everybody. Remembering the fiery discussions years later, Davis admits to having borrowed a lot of the second Doctor's mannerisms and attitudes directly from observations of Troughton himself!

The debut story, 'The Power of the Daleks' by David Whitaker, also features the Doctor's old enemies, but it is his two companions that Patrick remembers with greatest delight. 'Michael Craze and Anneke Wills were wonderful when I first joined the show, as it was obviously a very difficult thing to do – to slip into someone else's shoes who had been doing it for three years and was accepted by everyone. We knocked around together for the first six weeks or so in the various pubs in Fulham where they lived, getting to know each other well. They were marvellous . . .'

The trio also demonstrate the sense of humour and love of practical jokes which is to sustain them through any crisis by appearing on the set for the first day of shooting wearing T-shirts on which are emblazoned the words: 'Come Back Bill Hartnell – All Is Forgiven!'

MIKE GOODMAN

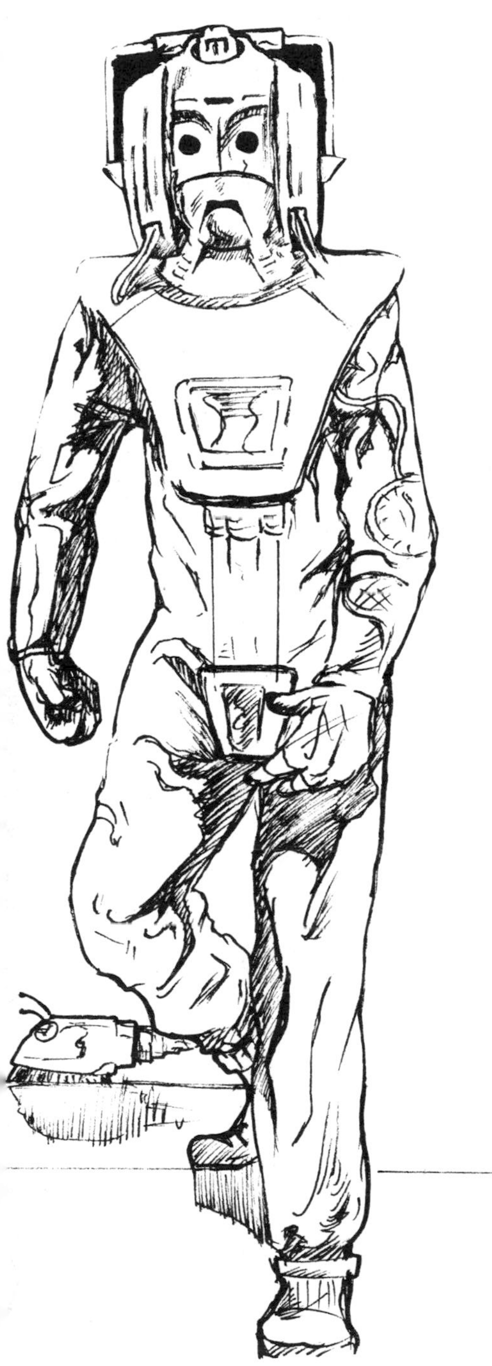

December 15

Despite his natural aversion to publicity, Patrick Troughton gives a rare interview to Ernest Thomson of the *Radio Times* which captures his personality neatly.

'Who is Doctor Who?' Thomson asks. 'In plain terms the answer is Patrick Troughton, an actor most people think they know, but one with so chameleon-like a range of character portrayals that there seems only one way to pin him down. You squat behind a TV camera during rehearsal. He knows you are there because, being Doctor Who, he knows practically everything. He even waves a welcome, looking like a Beatle reverting to type with his frizzed-up hair and the shard-shaped coat-tails flapping as he dances from camera to camera. "I'm having a whale of a time," he says, when at last the rehearsal breaks and there's a moment for a quiet chat. And then you realise that Doctor Who's journeyings through time and space perfectly express the yearnings of Patrick Troughton.' Recapping the actor's career, Thomson says that the part of the Doctor is 'for him an uncommonly sympathetic part, giving scope for sly fun and even a bit of clowning if it will fool the enemy and fox his friends.' Confessing that he likes dressing up and would have been happy as a novelist or a school teacher, Troughton himself says, 'Yes, I'd have liked teaching – children keep one young.' And Ernest Thomson remains none the wiser about his subject: 'Troughton's face spreads into a smile at the thought that, as Doctor Who, he can inject some fun into life and entertain the whole family. But under the surface, you feel, he remains as near a mystery as Doctor Who himself.'

December 17

A new companion for the Doctor, the Scottish piper Jamie McCrimmon, played by Frazer Hines, who joins the group in 'The Highlanders' co-written by Gerry Davis and Elwyn Jones. This story of the defeat of Bonnie Prince Charlie in 1746 is to prove the last purely historical story in the series for sixteen years – a fact that does not upset Patrick Troughton. 'No, they weren't my favourite ones,' he says, 'I didn't like going back in time. All they could show you was how history had gone.' The partnership with Frazer is to last until he himself leaves the series. 'He was marvellous, Frazer. They were wonderful years with him,' says Patrick, at the same time giving away the secret about what the young Scotsman wore under his kilt – a secret he preserved by insisting on no low-level camera shots. 'Yes, he *did* wear something: khaki shorts.'

Interviewed by the *Observer,* Innes Lloyd says, 'We have to recognise that millions of very young children do watch the programme – often wide-eyed from *behind* their chairs. So we must aim for good, clean, adventurous, *enjoyable* fear.' And of the decision to drop historical stories, 'They are obviously the weak ones, when the Doctor's time-machine travels into the past. I want the new stories to have less obvious history, more guts.' The *Observer* claims that 'Twelve million people watch *Doctor Who* if the Daleks are in it, only seven to eight million if they're not.' In actual fact, the figures are nearer four million, which makes Innes Lloyd's decision all the more crucial . . .

MIKE TUCKER

1967

January 25

The initial reactions to Innes Lloyd's change of direction for *Doctor Who* are not good. Mid-way through Geoffrey Orme's 'The Underwater Menace', directed by Julia Smith, the *Daily Worker*'s Ann Lawrence complains that watching the series is 'becoming increasingly painful'. She writes: 'The absurdity of the futurist stories in this series has always been noticeable. Somehow, however, William Hartnell's Doctor always managed to give a certain dignity to the part, in spite of all the nonsense, and one could not help believing in him. Patrick Troughton's Doctor Who is a clown, looking and acting something like one of the Marx Brothers. Instead of modifying nonsense, his interpretation of the part only heightens it. Still, he has my sympathies, wrestling with a script like that!' And Miss Lawrence concludes: 'Considering how good most of the BBC children's programmes are, I feel that the futurist stories of *Doctor Who* are an awful let-down. They are just not good enough for the children, and my own youngsters' interest has declined markedly.' Remarkably, within a month she is to revise her opinions completely . . .

February 11

The Cybermen return to *Doctor Who* in the serial – 'The Moonbase'. Slightly taken aback by their overnight success in 'The Tenth Planet', Innes Lloyd decides on a gamble with them, electing to reintroduce them totally redesigned but looking as though 'money has been spent on them'. In fact, being even cleverer, Lloyd chooses not only to have the Cybermen redesigned, but also to bring them back in a serial that is almost a carbon copy of 'The Tenth Planet'. The theory behind Lloyd's judgment is that, given the risks involved in asking an audience to accept a totally redesigned monster that had been successful in its original form, a virtual retelling of the original plotline would serve as something of a relaunch. Therefore, if you lose the audience loyal to 'The Tenth Planet', you would pick up a new audience that would see, in 'The Moonbase', the same production values that made the first show popular, but with, in Lloyd's eyes, better-looking villains.

ROBERT SHAW

The ploy works, with 'The Moonbase' now standing as the watershed marking the end of the lowish ratings the show had seen towards the end of Hartnell's era and the early serials of Patrick Troughton. It succeeds with the critics, too, among them the previously disappointed Ann Lawrence. She writes: 'The present futuristic episode of *Doctor Who* is of a much higher quality than we have been used to for some time. Written by Kit Pedler, himself a scientist and research worker, the present adventure of the crew of the TARDIS has a better balanced mixture of science and fiction.' She does, though, have one complaint. 'But I wish we could have a little less screaming from Anneke Wills as Polly. Her screams are all too predictable. "Here we go again" is the wry comment from my family. Isn't it possible to allow her a slightly more intelligent reaction to sudden shock?'

DAVID ADAMSON

March 4

Doctor Who's first 'optical effect' is seen by the viewers as the Cybermen fire a laser-beam from their cannon trained on a Moonbase. The base, however, is protected by an invisible gravity-shield and the beam is deflected harmlessly into space. Optical effects is a difficult, and very broad-based, area of special effects to quantify. Basically, any visual effect seen on the finished picture which is not manually built for the programme's filming or recording is judged to be an optical. Optical effects are either added to a film or tape in post-production, or are added to the picture electronically during recording. In the case of the laser effect in episode four of 'The Moonbase', this is added to the film footage after it is processed. The sequence in question is filmed at Ealing with the Cybermen firing the gun and then reacting to the beam flying up into space. Then a separate strip of film is made showing nothing other than a white beam of light extending along the frames and then deflecting. This has to be done using the finished live-action film both for reference and to ensure synchronisation of the two images. Once completed, the two pieces of film are run together through a device known as a triple-headed printer, which generates a third piece of film with the two sequences blended and perfectly 'synched'.

March 11

The BBC's Visual Effects Department delivers its most ambitious monster to date, for the story 'The Macra Terror' by Ian Stuart Black. Due to earlier wranglings about *Doctor Who* – in the wake of Sydney Newman's arrival at the BBC – the BBC Visual Effects Department had declined to work on the show, thereby leaving it up to the designers to plan and execute the monsters. These differences have now been resolved, and Jack Kines's department find themselves having to dream up ever more impressive creations for the three-year-old series. The Macra tests their resources to the full. Described by the director as a giant crab, that is just what Visual Effects deliver – a giant crustacean so large and bulky that it has to be mounted on the back of a lorry-cab chassis to give it movement. Inside the huge costume the operator, Robert Jewell, has to contend with working, by levers, the huge claws, the mandibles, the illuminated brain-case, the quivering mouth and the eye-stalks. Further out of vision, the visual effects technicians control the hand pump which feeds down plastic pipes large quantities of a green, viscous ooze that emerges foaming from the Macra's mouth!

As monsters go, the Macra is impressive – but to solve the problem in the studio of needing to see more than one, special mirrors and screens have to be set up at strategic points to reflect the image of the static Macra prop into desired locations, i.e. seen through a window, glimpsed down a mine tunnel. Patrick Troughton will certainly never forget it. 'You know it cost as much as a Mini did in those days,' he said later, 'and we could only use it once! It was very difficult to shoot with its enormous mouth and claws. In fact, there wasn't very much you could do with it – but we covered it in smoke and darkness and it came rumbling out towards us. It was very impressive, though!'

MICHAEL G. CLARK

April 8

The first appearance of the now-familiar title graphics for the show featuring the Doctor's face – in the perhaps inappropriately titled story 'The Faceless Ones' by David Ellis and Malcolm Hulke! Bernard Lodge, the graphics designer who had created the original opening sequence of lettering over an electronically-generated pattern of pulsating shapes, explains how this striking new effect came about. 'We had noticed when making the original sequence that if a face was used instead of lettering the same effect was achieved – an amazing distortion. When the Patrick Troughton version of the Doctor came along we used this face distortion as the main element.' Speaking again later about the enduring impact of the titles, Bernard says: 'I've tried not to make them horrific. I want to give an impression of space-and-time travel, and a sense of magic, too. The music itself has a sinister quality and I didn't want to add to that.'

The change of graphics is not the only interesting feature of 'The Faceless Ones', for director Gerry Mill elects to use the most ambitious location so far for the story – Gatwick Airport. Where stories like 'The Dalek Invasion of Earth' and 'The Smugglers' have been shot 'far from the madding crowds', this one is shot in a very public place, demanding a great deal of ingenuity from the crew to hide the public's tendency to gawp at cameras, especially in busy thoroughfares like the airport concourse. Leaning on his experience as a film director, Gerry Mill solves most of his problems during the week of location work by arranging with the airport authorities to close off sections of the concourse and then

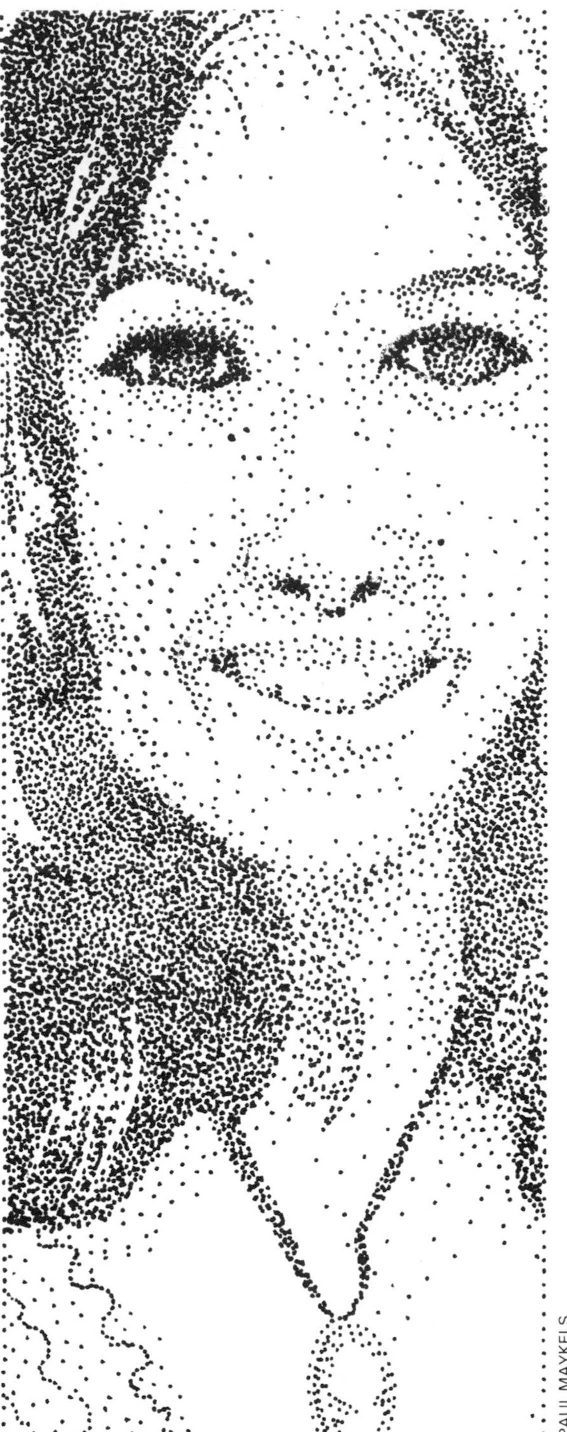
PAUL MAYKELS

filling them with thirty or so extras hired to mill around like members of the public. Thanks also to the authorities, the crew are able to shoot in less exposed areas – such as the hangars – but where the public cannot be avoided, the cameras are hidden on high balconies and fitted with zoom lenses so few people realise they are being filmed.

One in-studio shot causes Innes Lloyd quite a different problem, however. He explains: 'We had a scene where one of the Doctor's friends received an injection. After that episode I received a phone call from a nurse saying did I realise how many children were due to have vaccination injections that Monday? And so I was worried for a time that I might have unduly frightened a lot of youngsters by linking, in their minds, injections with invading monsters.'

May 13

The Doctor loses his two companions, Ben and Polly, and Patrick Troughton says goodbye to Michael Craze and Anneke Wills, who have become close friends. Michael speaks for both of them when he says, 'We became almost like relatives, and I think it showed in the stories. It was marvellous working with Pat.'

With their departure, a new companion is announced: delectable Deborah Watling, youngest member of the well-known acting family, who is to play a demure young Victorian lady appropriately named Victoria Waterfield. Although she is a determined and self-confident young woman, Deborah says, 'I'm supposed to be a rather timid soul who screams at the first sign of trouble. But it does sound fun all the same . . .'

July 1

In an explosive climax, what is intended to be the final meeting between the Daleks and the Doctor takes place as David Whitaker's 'The Evil of the Daleks' draws to a close.

Although never intended as an effects-orientated show, this final episode of the seven-week Dalek classic gives a powerful demonstration of just how ingenious and sophisticated effects can be. The sequence in question occurs in the last ten minutes of the final episode as the Doctor instigates a situation of civil war between two opposing factions of Daleks. As the two sides blaze into each other, the fiery destruction of the Daleks, their Emperor and their city is truly impressive. So heavy are the demands for the effects in these scenes that director Derek Martinus has to appoint an assistant director, Tim Combe, to oversee the work.

Visual effects designers Michael Harris and Peter Day systematically construct and destroy almost a dozen lightweight Daleks made from balsa wood and vacuum-formed plastic. Each Dalek, when destroyed, is filmed from several angles to give the impression, when edited together, of whole legions of Daleks being exterminated. Not happy with just destroying the robots, Harris and Day also consider the organic Daleks inside the casings and give them a grisly fate as well. Several domes, when blown up, exude a frothing mass of foam meant to indicate the death throes of the creatures inside. Several model stages are also built and explode on cue, with the big finale reserved for the destruction of the Emperor's quarters. Not to be outdone, sounds effects creator Brian Hodgson prepares a multi-layered soundtrack of Dalek voices, klaxon alarms, explosions and gun shots to give the final minutes of 'Evil of the Daleks' an impact few will forget.

August 14

With a two-month gap between *Doctor Who* recording dates in the studio, a cast and film crew are dispatched to Snowdonia in North Wales for a week to shoot the location footage for 'The Abominable Snowmen'. Ideally, the script calls for a snow-covered setting to suggest Tibet but, recording schedules being of paramount importance during the rest of the year, August is the only month when shooting a story with this amount of location work is feasible. Hence no pretence at snow is attempted. What the cast and crew find in Snowdonia, though, is rain – lots of it and sufficient, over two days, to call a halt to any attempts to film, leaving everyone stranded in their hotel. By the time the weather dries sufficiently, the temperature up in the mountains has dropped far below the seasonal norm, with gusts of wind making it feel even more uncomfortable for anyone aside from the three actors warmly ensconced in their Yeti suits. Greatest of all the suffering is experienced by Frazer Hines who, as Jamie McCrimmon, is obliged to wear his Scottish kilt throughout!

Another penalty wrought by the weather is the slippery nature of the ground, a bad enough hazard for the normally dressed actors, but absolute purgatory for the three Yeti whose latex rubber feet lead to director Gerald Blake's returning to London, after the week's shooting, with several hundred feet of hilarious footage showing Yeti

RAY D. BROOKING

skidding and falling over on the soft Welsh turf. Ironically enough, the *Doctor Who* film crew find themselves being filmed for a feature on the local news service *Wales Today*, and Troughton himself gives a brief interview.

September 2

The Cybermen return for the second time in the year to open the fifth season of *Doctor Who* in 'The Tomb of the Cybermen'. This story by Kit Pedler and former script editor Gerry Davis (who left in the summer to give way to Victor Pemberton) also introduces vicious little creatures named Cybermats.

However, the violence in some of the scenes causes the story to be criticised by the press and also get numerous complaints from the public. Although the Cybermen are believed to be the cause of this outcry, there is no denying their popularity, and just as they had done with the Daleks, newspaper writers try to explain why. The *Daily Worker*'s Ann Lawrence finds the answer: 'I did not understand why these robots in human form with distorted faces were so universally popular with children until my daughter had nightmares about them,' she writes. 'When I asked her why she was frightened of the Cybermen but not of the Daleks, she replied that the Cybermen looked like terrible human beings, whereas the Daleks were just Daleks. So it seems that as long as children can't identify any of these studio-made monsters with something they know, they are not disturbed by them.'

ROBERT SHAW

September 3

A feature story by Kenneth Bailey in *The People* describes Patrick Troughton as 'the great unknown of outer space – as soon as you want to talk to him he goes invisible, unget-atable, unspeakable-to. 'Yet,' says Bailey, 'as soon as his name is mentioned he *materialises* in the enthusiastic talk which immediately erupts among fellow television workers.' 'You never forget

DAVID J. HOWS

working with Pat,' one TV producer tells him, 'he etches himself on your brain.' Troughton's reticence makes his period as the Doctor the least publicised, as Bailey explains: 'When he leaves the studio after a day's work, he's often roaring his head off over some salty crack he's made at the cast – which nevertheless adores him. Yet where he goes is his iron-fast secret. He's never let escape facts about his private life. He thinks actors should be known only by their parts. At the moment he is Doctor Who. That, he thinks, should be sufficient.'

September 26

The BBC screens the first *Talkback* programme, hosted by David Coleman. The show goes out live and features a debate with the audience on *Doctor Who. Talkback* is designed to be a programme wherein the public can come into the studio and give their views, on air, about BBC Television, so *Doctor Who* is almost a mandatory topic for inclusion in the opening show insofar that it is currently attracting a lot of criticism over the horror elements in the series. This has happened especially following the Visual Effects Department's discovery of foam-generating equipment. By mixing the foamable chemicals with various other ingredients – cocoa powder, wood chippings, paint, etc – different textures of the foam can be achieved. This has, so far, resulted in the slime of the Macra crabs, the fizzing brains of the Dalek creatures and, most recently, the disembowelled innards of a Cyberman. All three of these effects have, apparently, been exceptionally disturbing to younger minds and, for the *Talkback* prosecution, several mothers are invited by Coleman to give their views on *Doctor Who*'s content and to suggest solutions to the problem. Acting for the defence is the series' unofficial scientific adviser Kit Pedler – co-creator of the Cybermen, and a medical doctor in his own right. However, the programme is not at all well handled by its presenters, with many of Pedler's comments either being shouted down or chopped in mid-sentence by Coleman.

One suggestion put forward for further debate, though, is that *Doctor Who,* and other programmes of similar ilk, should carry certificates similar to those awarded to cinema films. This is later to be objected to by the Corporation Directors who feel that to impose such classifications would lessen the public's own right to discern what makes good and bad television.

September 30

'The Abominable Snowman' begins – one of the major stories to earn Patrick Troughton his enduring reputation as the 'Monster Doctor'. This story of the Yeti, by Mervyn Haisman and Henry Lincoln, based on an old Himalayan legend, is also one of Patrick Troughton's favourites. When asked years later if he ever had any trouble working with monsters, he replies, 'No trouble at all. There were some beautiful monsters. *They* were the ones who had the problems being shut in very hot and claustrophobic skins. They caught fire inside. I'm always asked if I have a favourite monster. I can't see how one can, really, although the Yeti were lovely and scary.'

STUART J. M. HILL

TIM PIERACCI

November 4

DEAN MOSTON

The first 'custom-made' *Doctor Who* trailer goes out on the air. It follows transmission of the final episode of 'The Abominable Snowmen' and heralds Brian Hayles's 'The Ice Warriors'. The trailer features Peter Barkworth as Leader Clent and Peter Sallis in his role of Penley. Barkworth does a short monologue introducing himself and the job he has to do as commander of the European Ice Station. He describes it as a tough job that needs to be tightly controlled, with no room for irregularities or the undisciplined mind. Penley is shown as a representative of an 'undisciplined mind' – a brilliant scientist who has dropped out of the procedure-bound society. However, his monologue is more in the way of a warning to the audience that Clent might be in for a few unsuspected shocks. The trailer closes with a short piece of film showing the vague outline of Varga the Ice Warrior's head within its cocoon of ice . . . Although trailers for 'Next week's *Doctor Who*' have been done since 'The Macra Terror', this is the first one to use a sequence not later seen in the forthcoming programme itself.

November 11

The terrifying shape of Varga the Ice Warrior is seen on television for the first time, and within a couple of weeks the Ice Warriors are established as one of the Doctors's four most popular enemies – the other three being the Yeti, Daleks and Cybermen.

Part of the reasons behind the overnight success of the Ice Warriors can be attributed to the novelty of their design. Instead of a full mask – as worn by the Sensorites, the Cybermen or the Monoids, the Ice Warrior helmet leaves the mouth visible. Once the mouth has been made up with latex rubber to look reptilian, the finished head is both alive and capable of a wide range of expressions – a key point in establishing the cruelty of these Martian invaders. No less impressive is the Ice Warrior costume, designed by Martin Baugh, who was also responsible for the Yeti. With a bodyshell constructed of fibreglass and with Bernard Bresslaw's height and build to support it, the finished creature stands nearly seven foot in height.

Reviewing the serial, Francis Hope writes gloomily: 'It is just too frightening for some children. For a start, I know one four-year-old who stood rigid with terror in front of the soft-whispering Ice Warriors, inviting his mother to come and hold his hand in case she was frightened. But I know many more households where the programme's name is forbidden in case the older children acquire a taste for it and the younger ones refuse to be excluded! There is nothing like being dragged out of bed by juvenile nightmares for blunting the finer edges of one's aesthetic judgement.'

December 14

Doctor Who's newest gadget is unveiled to the public via an appearance on the children's magazine programme *Blue Peter.* The gadget in question is a British-built VCS III monophonic synthesiser, one of the first instruments of its kind and demonstrated by *Doctor Who*'s resident sound effects creator Brian Hodgson. Up until the dawn of the synthesiser, all of the programme's special sounds – TARDIS dematerialisations, ray-guns firing, background atmospherics, etc – have had to be done by electrical rather than electronic means. The arrival of this synthesiser extends the capabilities of the Radiophonic workshop almost a hundredfold, and makes a lot easier the creation of the science-fiction effects for *Doctor Who.* One of the first uses the synthesiser has been put to is to make the bleeps for the robot spheres inside the Yeti.

December 23

'The Enemy of the World' begins its run on television – the six-part serial by David Whitaker marking a major step forward in *Doctor Who*'s production technique. Still some years away from being producer of the series, Barry Letts, director of this story, is the first man to break the mould of shooting *Doctor Who* episodes in consecutive scene number order. With recording equipment at the BBC now more sophisticated than its 1963 counterparts, Letts is one of the first directors to appreciate the advantages to be gained now that the stopping, starting and editing of video-tape is much easier.

So, for the first time in the show's history, scripts with differently coloured pages begin making their appearance. To explain: in ordinary terms a camera script (that which is seen and followed in the recording

COLIN HOWARD

studio by all the technicians and staff) is yellow in colour. A blue or pink page denotes a sequence that will be shot that day but not for that particular episode. This enables, for example, Patrick Troughton's scenes as the Doctor in episode three to be shot during episode two. This removes the need to have him made up as the Doctor for episode three's recording – thus he requires only one make-up session to turn him into the villain of the show, Leader Salamander. The distinction of playing the Doctor *and* his main enemy earns him this tribute in the *New Statesman:* 'Patrick Troughton was admirable playing both Doctor Who and the evil Salamander. First the cast and then the audience were kept in breathless suspense as to which twin had the megalomania.'

December 28

Once again, in the giant halls of Olympia at Earls Court, London, the *Daily Mail*'s Boys' and Girls' Exhibition opens to queues of youngsters stretching almost back to Olympia Underground station. As in the previous three years, one of the prime attractions at the event is the large *Doctor Who* display which, this year, thanks to the policies of Innes Lloyd and Peter Bryant, sports an even wider selection of monsters than before. Principal among these are the Yeti and the Cybermen, each costume being worn by Exhibition staff in specially designed scenarios using some leftover sets from the *Doctor Who* series. According to a report published in the London *Evening News,* the only drawback to being a Yeti at an Exhibition filled to capacity with thronging children is the sheer heat generated inside the heavy costume. This perhaps accounts for one Cyberman's particularly ferocious attitude to youngsters approaching too near the rope barriers – the Cyberman, on several occasions, is seen stepping over the barrier and chasing the offenders out of the display area!

It is at this event that Patrick Troughton makes one of his rare appearances in costume for one afternoon in a publicity exercise. The Christmas/New Year 1967/8 Boys' and Girls' Exhibition is to be the last of its kind, and signals the end of any public displays relating to *Doctor Who* until the early Seventies.

VITALY SABSAY

STUART J. M. HILL

1968

January 27

For the first and only time in the history of the programme, the Doctor appears immediately after the final episode of 'The Enemy of the World' to deliver a message of warning to viewers. Against the background of an Underground set for the next story, 'The Web of Fear' by Mervyn Haisman and Henry Lincoln, he tells the audience, 'Oh, it's you! I thought for one moment . . . Goodness me, I must sit down for a minute. I'm glad I've met you. As a matter of fact, there's something I want to tell you. When we start out on our next adventure, Jamie, Victoria and I meet some old friends and some old enemies – very old enemies! The Yeti as a matter of fact. Only this time they are just a little bit more frightening than last time. So I want to warn you that if your mummy and daddy are scared, you just get them to hold your hand!'

ALAN ROWLEY

Doctor Who now has a new producer in Peter Bryant, who has taken over after several months of understudying Innes Lloyd. Says Bryant: 'I love the monsters in the show and as far as I am concerned we can never get enough of them. I always know how well they are doing by looking at my own children's reactions to the stories. My only regret is that they cost so much that you can never get as many of them as you want in a story.' Derrick Sherwin is appointed his script editor.

February 18

First appearance of Alastair Gordon Lethbridge-Stewart, military man *par excellence*, at present an Army Colonel but later to be promoted a Brigadier and become one of the most famous characters in the series, known more familiarly as 'the Brig'. For actor Nicholas Courtney this is his second appearance on the programme, having previously played Bret Vyon in 'The Daleks' Master Plan' – and with the passage of time he is to enjoy the unique distinction of being the only actor to appear with the first five Doctors. It was the director of the earlier Dalek story, Douglas Camfield, who

DAVID WRIGHT

cast Nicholas as Vyon and then called him up again for 'The Web of Fear'. But the part which is to make him famous is almost given to someone else, as he recalls: 'When Douglas asked me to do "The Web of Fear", originally he asked me to play a captain – Captain Knight. Colonel Lethbridge-Stewart, as he was then, was going to be played by David Langdon. But then something happened and David was offered another part so he couldn't do it. So, I got dragged up and asked would I mind very much playing the colonel instead of the captain? Well, to my way of thinking it was firstly a better part and, secondly, it was promotion! So I said, "Of course I don't mind!" And Colonel Lethbridge-Stewart was born there and then in episode three.'

March 16

The Doctor first uses his remarkable sonic screwdriver in Victor Pemberton's story 'Fury from the Deep'. This small, pencil-shaped device is able to perform a multitude of tasks, from detecting radiation to detonating landmines, and is here employed to open an inspection hatch on a North Sea gas-refinery pipe. As he completes the job, the Doctor grins broadly about his invaluable piece of equipment: 'Neat, isn't it?'

SIMON LEWIS

March 22

The first suggestion that *Doctor Who* is becoming a cult is made by critic Francis Hope in an extensive review of the programme in the *New Statesman.* Describing the series as the 'greatest of all children's-programmes-really-for-adults – the all-time Daddy's electric train', he writes: 'To become truly modish, a cult on the scale of *The Avengers* – a possibly undesirable consummation – *Doctor Who* would have to sharpen its visual style. The opening titles were picked out years ago by the *Times Literary Supplement* in a special number devoted to the avant-garde, and Ron Grainer's backing is as weirdly memorable as anything since *Journey into Space*. But once in the main body of the story, the camerawork dwindles: the Underground, even the deserted Underground, is a familiar property, and last Saturday's episode included some ludicrous larking about on a beach, which was the soggiest possible echo of the obligatory seaside scene in the working-class melodramas of the Fifties.'

Mr Hope has some suggestions for what he sees as 'the strains of constant production': a schedule of six weeks on and six weeks off and perhaps a more regular change of companions. He continues: 'One of the things we would also like to learn is what set the Doctor on his Flying Dutchman travels in space and time in the first place. Like Captain Nemo, he is sometimes a little ostentatiously secretive about his central mystery. Children are not much concerned with such things, and apparently swallowed the change from one actor to another without much difficulty, but adult palates are choosier. Not too choosey, however; *Doctor Who* is obviously one of the BBC's great box-office successes, and no amount of peripheral niggling will alter the fact. It owes little of this to its timing: if anything 5.25 on a Saturday afternoon is an inconvenient slot for adults. It is an inconvenience that some of them have learned to live with. By comparison with

PAUL MAYKELS

much of the literary science fiction available, *Doctor Who* is crude indeed, but a new medium doth make children of us all. *Doctor Who* in colour will be able to get away with anything – for a while.'

April 20

Another companion, Deborah Watling's Victoria, leaves the series after the Doctor's triumph in 'Fury from the Deep'. She has completed 26 episodes, and tells the newspapers: 'It was a great break for me, but from the start I was determined not to stay too long.' Her replacement is to be the elfin-featured Wendy Padbury, who reveals: 'Patrick Troughton has been my favourite actor since I was a child and it is a marvellous opportunity to be able to work with him. I'm hoping to be a bit more in control and a bit less of a screamer than some of the other girls.'

DIANNE BEDFORD

'Evil of the Daleks' starts it second run on BBC Television and becomes the first *Doctor Who* adventure to be reshown in its entirety in this country. Conscious of its status as a repeat, producer Peter Bryant and script editor Derrick Sherwin devise a clever way to introduce the re-run. The previous week, in the last episode of David Whitaker's 'Wheel in Space' the Doctor's newest girl companion, Zoe Herriot (Wendy Padbury), steals aboard the TARDIS. Anxious that the girl should not find herself getting into depths she cannot get out of, the Doctor elects to show her the kind of situations she will be faced with if she travels with him. To this end the Doctor connects himself to an image-producing device and screens for Zoe a vision of his deadliest foes. This leads neatly into the re-run of 'Evil of the Daleks', episode one carrying a voice-over by Patrick Troughton in the opening minute, explaining the sequence of events leading up to the start of the serial. Remarkably perhaps, this repeat showing gains higher ratings than the first run!

Doctor Who fan and newspaper critic George Melly uses the repeat to castigate BBC's summer replacement, the American-made series *The Time Tunnel,* which is described as 'a new adventure series into the fourth dimension'. He calls it a 'four-star bore' with 'cardboard characters, limp dialogue and perfunctory motivation', and goes on: 'It isn't a patch on *Doctor Who,* where quirkiness, bad temper and a respect for the individual more than compensate for the occasional cut-price monster.'

August 10

Three schoolboys fulfil what must be the ambition of millions of young *Doctor Who* admirers – they play the monsters in the Doctor's adventure which opens the sixth season. Because of the diminutive size of the alien Quarks in 'The Dominators' a five-part story by Norman Ashby, director Morris Barry recruits three boys, Gary Smith, Freddie Wilson and John Hicks, to occupy and operate the machines. Even though the youngsters find it difficult to manipulate the tiny Quarks in their cramped interiors, acting in the series proves an unforgettable and unique experience for them!

September 14

Part one of 'The Mind Robber' by Peter Ling is screened on television, marking the culmination of much hard work for Derrick Sherwin. Like one of his predecessors, David Whitaker, Sherwin has found himself on the receiving end when problems with a storyline require the script editor to step into the breach, lock himself away in a room with a typewriter and emerge, a day later, complete with a workable script that uses no extra sets, no locations, no new monsters and no guest cast.

STEPHEN McKAY

The problem arises when 'The Dominators' proves to be unworkable as a six-part script. As money had already been spent on the show designing and building the Quarks, 'The Dominators' cannot be cancelled and so, in a bid to tighten up the action, an episode is hived off it. Thus left with an embarrassing one-week hole in the schedule before the start of 'The Mind Robber', Sherwin elects to graft an extra episode onto the front of Ling's storyline. However, with no sets from 'The Mind Robber' yet available, all Bryant, Sherwin and Director David Maloney have between them is an empty studio, a few stock sets (e.g. the TARDIS) and a couple of old robot costumes from an earlier BBC 2 production. That the finished episode – which bears no credit for a writer – succeeds in becoming one of *Doctor Who*'s most powerful narrative performances says a lot for the skills of Derrick Sherwin, the technical expertise of David Maloney and the acting talents of Patrick Troughton, who recalls later: 'It certainly was a wonderful story. I remember the awful white of the place and those strange robots. Yes, it was marvellous.'

September 19

A Cyberman in the heart of London draws looks of amazement from passers-by. It is not another invasion from space this time (although the Cyberman invasion of London story is only a month or two in the future), but a serious attempt by Kit Pedler to raise money for the blind as part of his campaign *Fight for Sight.* When not involved in creating horrors for *Doctor Who,* or frightening adults with *Doomwatch,* Kit Pedler is a continual campaigner for more funds to aid research into the nature of eye diseases and their cure. A year ago the BBC loaned Pedler one of their Cybermen costumes which has since become a prime weapon in his fund-raising arsenal – frequently seen on the Euston Road holding a tin to attract passers-by. In these instances it is only the sometimes unsympathetic attitudes of policemen, worried about disturbances of the peace, which defeat the warrior from Telos!

September 28

Stop motion animation is used for the Medusa scenes in part three of 'The Mind Robber.' Although this is not the first time animation has been used in the series – hand animation being used for the map sequences in 'Marco Polo', and rostrum camera animation for 'The Moonbase' – this marks the first utilisation of the technique more commonly employed by Ray Harryhausen in films such as *Jason and the Argonauts.*

The short sequence of animation in 'The Mind Robber' – short due to the time and expense involved in using such a technique – focuses on the Medusa's hair, a nest of snakes which gradually come to life to menace Zoe and the Doctor. The frame-by-frame shooting of the Medusa's hair was, for reasons of controllability, shot on film at the BBC's film studios in Ealing. To match this film footage of the Medusa to the studio-recorded scenes involving the Doctor and his companion requires the skills of the inlay operator, whose desk, up in the control gallery, has a bank of switches and buttons that can mix two separate pictures to achieve a composite third.

November 2

Kit Pedler comes up with another winning idea – the creation of UNIT (United Nations Intelligence Taskforce), which is turned into an eight-part serial, 'The Invasion' by Derrick Sherwin, with Brigadier Lethbridge-Stewart as a central character who is to grow ever more popular in the Seventies. Nicholas Courtney says of his role: 'The Brigadier was based on General "Mad Mitch" Mitchell, who was in the news at the time. Like all good officers, he would lead his men from the front and never ask them to do anything he couldn't do. One problem we had to overcome was that Douglas Camfield thought I looked too young to be a colonel, so he insisted I wear a moustache to make me look older. And it has literally stuck with me ever since! It was always a make-up moustache because the kind of moustache I could grow myself never looked Brigadier-ish. So we went through quite a wardrobe of moustaches trying to get the image right. You've perhaps noticed how they've changed over the years?'

'The Invasion' is to become, unintentionally, the blueprint for the way *Doctor Who* is to develop in the 1970s. Much of its success is due to the work of director Douglas Camfield. It was he who arranges for the participation of a battalion of.Coldstream Guards for the major battle sequence in episode eight, as the UNIT troops fight ray-guns with grenades and bazookas in a dazzling display of pyrotechnics. In a classic example of 'not-what-you-know-but-who', Camfield, persuades the Ministry of Defence with help from his friend Lord James, who then commands the barracks at St James, to let him have the soldiers. Happy that the story shows the Army in a sympathetic light, the Defence Ministry grants permission for the battalion to travel to the BBC's training centre in Devesham where the battle scenes are shot.

With this story, Terrance Dicks takes over from Derrick Sherwin as script editor and is to become the longest-serving person in that position. He is also to novelise more Doctors' adventures than any other writer.

PHILIP WAGSTAFF

1969

February 9

MICHAEL P. PAGET

Midway through the screening of Brian Hayles's 'The Seeds of Death', Patrick Troughton announces that he is to retire from playing the role of the Doctor. 'Three years was long enough,' he says later. 'I didn't want to get "typed" and had to get out while the going was good. Peter Bryant had asked me long before how long I would play the part and I had said – three years, no more. You see, say it had gone on for ten years and the BBC had decided to drop it, I would have been sunk. Because after ten years you can't just walk into something else. They'll all say, "Oh, look – its Doctor Who", straight away. Even though before I did *Doctor Who*, I had done a long line of character parts – thirteen years of one part would have been professional suicide. Unless of course, you can go on forever – that would have been all right – but there was no guarantee that the BBC were going to keep it on forever! So I had to decide – three years and I'll get out.'

Initially, it is planned that Patrick will leave in March, but production difficulties cause him to agree to stay until June. In the interim, a successor is found for the role, but information is deliberately withheld . . .

March 1

The last episode of 'The Seeds of Death' finishes on BBC 1 with only one aspect of its production left outstanding – a possible insurance claim against the BBC for a road accident on Hampstead Heath. The Heath is the location chosen by director Michael Ferguson for the scenes of an Ice Warrior ploughing through a fungus-encrusted landscape in search of the Weather Control Centre. The fungus – in reality a further use of the BBC's foam generator – takes some time to set up, leaving the cast with some free time between takes. Still in full costume, Ice Warrior actor Tony Harwood finds he had wandered a little distance from the location and is in full view of the public road. This fact is noted by a woman driver who, on catching sight of the giant green behemoth, is distracted long enough for the car to hit a kerb and go careering into a ditch. To this day no one can recall if the insurance claim was ever made!

March 14

The news of Patrick Troughton's departure from the series has led to inevitable speculation in the press, former BBC man Stuart Hood capturing the mood of the country very nicely in his piece for *The Spectator*. 'What gives added frisson to the present series', he says, 'are the newspaper reports that Doctor Who is to retire at the end of the present season. This means – if the reports are true – that sooner or later this latter-day man of many wiles is not going to get away with it any longer. My circle of child-viewers had prematurely decided that he could not survive the detergent (in "The Seeds of Death"). They are now in a state of agreeable tension over his chances in space. What is interesting is that they are perfectly aware that if the Doctor dies it will be because of decisions taken in the real world by the real man who acts the part. They are perfectly capable, in other words, of distinguishing between the worlds of fantasy, to which they look forward with such anticipation each Saturday, and everyday life.'

Stuart Hood also takes some time to compliment the production team on the superb models in the new story, 'The Space Pirates' by Robert Holmes, and draws an interesting conclusion, referring to what is going on in actual space exploration. (These models are actually made by the BBC's Space Unit, set up to provide special effects for the coverage of the Apollo Moon Shot, in spring 1969.) 'It would not, I think, have been possible to achieve a sequence like that in last Saturday's episode showing men walking in space had we not all by now seen precisely such manoeuvres being carried out by Russian and American cosmo/astronauts. The effect was so excellently simulated that for a moment or two I was undecided whether what I saw was not perhaps a piece of documentary film fed into the programme. It is one of the great strengths of *Doctor Who* that, while it refers back to archetypal situations involving extreme danger and survival from it, it also aims at credibility in detail; for it is on the basis of this credibility that young viewers, who a couple of days before may have watched a space shot from Cape Kennedy or seen men in conditions of weightlessness, are bound to judge it.'

April 19

'The War Games' starts its epic run of ten weeks. This is to be a turning-point in *Doctor Who*'s history, with a lot about the Doctor's background revealed, and with the final episode marking the end of the series in black and white. What few realise is that 'The War Games' could so easily have been the final *Doctor Who* story of all!

The dreaded curse of inflation is beginning to bite heavily into *Doctor Who*'s budget, limiting the show's ability to come up with new and exciting monsters – the greatest expense element on the programme. For some time as well, ratings for the five-and-a-half-year-old series have declined to an average of between four and five million. With Frazer Hines and Wendy Padbury having decided to leave with Patrick Troughton at the end of the season, serious discussions begin taking place at the higher-management levels of the BBC as to whether it is an opportune time to wind up *Doctor Who.* After all, within a few months BBC 1 would be going into colour, introducing it is hoped, a whole new era for the Corporation.

The major problem, it is decided, is what should replace *Doctor Who.* The Saturday tea-time slot is now regarded as an almost obligatory spot for science fantasy/fiction and, while it has been arranged that *Star Trek* will commence its first run on British television after the *Doctor Who* season has finished, the BBC wants to instigate a production of its own to fill the slot once *Star Trek* has run for six months. Many authors are approached to suggest ideas and submit storylines, and these include Terry Nation and Nigel Kneale. During this interim period, though, while ideas are being considered, *Doctor Who* fills in with an open-ended serial that could go on for as long as necessary and then either be wound up, or given a bridge to a new season and a new Doctor.

As things transpire none of the suggested storylines and pilots carry the sheer flexibility of *Doctor Who,* and so producers Peter Bryant and Derrick Sherwin are authorised to seek out their new Doctor, and writers Terrance Dicks and Malcolm

Hulke are commissioned to adjust their final episode so that the Doctor will regenerate again into a new body in time for 1970.

June 21

The end of 'The War Games' and the promise of a new Doctor. But the outgoing holder of the office, Patrick Troughton, sighs with relief. 'We all knew that we were leaving, Frazer, Wendy and I,' he recalls later.' And it was rather like racing for the tape at the end of a long-distance run. And because you knew it was going to end you got terribly tired and giggly, and we hardly got through it for giggling. We suddenly got hysterical giggles by looking at each other. It was simply fatigue. We knew it was going to stop after three years of every Saturday, and then suddenly it would be all over. Still, *Doctor Who* has remained one of the most enjoyable roles I have ever played.'

Not all the members of the press are sure the programme should return, however, and Ann Lawrence of the *Morning Star* delivers another complaint against it. 'The present series of *Doctor Who* is marked by an uncalled-for degree of violence,' she writes. 'Bearing in mind that the programme is compulsive viewing for a very large number of children, and often very young ones at that, this wholesale killing of people in the "War Lords" (*sic*) is unsuitable, to say the least. Complaints were made about previous episodes, that some of the destruction of Daleks, Cybermen, or what have you, had upset younger viewers. But then the argument was that, since these were not humans, it was not quite the same thing. Why then not keep up the air of fantasy and give the children the opportunity to escape from war and destruction for once. There is enough of it in the news bulletin following *Doctor Who.'* And Miss Lawrence concludes: 'If the present series is an indication of the kind of new *Doctor Who* we shall be treated to later in the year, then I would prefer the whole thing to fold up and the Doctor never to be heard of again.'

July 1

Behind the scenes, producer Peter Bryant has lined up his new Doctor, Jon Pertwee, the radio and stage comedian, though not without some soul-searching as he is later quite ready to admit. 'Jon wasn't my first choice,' he says. 'I thought Ron Moody would have been tremendous for the part. But Jon was high up on the list and of course he could do everything – all those voices, all those mannerisms. He seemed to have everything I was looking for to give the show a more light-hearted approach. But in the end, of course, he played it straight – and what a success he was! I think it also established him as an actor in the television public's eyes.' Apart from being unable to get Ron Moody to play the Doctor, Peter Bryant is also to confess that he tried unsuccessfully to get actress Pauline Collins to play a companion. He himself now hands over the reins of the show to Derrick Sherwin, already well versed in the ways of the Doctor from his experiences as writer and script editor.

Sherwin makes his intentions for the show perfectly plain. 'What I want to do', he says, 'is to bring *Doctor Who* down to Earth because the time is ripe for a change. I want to mould the programme along the lines of

the old *Quatermass* serials, which I found so compelling. I want to establish the concept of having things happen down on Earth, with people with everyday lives coming up against the unknown.'

The BBC also decide because of the increasing demands on the programme in terms of technical details and special effects – as well as the pressure on the cast and production staff – a summer break in transmission of an average of six months is to be taken each year. (In future years, repeats of *Doctor Who* stories will be run during these breaks). Stories, too, are to be shorter in length to allow for greater expenditure in their making.

September 15

The colour cameras start rolling on the first episode of Jon Pertwee's story, 'Spearhead From Space', though not in the way the new producer, Derrick Sherwin, would have liked. 'We knew four weeks before we were due to start shooting that we'd lost our studios, so I had to make the decision there and then to do it all on film with the restraint of not being able to get any more money. All our props had to be rebuilt from scratch. We needed to film an episode a week and I had just five days to re-plan and re-script the whole set-up.'

The problem has arisen because of a strike by scenery builders at the BBC's Television Centre where the serial is due to be recorded using the new colour video cameras. Losing that facility means the whole thing has to be done on location and on film – calling for some of the tightest restructuring of a serial ever done for *Doctor Who.* There is, however, room within the production for the odd light-hearted moment, as Jon Pertwee recalls: 'Where we filmed that one was a magnificent seventeenth-century house in the middle of the countryside, used by the BBC as a training centre. While I was looking around one morning I came across this incredible shower unit that a previous owner had had installed. It was a tubular metal frame that enclosed you completely and had a royal crest at the top of it. The water passed through the tubes and so sprayed you from all angles. As soon as I saw this I sought out our director Derek Martinus, and suggested we use this in the story as a kind of visual ad-lib.'

VITALY SABSAY

MARGARET JONES

1970

January 3

The dawn of a new decade and a new era for *Doctor Who* as it is transmitted in colour for the first time, complete with a new Doctor, Jon Pertwee, who has been told to play the role 'as himself'. A long-time viewer of the series himself, Jon has very definite ideas about the character. 'I don't see him as such a clown as Patrick played him,' he says, 'more a folk hero, I suppose, a kind of interplanetary crusader. He'll be a bit like me, too – loving gadgets, driving fast, doing all kinds of devil-may-care things.' For a man who has once worked on a circus Wall of Death, the challenge of *Doctor Who* seemingly holds no fears!

BILL MARSH

This seventh season is to see a strong involvement with the Brigadier and the soldiers of UNIT, and 'Spearhead from Space' also introduces a new companion, Liz Shaw, played by Caroline John, whom the *Sun* newspaper promptly features and calls 'a rather cool scientific lady'. Miss John is said to take her work so seriously that she 'nipped out of the rehearsals when she first took the part to buy a scientific dictionary!' Caroline herself says, 'I had no idea what I was talking about half the time so I thought I'd better find out quick. Then I discovered that the script writers had made up half the scientific words anyway. I don't normally like science fiction, and would never go to watch it. I'm always scared of getting nightmares!'

The press reaction to these changes is enthusiastic: Matthew Coady of the *Daily Mirror* cheers, 'This *Doctor Who* adventure wins my vote as the best in the lifetime of the series so far. What it did was to suggest an authentic sense of the uncanny. Clearly, the tots can take it – although I have been told of some who wouldn't watch. Many of them, though, like adults, enjoy frightening themselves. That, after all, is what invented nightmares are for.' And Mr Coady also has praise for the new Doctor. 'Jon Pertwee's Doctor is wholly acceptable,' he writes. 'Where William Hartnell was comically irascible, and Patrick Troughton like a greying, worried schoolboy, the newest recruit is suave and confident: obviously a Harley Street doctor. At the same time, he manages to look like Danny Kaye while sounding like Boris Karloff – and that's a mixture for the connoisseur.'

January 31

Because of his love of speed and gadgets Jon Pertwee is behind the introduction of an Edwardian four-seater roadster named Bessie, which is to become the Doctor's main mode of transport. The car, one of a

limited edition made by the firm of Siva/Neville Trickett Ltd of Blandford in Dorset, is basically a Ford E93A chassis of the kind used in that company's Popular, Prefect and Anglia ranges from 1940 to 1958. Because the registration number plate WHO 1 is not available, the BBC register the car as MTR 5 for use on public roads and switch to the special plates when filming it on private ground.

Following the car's debut in Malcolm Hulke's 'Doctor Who and the Silurians' (the only serial to bear the Doctor's name in the title), new producer Barry Letts, who has taken over from Derrick Sherwin, tells the press: 'We think viewers will grow quite affectionate towards Bessie.' This proves an understatement and is echoed by the trade magazine *Custom Car*, which says: 'Its appeal is enormous and as a crowd-puller it has few equals.' While the *Daily Sketch* calls it 'the car that gives you 100 smiles an hour'. (Interestingly, the total cost of Bessie is just over £300!)

Jon Pertwee's development in his new role is further praised by Stuart Lane of the *Morning Star:* 'No longer labelled "For Children" – though I'll bet plenty enough will still watch it – and with previously "compulsory" adolescent characters in the cast eliminated, the series has been given a shot in the arm with the advent of Jon Pertwee. We wondered if a trend had set in, if *Doctor Who* would get progressively zanier with Pertwee an established comedian in the lead role. The danger here could have been that if the Doctor had been allowed to get too far-out, his observations on life, science and the universe would become less and less credible. So, with just a hint now and again of a near-slip into *The Navy Lark,* in the new Doctor Who we've got some charm, a suggestion of presence and a restraining pedal on the still-present humour. Given all that – I'd still like to watch him try and get that old banger of his through the door of that police-box spaceship when he takes off again.'

February 21

A process that will give *Doctor Who* a quantum leap forward is tried out for the first time in episode four of 'Doctor Who and the Silurians'. The effect, colour separation overlay (CSO), is used to show Liz and the Doctor in the same frame as a Tyrannosaurus Rex dinosaur. The technique, rather akin to inlay, blends two pictures together electronically: a picture from one camera's point of view, mixes with one from another camera. The trick is that camera 1 is set up not to see a certain colour – usually blue. Thus, on camera 1's set there is, somewhere, a length of blue curtaining which is invisible to camera 1. Camera 2, meanwhile, shoots a dinosaur on a totally blue set. When the images are mixed, camera 1 sees its own set plus only the dinosaur from camera 2's picture. Nowadays CSO is a widely used process on programmes as disparate as *Blake's Seven* and *The Nine O'Clock News,* and use of CSO is understood by virtually any technician at the BBC.

However, this has not always been the case as producer Barry Letts describes, remembering his debut on 'The Silurians': 'Visual Effects saw in the script a requirement for a twenty-foot monster which they then made in the customary way. They produced a man-sized dinosaur suit which was so heavy when worn that in order to support the weight of it, the head had a ring bolt through it, fixed to a line attached to the ceiling. Therefore the actor inside could only move within the narrow radius allowed by the length of the line. After that, they used CSO to make the creature seem large beside Jon Pertwee, and it wasn't until a while afterwards that it dawned on everyone that there was no need to have gone to all the time and expense of building a full-sized suit. They could have achieved exactly the same effect using a puppet two-foot tall operated by rods!'

March 18

The first major *Radio Times* feature on *Doctor Who* is published since the series has gone into colour, although a colour cover advertising the new series has been printed to coincide with week 1 of 'Spearhead from Space'. Unlike many articles before or since, this feature is a serious look at the production both from the point of view of the lead actor, Jon Pertwee, and the production team, headed by Barry Letts and Terrance Dicks. The article gives hefty coverage to the new serial, 'The Ambassadors of Death' written by David Whitaker, looking at many aspects of its composition including costumes, make-up and visual effects. Interviewed about the appearance of the ambassador aliens without their space helmets, make-up Supervisor Marion Richards explains how their hideous looks were achieved with the aid of very fine latex rubber with blue make-up foundation underneath. 'To make the face appear irradiated when the special colour separation overlay process was used, on some parts of his face we used tissue and

COLIN HOWARD

wet latex. Only the human eyes remained recognisable.'

With all of the stories this season being set on Earth more-or-less in the present day, costume designer Christine Rawlings gives her thoughts on the approach to clothing the alien astronauts: 'Because the story was set late in the seventies, I designed a simplified version of the sort of spacesuit we know today.'

But as ever with a *Doctor Who* production, the main field of ingenuity lies with the team handling the complex visual effects for the series. Anna Braybrooke outlines her contribution, the Tyrannosaurus Rex costume for 'Doctor Who and the Silurians', James Ward is complimented on the Silurian heads themselves, and Peter Day takes responsibility for the rocket seen in 'The Ambassadors of Death', belching smoke and steam as it lifts off with the Doctor for a rendezvous in space. Visual Effects boss Jack Kine adds: 'Our motto is "Anything that can be imagined can be made" – it has to be! This place may look like a schoolboy's dream but it can be very hairy and hysterical.'

March 21

'Havoc' brings a new generation of action scene filming both to *Doctor Who* and to BBC TV drama as a whole. Conceived by veteran stunt expert Derek Ware – whose *Doctor Who* track record stretches back almost to the first episode – Havoc is an association of stuntmen available for hire to television productions. For a set fee they co-ordinate and direct all the hazardous and dangerous scenes needed to bring a really exciting action sequence to life. In practical terms this can mean organising everything from a kung fu fight scene in *Steptoe and Son* to a car crash in *Doomwatch.*

Impressed by their portfolio, producer Barry Letts has no qualms about engaging Havoc to handle some of *Doctor Who*'s more demanding set pieces. 'The Ambassadors of Death' is one of their first assignments, the brief for episode one being to conduct a lengthy fight sequence between UNIT troops and a gang of hired mercenaries in a deserted warehouse. The fight entails everything from brutal punch-ups to dramatic falls, but even this pales in comparison to Havoc's role in episode two.

Here, the script calls for a motorcyle-escorted convoy to be held up by a team of raiders using smoke grenades and a helicopter. In a four-minute sequence, Derek Ware is called on to co-ordinate a helicopter bombing-run, stunt crashes on motorcycles, a punch-up and a hazardous escape by the raiders with a UNIT soldier, clinging to the skids of the helicopter, being thrown off in mid-air. With hefty overheads of man hours, specialist equipment and hours of preparation Havoc's services are not cheap, and some of their bigger set pieces have to be confined to *Doctor Who*'s longer six- or seven-part serials. Nevertheless, impressed by their efforts, Barry Letts is keen to use Havoc stuntmen in as many shows as possible.

March 31

The lack of monsters in the current season of *Doctor Who* brings a complaint from *Sun* columnist Ramsden Greig after the second

TIM PIERACCINI

episode of 'The Ambassadors of Death' – despite its being splendidly filmed on location and featuring some superb space models. Mr Greig writes: 'What's gone wrong in the monster-making business at the BBC? Fings ain't what they used to be. Remember the Daleks, the Yeti, the Macra, the Cybermats, the creepy-crawly Mirebeast and the deadly Quarks who sent adult viewers scurrying behind their sofas while the children sat on the edge of their seats glued to *Doctor Who?* By comparison, it's a tame lot of monsters Jon Pertwee has to put up with these days. In the current capers all he has to contend with are creatures with the mundane name of 'alien astronauts'. They wouldn't frighten a highly strung cat.' A BBC spokesman responding to this charge says: 'The show has become so successful that we are now aiming it at adults as well as children. We've got to be more sophisticated.'

May 9

Caroline John begins her last serial in the role of Elizabeth Shaw. The show is 'Inferno' by Don Houghton, a seven-parter remarkable for being the only instance – allowing for the abrupt handover of Mary Tamm to Lalla Ward as Romana – where an outgoing companion has not been given a 'writing-out' scene. In this instance producer Barry Letts attributes the fault to his rapid takeover of the producer's chair from Derrick Sherwin. Due to the almost non-existent transition period, Letts has spent most of his first season picking up the reins of stories already commissioned and contracted. Only after several months' solid work on the show – which includes a lengthy spell of directing 'Inferno' in place of Douglas Camfield, who fell ill – is Letts able to consider his own approach to the series. By that time 'Inferno' is 'in the can' and any explanations for a companion changeover are left till the new season.

'The assistant I had inherited was Caroline John . . . a polymath who could answer practically any question on any discipline,' Letts explains. 'Caroline is a very good actress, and has played at the National and all that sort of thing, so the fact that we dropped her after a season has nothing to do with her ability. It had to do with the designing of the character who was supposed to be a brilliant Cambridge scientist . . . So the consequence was that when anything came up, she discussed it with the Doctor more or less as an equal. We didn't have anybody who could say, "Doctor, what's all this about?"' The way has been paved for the introduction of Jo Grant.

June 20

Havoc's work in *Doctor Who* receives its first notice of public acclaim in the *Daily Express* as 'Inferno' reaches the final episode: 'The present television series of *Doctor Who* comes to a finish with a bang, and helping to provide it, in a spectacular manner, is stuntman Roy Scammell, aged thirty-four,' reports the paper. 'In what is described as TV's highest fall yet Roy plunges 50 feet from a gasholder. Of course, it's a feat that needs careful preparation and Roy supervises from start to finish. Dozens of cardboard boxes are placed at the base of the holder and these are covered with mattresses and foam rubber. When everything is to Roy's satisfaction he then completes his blood-chilling leap. The stunt takes place at Hoo, near Strood, Kent, just another job in Roy's life of thrills.'

For his efforts on 'Inferno' Roy Scammell is awarded a mention in the current *Guinness Book of Records,* another first for *Doctor Who.*

For Nicholas Courtney, who is now well on the way to establishing 'the Brig' as among the most successful characters in the series, 'Inferno' proves to be a favourite story, as he later recalls: 'I very much enjoyed this fourth story with Jon because I got to play two parts, the Brig and his Fascist counterpart with the eyepatch, scar and bombastic attitude which, actually, I modelled very much on Mussolini. I particularly liked the story for its contrasts and for letting me play two parts.' He does not, however, share the fear of most actors

RONALD BINNIE

in *Doctor Who* of becoming typecast. 'It did cross my mind, of course,' he says, 'and I once said to Barry Letts that I wouldn't mind being written out of the series so long as they let me go in a blaze of glory. But he only said, "No, no, we want to keep you" – and so I've stayed ever since!'

August 20

During *Doctor Who*'s break from transmission, producer Barry Letts and script editor Terrance Dicks devise the character of a man who is destined – rather like the Daleks – to threaten even the Doctor's popularity as the most outstanding figure in the series: the Master. Letts and Dicks want a regular villian to play opposite the Doctor – a renegade Time Lord as hellbent on evil and destruction as the Doctor is on peace and justice. They find the perfect actor to play the role in Roger Delgado, a man of Satanic dark looks with a long history of playing villains. He is also blessed with a laconic sense of humour and an ability to mix charm with absolute ruthlessness when playing a role – in marked contrast to his gentle and charming nature off screen. Barry Letts is never in any doubt they have the right man. 'As soon as we thought of the character I knew who I wanted to play it. I'd known Roger for many years. I remember having a great sword fight with him in the surf near Hastings in a costume drama we appeared in together. He had the enormous capacity for villainy – and charm – that the part of the Master demanded.' Delgado is equally enthusiastic about the part. 'I like playing villains,' he says. 'I am often chosen by directors to play wicked men because I have a beard, a menacing chin and piercing eyes. I know from the letters I get that I'm the man people love to hate.' As one newspaper puts it, the man who has been a blackguard almost all his professional life is about to embark on probably his most successful role . . .

September 18

Shooting begins on the eighth season of *Doctor Who* at Chipperfield's Circus, where the first location filmed inserts for Robert Holmes's 'Terror of the Autons' are taken. Although no one knows it at the time the new serial is to prove a trend-setter for the series, with many of its production values still in operation today. To begin with, producer Barry Letts is able to modify the season-length of 26 weeks to include a balance between four-part and six-part stories. The four-part stories have dramatic appeal in the eyes of script editor Terrance Dicks, while six-parters are favoured by Barry Letts for the larger budgets they give to a serial. More significantly 'Terror of the Autons' inaugurates the practice of recording two episodes per fortnight, rather than one episode per week. This allows more, and sometimes larger, sets to be built, since all the sets for one episode do not have to be present as in the former continuous recording environment, where all the scenes for one episode are shot on one day. Under Letts's new format the UNIT laboratory set, for instance, only

NICK HARRIS

needs to be erected once over the fortnight. Thus all the scenes in episodes three and four can be shot in one evening, thereby freeing studio space for the following day to concentrate on a larger more elaborate set, the footage from which will be edited into the two episodes during post-production. The advantages are considerable. Set designers and builders have ten days instead of five to prepare, artists have longer to read and rehearse scripts, and directors are given more flexibility to plan and arrange exterior filming.

1971

January 2

The eighth season is launched with *Doctor Who* on the front cover of the *Radio Times* and a special feature inside, 'Doctor Who v the Master', which spotlights Jon Pertwee, Roger Delgado and Barry Letts. The producer explains he has been making some changes to the series: 'Like most of the cast I'm an avid science fiction man,' he says. 'I mean science fiction rather than science fantasy. And that means making sure it's believable.' Rather than having the Doctor 'zooming off on so many wild adventures', he is to have an opponent truly worthy of his mettle, the Master, described as Moriarty to Doctor Who's Sherlock Holmes.

'But I think he's more than a Moriarty,' says Roger Delgado who reveals that he three times previously tried to break into the series. 'In considering my approach to the part I've been very wary of repeating some of my past heavily accented baddies. Equally, though, you can't be too light-hearted – though I don't think that will happen. Why, I remember starting sixteen years ago in *Midday Matinees* and being faced with a quite unbelievable line, "Come in and put your feet up on the Algerian poof." If you can handle something like that, then you can handle anything!' he says.

The article reports that Jon Pertwee is his effervescent self, creating a happy, almost family-like atmosphere on the set when shooting takes place. He loves to regale people with stories of things that have happened to him since becoming the Doctor; a particular favourite dates from the previous year when he was in Morocco and was suddenly stopped by a policeman. *'M'sieur – un moment s'il vous plaît'* 'Oh, er – what is it?' *'Pardon, mais c'est* Doctor Who, *n'est-ce-pas?'* 'My God! I mean, yes!'

'Terror of the Autons' also introduces the new companion, Jo Grant, played by Katy Manning, twenty-one years old and just a year out of drama school. 'I'd watched the show since I was a kid and thought it would be great fun to do,' she says.

January 16

Instant fame for the Master after his appearance in his horsebox-shaped TARDIS. Philip Phillips of the *Sun* runs a feature on Roger Delgado headlined 'He Just Hates To Be Nice', in which he states: 'His name may not mean much to you, but when I tell you he plays the villainous Master in *Doctor Who,* you will, I am certain, know him and join me in a hiss, boo and a jeer. Delgado knows from the letters he has received from some of the millions of children and adults who watch *Doctor Who* that he's already a hit. But one or two kids have complained he is not wicked enough! This hurts the Master who, through me, issued this communiqué to them: "Trust me. You haven't seen anything yet. Two weeks from now I really get going!"' Prophetic words indeed . . .

January 18

A spectacular stunt that nearly ends in disaster and fierce controversy are part and parcel of 'Terror of the Autons', which producer Barry Letts also directs. The stunt involves the Doctor and Jo when they are

PAUL VYSE

saved from extinction by a car knocking an Auton over a cliff. Inside the Auton is Terry Walsh, who plans to have the car stop short and then bounce back a few feet. However, in performing the stunt he bounces back too far and hurtles headlong down many feet of a scree slope, providing what is still the most spectacular fall ever seen in *Doctor Who.* Terry, luckily, is unharmed.

It is the Autons, too, who are the subject of the controversy that has parents telephoning and writing to the BBC to complain, and Sylvia Clayton of the *Daily Telegraph* advances their arguments in her column: 'What level of horror is acceptable in a tea-time programme?' she asks. 'The present *Doctor Who* adventure makes this question pertinent by the very effectiveness of its attack on the nerves. These plastic monsters come from within the range of a child's domestic scene. There is a murderous mannikin doll with deadly fangs, a chair which inflates to suffocate the victim, a telephone flex which strangles the caller. Policemen with apparently normal faces whip off their masks to show a hideous non-face underneath. Small children of my acquaintance have found these devices terrifying in a way fantasy figures such as the Daleks and the Cybermen were not. It seems to me specious to argue, as the BBC does, that there are no specfic programmes for children at weekends, but all are designed for family viewing. *Doctor Who* is placed at a time when the smallest children will be watching, and adult frissons are best left to *Doomwatch.*'

Barry Letts later admits to faults in this story. 'It got us into quite a lot of trouble,' he says. 'You may remember that the alien life-form had the power to bring plastic to life. We had letters telling us of children who were afraid to take their teddy bears to bed in case they came to life and strangled them; and a pained letter from Scotland Yard complaining that our plastic killer-policemen were undoing all their efforts to persuade children to see the local constable as a friend. Though we went too far on this occasion, I was always very keen to relate the stories to reality.'

February 6

As a small extra in his script for part two of 'The Mind of Evil', witer Don Houghton includes a minute-long section of dialogue to be spoken in Chinese. Although not fluent in Chinese himself, Don Houghton's wife is the actress Pik-Sen Lim, who also guest stars in this story as Captain Chin Lee, the Master's servant. This section of authentic dialogue was carefully rehearsed by Jon Pertwee and Kristopher Kum under the coaching of Pik-Sen Lim, who suggests this introductory exchange between the Doctor and Chinese delegation leader Fu Peng to lend credence to the Doctor's supposed powers to speak any language. So that the audience is not left out during this sequence, director Tim Combe arranges to have a set of subtitles flashed onto the TV screen. To date this remains the only use of formal subtitles in the series.

March 20

The second complaint of the year about *Doctor Who* – this time from a most unexpected source, the Doctor himself! Or to be precise, the first Doctor, William Hartnell. In an interview with Shaun Usher of the *Daily Sketch,* he says that he no longer switches on with millions of other viewers each Saturday afternoon to watch the series. 'I haven't done much television since leaving,' he says from his Sussex home, 'but I don't regret going. I'm over sixty and it's time to start taking things a bit easier. But what I do regret is the way *Doctor Who* is no longer a programme for children. That's why I hardly ever watch it.'

M. HYLAND

Describing Hartnell as 'the first, and for some of the show's addicts, the best of the time-travelling Doctors' – Usher reflects that it is probably being a children's favourite that 'deep down is what he'll be missing this afternoon.' And of Hartnell's faith that the show would run for at least five years, he adds: 'Now, the better part of eight years later, he has been proved pessimistic, if anything. But the veteran actor gets little satisfaction from the victory.' Evidently, Shaun Usher knew nothing of the debilitating illness that was afflicting the original Doctor . . .

March 27

The interior of the Doctor's TARDIS is seen again, for the first time in the Jon Pertwee era, in 'The Claws of Axos' with hefty modifications having been performed on the console. The original console, designed and built for the series back in 1963, lasted right through to the serial 'Inferno' in 1970, though by then much of its electrically driven apparatus had long since ceased to function. Features of this original console included banks of sequentially flashing lights, a series of working dials and indicators, two rotating strobe-effect lanterns and, most impressive of all, a central illuminated perspex time-rotor which could rise, fall and rotate on cue. A combination of damage and age decreed that the old console be finally scrapped in 1970, and for its successor the designers put the emphasis on durability and ease of repair.

Slightly smaller in diameter than the Mark I version, the new console is painted white rather than pale green (under the right lighting conditions pale green, on a black and white picture, can look more gleaming white than white itself); it has a similar configuration of knobs and dials though fewer of them are working props; and a far more simple central column, capable only of up and down movement. The operation of the central column provides the designers with recurrent headaches brought on by attempts to devise a robust mechanism that will not break down. Over the next few years many methods will be tried including a camshaft device, a compressed-air-driven piston, an electromagnet, and even, on one occasion, a studio technician, hidden out of camera shot, pushing the column up and down manually!

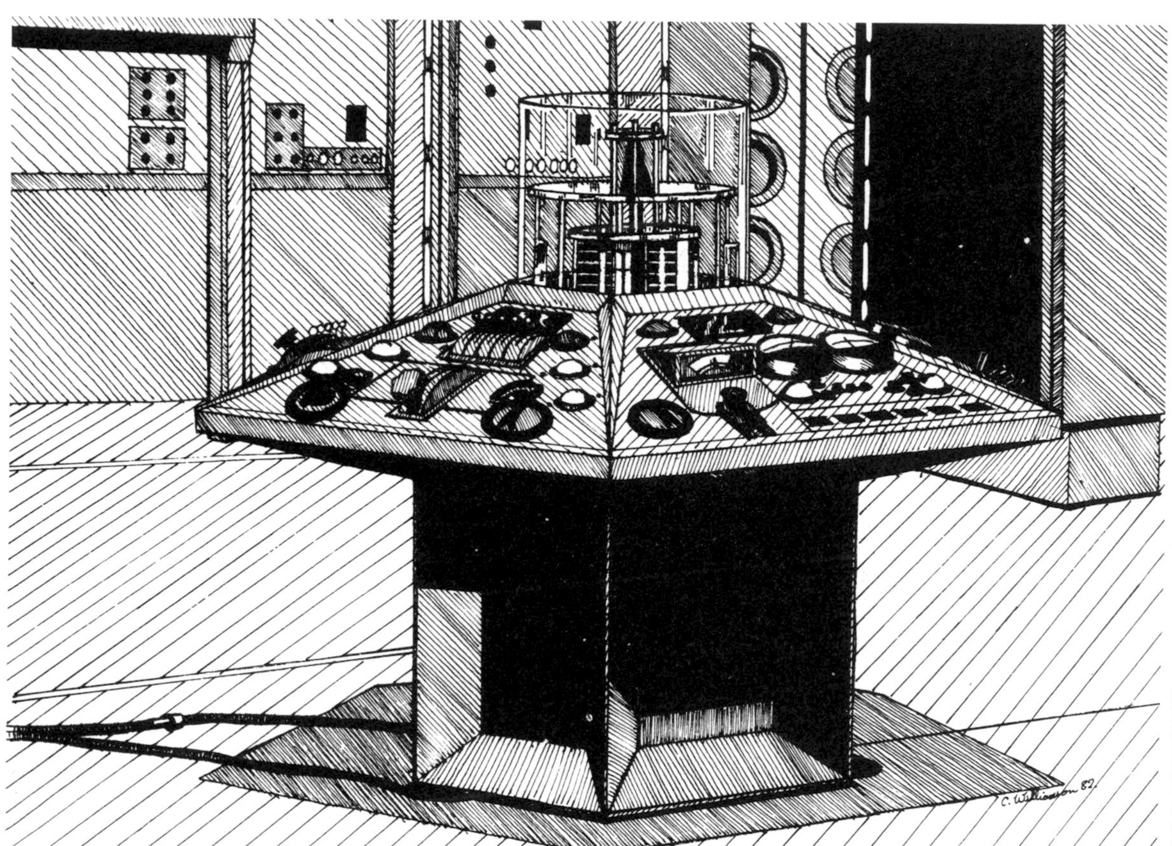
CLIVE N. WILLIAMSON

April 10

Episode one of 'Colony in Space' by Malcolm Hulke begins, and for the first time in nearly two years the Doctor is given a temporary reprieve from exile and allowed to make a journey in the TARDIS. To commemorate this long-awaited occasion, the *Radio Times* publishes the opening half of the episode as a lavishly illustrated strip cartoon, with two pages in full colour as part of its feature on *Doctor Who* for the week of 10 April. The strip is by artist Frank Bellamy, well known to readers of *Look and Learn* and *TV 21* for his richly illustrated features on the life of Winston Churchill, and the *Thunderbirds* television series. So impressed are the editors of *Radio Times* with Bellamy's work on the 'Colony in Space' strip that he is commissioned to produce one panel of *Doctor Who* artwork per week to go with the formal credits section – each issue, starting the next season with 'The Day of the Daleks'. In each case Bellamy draws a full A3-sized panel of artwork, but this is always reduced to the size of a postage stamp for publication. Between 1972 and 1977 Frank Bellamy is a regular contributor of artwork, especially for *Doctor Who,* to the *Radio Times.* Only his untimely death that year ceases the flow.

After all the recent criticism in the press, reviews for 'Colony in Space' are enthusiastic. The *Sun* declares: 'Cape flapping and nostrils flaring, Doctor Who is off again on his inter-planetary travels to the relief of parents all over the country. The very popular series has been coming in for a lot of criticism recently because, instead of the reliable and basically unbelievable monsters from outer space, recent storylines have relied upon more earthbound subjects. While he fights Daleks and so forth, few children can be genuinely upset. It was when policemen turned out to be faceless monsters that children got worried and their parents disturbed. Now, however, sense seems to have prevailed and the Doctor and Jo are off once again on the interplanetary circuit.'

ANDREW FOURNIER

May 4

The Doctor learns he has one very distinguished fan indeed: the Queen. Her Majesty visits the Royal Festival Hall in London to be present at a radiophonic concert being staged by the BBC's Radiophonic Workshop. Formed in 1958, the workshop which actually pioneered electronic music in Britain, creates music for over two hundred programmes a year at its Maida Vale studios – among which is *Doctor Who.* And in being introduced to Desmond Briscoe, head of the Workshop, the Queen remarks, 'The Radiophonic Workshop? Ah yes, *Doctor Who?'* As *The Sunday Times* is to note later: 'The Queen neatly expressed everything most of us know about the workshop.'

May 22

There is a dramatic increase in the ratings when episode one of 'The Daemons' written by Barry Letts and Robert Sloman under the pen-name of Guy Leopold, is transmitted at the later time of 6.15. For this story, director Christopher Barry is allowed a luxury accorded few of the series' directors: on location shot scenes – which

ANDREW MARTIN

DAN SCHAEFER

comprise almost half the five-part story – he is granted the use of four film cameras instead of the usual one. Thus, for each action sequence – such as the attack on Bessie by a hijacked UNIT helicopter – each shot is captured by four cameras positioned to cover different angles. Very expensive in terms of film and film-processing costs, the dividends prove to be enormous, the extra cameras assisting the flow of the serial and giving it a finished gloss akin to more accepted film series like ITV's *The Persuaders.* In addition Barry is also permitted to film several night-time scenes – again an expensive venture, due to the cost of paying actors and technicians unsocial hours overtime rates. This proves to be the first time in *Doctor Who*'s history that extensive night filming is done, but it turns out likewise to be a factor towards according this serial a classic status even among other outstanding serials.

July 6

On location filming scenes for the forthcoming 'The Day of the Daleks', Jon Pertwee takes time off from the set to talk to journalist Ann Pacey about the BBC's plans for *Doctor Who* when it returns in January 1972. The emphasis, he says, will be to aim for the grown-up audience – just what Barry Letts, Derrick Sherwin and Peter Bryant had intended. 'Seventy per cent of our viewers now are grown-ups. The viewing figures have been going up and up, particularly since we switched times. The show now goes out about an hour later than the earlier series. When we come back in January we could be later still, which could have some interesting results. We might lose some of the remaining child-viewers, but we could gain a whole new adult audience.'

With the series now firmly assured of a future, thanks to the success of the past two seasons, work on the five shows that now comprise a season still takes up three-quarters of the year. But to the regular cast and crew alike it is an easier arrangement than the year-round treadmill of the series' black-and-white days. 'It is the best job on television,' says Jon Pertwee. 'I'm working nine months a year with the BBC. On ITV you'd probably get double the money, but not work for nine months of each year.'

ALAN ROWLEY

July 9

BBC 1 elects to repeat 'Spearhead from Space' over four consecutive Fridays, thereby making it the first *Doctor Who* serial to be re-run outside the conventional Saturday slot, and featuring, somewhat against the BBC's subsequent policies on *Doctor Who,* a companion other than the one involved in the current series. The choice of 'Spearhead from Space' for re-running is a popular one, brought on, in the main, by the exceptionally favourable response the show received on its first transmission back in January 1970.

October 26

As part of their week-long filming down at Portsmouth and the Isle of Wight the *Doctor Who* production team shooting

Malcolm Hulke's 'The Sea Devils' is allowed aboard *HMS Reclaim* to do the underwater diving scenes required for the story. This is to prove the most hardware-orientated serial in the series so far, superceding even 'The Invasion', with its inclusion of scenes involving a helicopter, a hovercraft, a turret-mounted 'pom-pom' gun, two one-man speed-boats, a diving bell, and *HMS Reclaim* itself. The Royal Navy agree, some months previous, to Barry Letts's request for help with this story, subject to the scripts' showing the Navy in a favourable light, which is often a pre-condition for any drama or documentary production requiring the co-operation of the armed forces. For their part, the Navy arranges for director Michael Briant and his team to shoot scenes showing the diving bell in action, and, later, the 'pom-pom' gun being fired.

MIKE GOODMAN

December 29

Encouraged by the success of the 'Spearhead from Space' re-run during the summer, BBC 1, as part of its Christmas fare, repeats the phenomenally successful story 'The Daemons'. However, instead of showing all five episodes the material is condensed down into a ninety-minute edition, thereby losing almost a full episode's worth of narrative. The venture is, nonetheless, well received and the practice of repeating *Doctor Who* serials in ombinus form continues, off and on, throughout the next five years. Other serials repeated in one-off omnibus form are 'The Sea Devils' (shown twice), 'The Day of the Daleks', 'The Green Death', 'Planet of the Spiders', 'The Ark in Space', 'The Genesis of the Daleks', 'The Sontaran Experiment', 'The Pyramids of Mars' and 'The Brain of Morbius'. 'The Seeds of Doom', originally scheduled to be re-shown as an omnibus edition on 11 December 1976, is cancelled in favour of screening a special Gerry Anderson pilot show called *Into Infinity.*

1972

January 1

Bringing a happy new year to many nostalgic *Doctor Who* fans, the Daleks at long last return to the series in part one of 'The Day of the Daleks' by Louis Marks, carrying on the Dalek tradition of not being fully revealed in the plot until the last minute of the episode. Not allowing for the re-run of 'Evil of the Daleks', this is the first appearance of the Daleks in *Doctor Who* since 1967 and their return helps to boost the series ratings even higher – to nearly nine million – spawning a whole new range of Dalek and *Doctor Who* merchandise over the next few years, and counteracting the dearth of material since the petering out of Dalekmania in 1966.

PAUL MAYKELS

Keen to boost public interest in *Doctor Who* Jon Pertwee and Barry Letts are guests at a Christmas show at the London Planetarium, at which the Daleks, along with the Ogrons and the Sea Devils are unveiled to an audience of enthralled youngsters.

The return of the Daleks to *Doctor Who* also marks the beginning of the BBC's domination of Saturday evening viewing, a reign that will last for the next six years. With great foresight of things to come the *Daily Mail* predicts, in an article published 1 January: 'Saturdays belong to the BBC. It is the heaviest viewing night of the week and old Auntie BBC lifts her skirts to pitch unashamedly after the audience ratings. This evening, for instance, Paul Fox, the BBC 1 Controller, gives the viewer absolutely no excuse for switching to the opposition. From 5.00 p.m. to midnight it is a solid slab of undemanding entertainment. The 'secret weapon' that Fox has been guarding this past month is finally unmasked with the return of *Doctor Who* (5.50 p.m.). It is, of course, those atrophied, metallic monsters the Daleks, programmed to AN-NI-HIL-ATE the enemy, particularly on ITV. Those lovable horrors are nine years old, which means that some of the original young viewers will now be watching with their own children.'

January 22

With the ending of 'The Day of the Daleks', *Sun* critic Chris Kenworthy examines the latest adventure and looks to what the

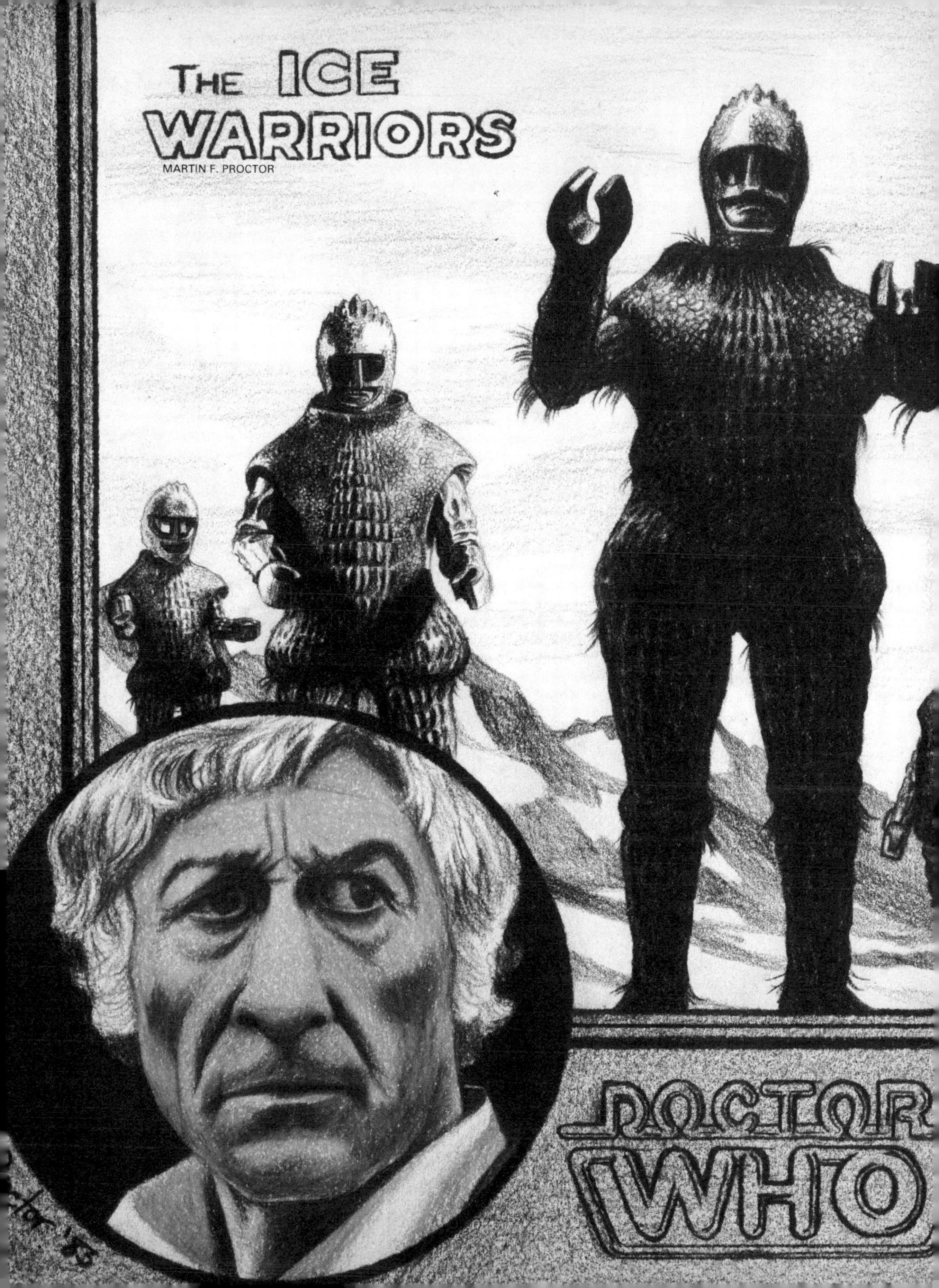

THE ICE WARRIORS

MARTIN F. PROCTOR

DOCTOR WHO

future holds: 'Those preposterous pepper-pots, the Daleks, have been decidedly annoying a lot of people who think it's about time the BBC exterminated them once and for all,' he writes. 'After all, the Daleks have had nine years, half a dozen previous TV series and two films in which to demolish the Doctor. Each time they've muffed it and ended up with a set of severely blown fuses.' Why, he asks, don't the BBC do away with them and look for a new idea? 'Well, they did try to put the Daleks on the scrapheap. The trouble is that the kids wouldn't let them. In fact, there have been no new Dalek adventures on TV for five years and in that time the BBC have had a steady trickle of requests that they should be brought back. When the tin-plated horrors finally did reappear at the beginning of the year, audience figures for *Doctor Who* doubled.' Kenworthy is therefore in no doubt that there are plenty of people who *do* like the Daleks – and cites all the available merchandising: Dalek suits for children, plastic Daleks in cornflake packets, and 'many other home-spun Daleks'. Terry Nation, he says, even keeps four in his garage to lend out to church fêtes and similar functions. 'Oh, yes,' he concludes, 'The BBC were right to bring back the revolting, deeply loved Daleks. The real question is: should we be quite so glad to see them?'

January 29

One of only two Jon Pertwee stories not to use any exterior filmed locations is transmitted as the Doctor and Jo arrive on a wind-swept planet in part one of 'The Curse of Peladon'. Although all of the serials can afford to 'go outside', if only for one day's shooting, Brian Hayles's ghost-story is set firmly inside the walls and cave galleries of a royal castle – the only exterior scenes required are the initial ones, as the TARDIS arrives on a mountain slope. All these sequences are done without setting foot outside BBC premises. The initial materialisation of the TARDIS is filmed on a model stage at the special effects workshop at Television Centre; the scenes of Jo and the Doctor climbing the mountain itself are done at Ealing film studios, and the distance shot of the TARDIS tumbling off the slope and falling hundreds of feet is a gallery-controlled scene combining film, a caption slide and CSO.

The only other Jon Pertwee serial not to use exteriors is Hayles's sequel story, 'The Monster of Peladon', two years later.

'The Curse of Peladon' re-introduces the Ice Warriors for a successful third time, and also provides a leading role for the 'Son of Doctor Who', David Troughton, eldest son of the second Doctor, who plays King Peladon.

January 30

Doctor Who on the BBC's 'black list'? Yes, according to a report in the *Daily Express* which says: 'Of all the out-of-this-world places to find Doctor Who, none is more unbelievable and fantastic than his arrival this week in the BBC's top ten "black list" of most violent TV programmes. Even more stunned by the event is the good Doctor himself, Jon Pertwee, whose seven-year-old son is understandably a devoted fan of the series. To this development, Pertwee replies: 'Rubbish. Our programme isn't violent, it's all just fantasy. There is no blood, no pain – it wouldn't upset an eighty-year-old maiden aunt and my young son loves it. Of course the whole point of science fiction is to be a bit scary, but I think the most alarming item in the programme is our electronic theme music at the beginning. And that is always shown with a rather benign picture of me to reassure the viewers.'

RONALD BINNIE

February 12

A nationwide strike by electrical workers begins to bite hard as many areas across the country are hit by random power-cuts, some lasting over an hour. Among those feeling particularly hard hit by the continuing industrial action are followers of TV serials like *Coronation Street* and *Doctor Who.* Both TV channels, answering letters to the newspapers, state they will not be able to find repeat slots to show episodes missed by viewers experiencing power cuts. But a report in the London *Evening Standard* states: 'Each new *Coronation Street* or *Doctor Who* will start by putting you in the picture about the previous episode.'

Most affected of the *Doctor Who* episodes is part three of 'The Curse of Peladon', which is blotted out through most of South West England and South Wales. Desperate to maintain their collections, some *Doctor Who* fans resort to fail-safe methods of securing their episodes – plugging portable television sets into car batteries and recording the show on battery-driven tape-cassette machines!

April 20

The first book to look seriously behind the programme's cameras is published in the form of *The Making of Doctor Who* by Malcolm Hulke and Terrance Dicks.

The book is, by admission of author Terrance Dicks, inspired by the Whitfield/Roddenberry publication *The Making of Star Trek,* itself a pioneer in

TIM PIERACCINI

going behind the scenes on a modern TV science fiction series. Significantly in paperback form, and with a retail price of only 25p, the book is the first work to document the travels of the Doctor up to *The Sea Devils,* and to show the way in which a story evolves right from the opening discussions between the producer, script editor and writer, to final transmission of the completed episodes. Coming in the wake of the new upsurge in *Doctor Who*'s popularity, the book is an instant hit, opening up a market for *Doctor Who* books and publications that will be fulfilled more and more in the coming years.

June 24

The final episode of Robert Sloman's 'The Time Monster' is shown, the last serial – though no one realises it then – in which the complete line-up of Jon Pertwee regulars is mustered. In many subsequent interviews for television and magazines the cast involved at this period in the show's history cite this as a very happy time in their careers; working together more as a family than a team to push forward what was becoming an increasingly popular programme. The regulars comprise Jon Pertwee as the Doctor, Katy Manning as Jo Grant, Nicholas Courtney as the Brigadier, Roger Delgado as the Master, Richard Franklin as Captain Yates and John Levene as Sergeant Benton. Although Yates does not appear in the final episode of 'The Time Monster' – thus making episode four the last occasion when all six regulars are present – another actor who does appear is Dave Prowse, playing the Minotaur – and four years later he is destined to become world famous as the evil Darth Vader in the blockbuster film *Star Wars.*

SIMON LEWIS

July 1

Some seven years after its first release in the cinemas *Doctor Who and the Daleks* is shown for the first time on BBC 1, the weekend following the last episode of the ninth season. Several reasons account for the relatively long delay in getting these still-popular matinee films onto television. First, it has until now been considered unwise to screen them as they are, technically, 'out of Doctor', featuring Peter Cushing instead of Jon Pertwee. Secondly, it takes till 1972 to renegotiate the BBC's agreement with Terry Nation's agents about not screening Dalek material. And,

thirdly, despite being seven years old, the film, and its sequel, *Daleks – Invasion Earth 2150 AD*, have been pulling in young audiences at cinemas, thereby making the distributing company wary about releasing them for television.

The screening of the film is preceded on Friday and Saturday by airings of the little-seen trailer for *Doctor Who and the Daleks* – a dynamic montage of Dalek scenes from the film, with a specially dubbed voice-over by Peter Hawkins, using the Dalek ring modulator, who warns the audience that every sound they utter the Daleks can hear, every move they make the Daleks can see . . .

December 27

As a commercial for the forthcoming tenth anniversary season, BBC 1 airs a thirty-second trailer for 'The Three Doctors' which features what was to have been the new theme music for *Doctor Who.* At Barry Letts' request, the Radiophonic Workshop re-arranged Ron Grainer's famous theme using their new generation of music synthesisers. The finished piece is applied to several of the new season's stories before Letts decides that the theme does not carry enough weight to do justice to the series. Hurriedly the old theme is grafted onto the episodes due for transmission – though the trailer, prepared some weeks earlier by the BBC's Presentation Wing, retains the new music. Oddly enough, the second episode of 'Carnival of Monsters'

The Master (Roger Delgado), the greatest of the Doctor's humanoid enemies

Above: The futuristic Whomobile demonstrating its capabilities in 'Planet of the Spiders' (1974)

Left: The Doctor's veteran tourer, Bessie, in 'Inferno' (1970)

Left: The girl who brought sex appeal to Doctor Who, *Louise Jameson, in 'The Robots of Death' (1977)*

Below: The Doctor's redoubtable robot, K9, and Sarah Jane Smith (Elisabeth Sladen) in K9 and Company

Right: The fourth Doctor, Tom Baker, giving a remarkable impression of Sherlock Holmes in 'The Talons of Weng-Chiang' (1977)

Overleaf: The Cybermen, another of the Doctor's most popular enemies, in 'Revenge of the Cybermen' (1975)

supplied to Australia retains the new theme and is the only instance of this version being heard by the public except on the BBC trailer.

December 30

Having kept details carefully under wraps, Barry Letts and Terrance Dicks unveil their unique story to mark ten years of the programme, 'The Three Doctors', which brings William Hartnell, Patrick Troughton and Jon Pertwee all together at one time. The story is given widespread press coverage in the Saturday papers, and the *Radio Times* provides a main feature story by Michael Wynn Jones, in which he describes the Doctor as 'seemingly everlasting – a space- and time-traveller, meddler and fixer extraordinary.' He has, says Jones, 'at the ripe old age of 755, grown not older but ever more youthful, jollier rather than more intolerant, more athletic rather than decrepit.' The piece also describes how this transformation has taken place through the work of the three actors involved, by interviewing each of them. 'The original Doctor was pig-headed and irascible, certainly,' says William Hartnell, 'but there was almost an element of magic in him – and that was what I tried to bring out.' Patrick Troughton who took over continues: 'It was perfectly feasible. We are all different aspects of the same character. Of course it's bound to be a bit of a mystery to us, but in the Doctor's space-time machine the so-called past just doesn't exist.' Jon Pertwee sees more than a little of his own love of adventure in the character, and also takes the opportunity to refute suggestions that because of recent achievements in space-flight the programme has lost some of its appeal. 'If anything,' he says, 'they've made it more appealing. They've stimulated imaginations. What, just because we discovered that the moon is uninhabited? How do you know there aren't "dust animals" that we can't even conceive of? We tend to think of life on other planets in forms we know. But why?' All three Doctors, in fact, share this view; William Hartnell speaks for all of them: 'Certainly I believe there is life on other planets – and they know there's life there but don't have the technology to get through.'

The 'lost' Doctor Who *story, 'Shada', made in 1979. The Doctor and Romana II (Lalla Ward) study the mysterious book* The Ancient Law of Gallifrey

There has to be a great deal of last-minute rewriting of the script by Terrance Dicks as neither he nor Barry Letts are aware of how fragile is William Hartnell's health until just before shooting commences. His scenes are all pre-filmed at Ealing Studios in what is to prove his last performance as an actor. In the original script, instead of merely appearing on a monitor screen, the first Doctor was to have made a dramatic appearance in the flesh during the last episode as all the Doctors confront the renegade Time Lord Omega for the showdown. As it is, the three performers only meet briefly for a press photocall.

After completing 'The Three Doctors', Patrick Troughton is to bemoan the fact that his beloved recorder was blown up during the filming. Nevertheless, he can take comfort from the widely held belief that his adoption of the instrument has done much to revive interest in it among school-children!

IVAN JOHN PHILLIPS

1973

January 1

There is widespread approval among the TV critics for 'The Three Doctors', led by Richard Last in the *Daily Telegraph*: 'When the definitive treatise on television durability comes to be written,' he says, 'a special chapter will have to be devoted to *Doctor Who.* This apparently indestructible series, ten years old this year, returned with a promising new breed of monsters, a destructive force which manifests itself as a paint blob, and an ingenious plot device whereby the two previous Doctors appeared simultaneously with the present incumbent. What keeps *Doctor Who* forever young, as opposed to some half-hearted adult excursions into science fiction, is the absolute conviction. You feel that for the twenty-five minutes of the programme at least everyone concerned believes fervently in time-slips, space lords, and the dread perils that menace us from galactic space.' Even the *Daily Mirror*'s Matthew Coady, who had been complaining about the lack of imagination in the series a year before, sees a great improvement: 'The significant thing about Saturday's opener', he writes, 'was an increased reliance on technological tricks. For ten years now, this has been predominantly an actors' serial, tarted-up with horror movie props and a lot of ingenious machinery. Its long gallery of villains and monsters bent on dominating the world, has always been recognisably human. Even in the heyday of the Daleks – the serial's high peak – it was impossible to forget that behind the armour plating there was a perspiring player. This time it looks as though it is the director, Lennie Mayne, who is having the ball. The "powerful

BILL MARSH

organism" is a piece of pure movie technology, a shape wriggling across the screen, crudely done, perhaps, but instantly effective because it lacks all trace of human identity. It is this kind of change that gives the show a lift.'

January 10

In a unique 'double act', Jon Pertwee and Patrick Troughton appear on the BBC's *Pebble Mill at One* programme to promote the series. Both Doctors are dressed in their respective costumes, with the TARDIS as the backdrop to their conversation. The tone of the interview is set right from the outset as both Doctors jostle with each other to be first out of the TARDIS to greet the interviewer. Then, to the astonishment of Jon Pertwee and the Pebble Mill crew,

Patrick Troughton proceeds to send up the whole venture, offering to demonstrate for the viewers his impersonation of a Dalek; he tugs his coat over his head, and runs around the studio, arm outstretched, telling the audience, 'I am a Dalek.' It is, to date, Patrick Troughton's last appearance at Pebble Mill in a *Doctor Who* capacity.

January 27

At the conclusion of 'The Three Doctors', the Time Lords lift the sentence of exile on Jon Pertwee's Doctor, leaving him free to roam space and time at will. Producer Barry Letts speaks enthustiastically to the press at the start of a new four-parter 'Carnival of Monsters', which he himself has directed from a script by Robert Holmes. 'We have two lots of new life-forms in this adventure,' he says. 'One lot are called the Minorians. They are grey-faced and humanoid. The other is the Drashig. It is a fearsome monster. In fact, we think he's one of the most striking and original ones we have produced in some time.' The comic element in the adventure delights viewers, and Jon Pertwee remembers the story with affection because it re-unites him with a friend from his years on the radio comedy show *The Navy Lark,* Tenniel Evans, the man who had actually suggested he should apply for the part of the third Doctor. A suggestion which, as he was later to recall, he thought quite absurd!

An original member of the *Doctor Who* team, Brian Hodgson, who has been the designer of the series' special sounds, leaves. Hodgson has been on the programme since the very first episode, constructing and recording all the strange sound effects that could not come from stock discs and tapes. Everything from TARDIS hums to Dalek voices have been his speciality and to mark his departure from *Doctor Who* (Hodgson leaves the BBC to found his own company *Electrophon*) he devises a chilling sequence of multi-layered screams for the Drashig monsters' howls. Hodgson's successor in the area of special sounds will be Dick Mills, himself no stranger to providing sound effects for *Doctor Who,* having worked with Hodgson on the programme virtually since the beginning.

March 3

ALAN MORTON

A rare piece of national publicity for more people at the heart of the *Doctor Who* success story – John Friedlander and his team in the BBC Special Effects Department. In an article headlined 'Doctor Who's Great Green Monster Machine' carried by the *Sun* after the opening episode of Malcolm Hulke's 'Frontier in Space', which produces another memorable enemy for the Doctor in the shape of the Draconians, Friedlander reveals that their terrifying faces are actually based on the comedian Dave Allen! 'Monsters are very much a team effort,' he explains. 'I go along and see the director who explains the effect he wants. Then we get together with the costume department and make-up and work the thing out.' The Draconians as seen on television actually came about because of a make-up problem, Friedlander goes on. 'Sandra Shepherd from make-up found that at one point they needed twelve Draconians to be on set at once. Since it takes literally hours to do one, obviously she couldn't manage twelve in one day. So we decided the make-up would have to be a mask. We got together with Barbara Kidd of the costume department and together we worked out what a Draconian ought to look like. We made a mask which fits over the actor's head, leaving his eyes and chin free to move. And I modelled it on a sculptured head of Dave Allen because we had one in the workshop at the time!' John Friendlander also explains that the ideas for monsters often come from very ordinary things – the Ogrons bearing a striking resemblence to Neanderthal man. Currently, he says, the team is working on a swarm of two-foot-long maggots for a forthcoming adventure, 'The Green Death'. The man in charge, Ronald Oates, explains, 'We are making them out of flexible tubing, covered with cotton wool, painted green and finally covered with a nylon stocking to make them shine. The only trouble is – I can't stand the sight of risotto any more!'

PHILIP WAGSTAFF

April 7

The Daleks return yet again in 'Planet of the Daleks', an imaginative script written by their original creator, Terry Nation. Ensconsed on the planet Spiridon, they have secured the secret of invisibility which makes them doubly formidable foes for the Doctor and Jo until they can be made visible again. Stanley Reynolds, TV critic of *The Times,* enjoys it all immensely. 'Of course the whole point of Doctor Who's adventures is that they are scary and menacing,' he says, 'the sort of thing fit to dominate the childhood pantheon of terror. Even though the Doctor has defeated the Daleks countless times, they still represent the ultimate bogeyman. And they have had stiff competition, lizardmen and all manner of warty, grotty space beings. Still, the Daleks are the boss space horrors, something to get the children hiding behind the sofa in happy anticipation of twenty-five minutes of fear . . . Somehow *Doctor Who* is just that bit more classy when you know the dustbins on wheels are tooling around behind the next time-warp.'

May 3

Paperback publishers Target Books begin their series of *Doctor Who* titles novelising stories from the programme, which has since grown into such an international success with the number of books approaching one hundred. The first three titles are, however, reprints of earlier hardcover books first published by Frederick Muller in 1965: *Doctor Who and the Crusaders* by David Whitaker, *Doctor Who and the Zarbi* by Bill Strutton and *Doctor Who and the Daleks* also by David

Whitaker. This last title enters the list of top ten best-selling children's books, and encourages Target Books to commission more works, many to be written by the original script writers. Later this same month, Polystyle Publications release the first *Doctor Who Summer Special* with articles, comic strips and photographs.

May 12

Doctor Who comes full circle as one of the Daleks from the *Doctor Who* films, themselves spawned by the TV series, makes an appearance in the final episode of 'Planet of the Daleks'. The Dalek in question is one of two given to author Terry Nation on completion of the films in 1966. Disguising its origins, the visual effects team for 'Planet of the Daleks' modifies the casing, giving it a different set of head flanges, an illuminated eye-unit, flat-topped cylindrical head-lights and a paint livery of gold and black. Presented in the story as a Dalek Supreme, this new Dalek appears only in the final episode, bringing to a climax the twelve-week saga which had begun with 'Frontier in Space'.

May 19

After some months' absence from the *Doctor Who* series, Bessie, the Doctor's car, re-appears in the opening episode of Robert Sloman's 'The Green Death' complete with a few modifications. Bessie's problem has been that while on screen she looks the perfect combination of elegance and speed, the weight of the extra subframes and supporting brackets underneath the fibreglass body shells restrict her speed to just over 30 mph – a point frequently noted by Jon Pertwee. Hence, trick photography has to account for all cases of her being seen driving at speed. With Barry Letts's blessing, Jon Pertwee has Bessie modified by a group of engineers who fit a more powerful engine into the car, plus a corresponding gearbox and cooling system. However, this extra engine adds nearly eight inches to the length of the engine compartment, with the result that the old square bonnet will no longer fit. To compensate for this, Bessie is returned to the BBC with a new radiator and a raised, rounded bonnet that both covers the engine and allows enough space underneath to aid air-circulation and cooling.

June 7

An appeal is made through the national press and on *Blue Peter* to help in the recovery of two Daleks that have gone missing! The two machines have been sent from the London TV Centre warehouse to Wales for a regional programme, but when the *Doctor Who* production team go to reclaim them there is no sign of them. 'It's a bit of a mystery,' Barry Letts tells newspaper reporters. 'It's possible the Daleks were misrouted on return from Wales. Maybe they were picked up by the wrong lorry, and are sitting in a warehouse somewhere. I do hope somebody can find them – we'll need them again fairly soon!'

Two days later, the newspapers carry a terse report:' The BBC's two missing Daleks were recovered in London yesterday. Police would not say how they were found.' It later transpires the Daleks were stolen while awaiting collection for a fête appearance. One was spotted by two nurses behind a garage, while the other was discovered by a businessman hidden underneath the plastic tarpaulin covering his car when he took it off to go to work!

June 18

TIM PIERACCINI

The first tragedy for *Doctor Who* – while on location in Turkey making a feature film, Roger Delgado, the Master, is killed in a car crash. He had last been seen on 31 March in 'Frontier in Space' when his success in the role had lead to suggestions that his popularity even overshadowed that of the Doctor. Delgado, aged fifty-three, was travelling with two Turkish film technicians when their hired car ran off the road into a ravine near Neveshir. One technician was killed, while the driver and the other technician were badly injured. All were to have been involved in the making of a Turkish-French television film entitled *Bell of Tibet*. Police at the scene of the accident say the car ran off the road at a bend because it was going too fast.

The national newspaper obituaries on Roger Delgado all highlight his role as the Master even though during a career spanning thirty years he has appeared in many radio dramas, television plays and numerous feature films. *The Times* runs a photograph of him from the series and states that he was 'known to millions of television viewers for his vivid portrayal of the Master in *Doctor Who.*' The report continues: 'A dark, strikingly handsome man, he played with great panache the sinister scientist, versed in all the black arts, who repeatedly plots to do down Doctor Who (Jon Pertwee). Though entirely convincing in his sudden Mephistophelean appearances and disappearances and his blood-curdling threats of disaster for the Doctor, he was a villain whom it was hard to hate.' Indeed, Delgado was a man much loved by his fellow workers on the programme, and his death is to have far-reaching effects amongst them . . .

June 23

Jo Grant leaves the Doctor and her job with UNIT to marry Professor Clifford Jones at the resolution of 'The Green Death'. Katy Manning, however, finds her role a hard one to follow and in 1978 tells a reporter: 'Even now, five years later, I'm still known as a Doctor Who girl. I live for the day when I'm known simply as Katy Manning, actress.'

October 16

Adding further to the events marking the tenth anniversary of *Doctor Who,* a *Radio Times* Special is published, retailing in the shops for 30p. All pages in full colour, the magazine comprises a photo-illustrated guide to the ten seasons, interviews with some of the companions and all three Doctors, a specially written story by Terry Nation, and plans for how to build a Dalek. The plans illustrated, however, are not those used by the BBC nor by Shawcraft but are, instead, the design of two fans, Deirdre MacDonald and Nigel Holmes, and only approximate, not duplicate, the plans drawn up in 1963 by Raymond Cusick.

November 8

In celebration of ten years of *Doctor Who, Blue Peter* devotes the final half of its Thursday programme to a review of the entire series. The opening part of the survey takes the form of a look back at the programme illustrated with a range of caption photographs and a film of extracts from various *Doctor Who* episodes. Among the clips is a segment from the last episode of 'An Unearthly Child' (which is played not with the original soundtrack but with a short passage of music), two clips from 'The Daleks' Master Plan', and the regeneration scene from 'The Tenth Planet' (the latter three clips all being from episodes now missing from the BBC's archives).

The second half of the commemoration features Jon Pertwee in the studio demonstrating his latest vehicle soon to come into the programme – the Whomobile. All the machine's special gadgets are shown off, including the twin electric aerials, the intricate system of indicator lights, the TV screen, the telephone, and even the on-board computer. Viewers are told to watch out for the Whomobile in the forthcoming story 'Invasion of the Dinosaurs.'

One result of the programme is an immediate flood of requests for earlier stories from the series to be re-shown. Ronald Marsh, Head of BBC Television Serials, replies in the *Radio Times*: 'Some *Doctor Who* stories have been repeated very successfully as single programmes, and we certainly hope to show others this way in the future. However, writers' and artists' contracts include an agreement that repeats may only take place within a specified period, and this has expired as far as the very early stories are concerned.' However, both William Hartnell and Patrick Troughton later confirm they would have no objection to any of their stories being shown.

December 15

A new season of *Doctor Who* – the eleventh – introduces two new elements to the series in 'The Time Warrior' by Robert Holmes. The first is a new set of title graphics, again designed and executed by graphics specialist Bernard Lodge but this time using rostrum camera animation for

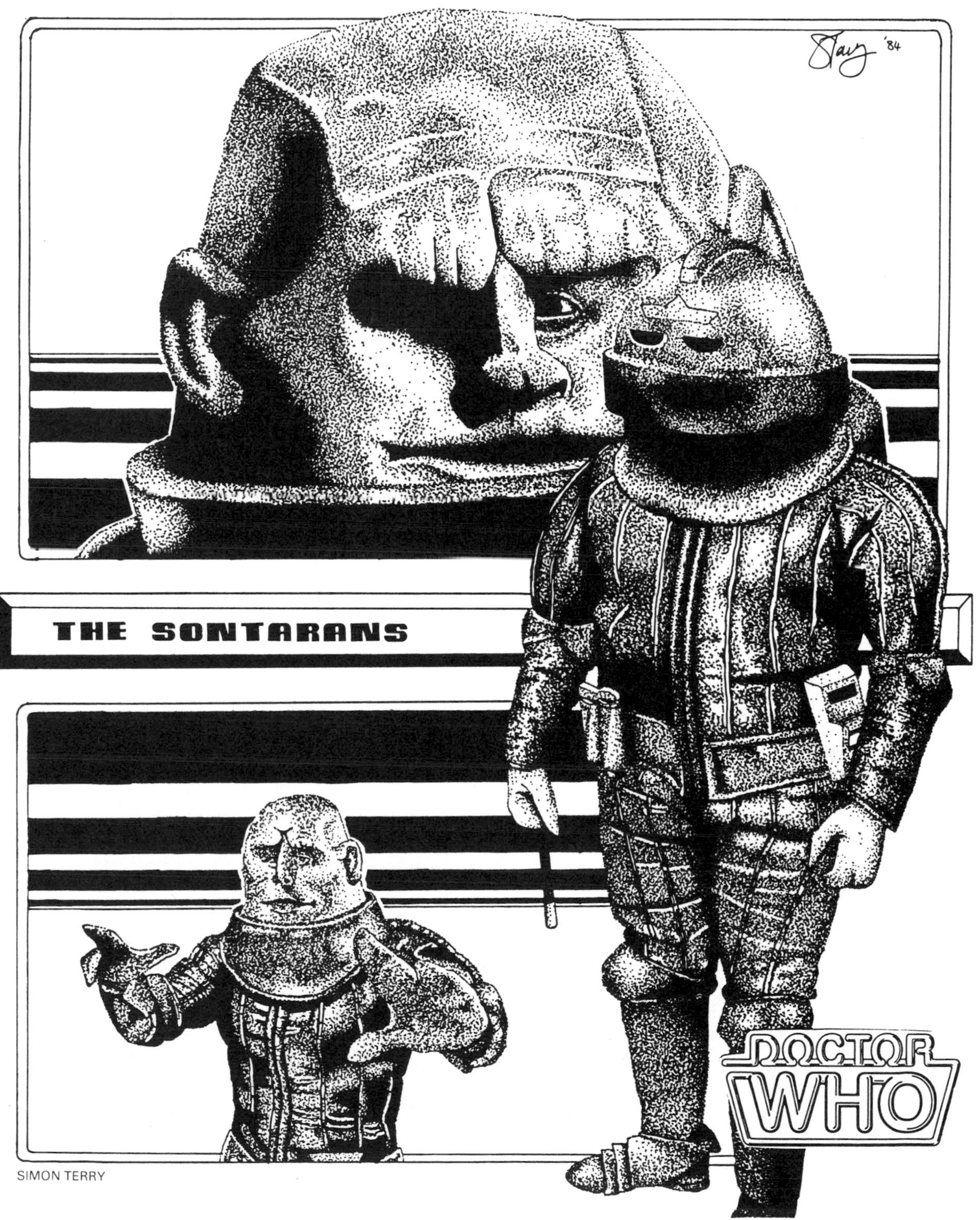

SIMON TERRY

the 'time tunnel' background rather than the video feedback technique used in the previous three graphic sequences. Interviewed about the techniques employed in generating the images, Lodge confesses to being influenced by Douglas Trumbull's 'Star Gate' effects in *2001*, and to using the same technique to create the patterns which swirl out of nowhere, towards and past the camera for the *Doctor Who* titles. Lodge is also responsible for the radically different *Doctor Who* logo now shaped in the form of a diamond, which will symbolise the show for the next six years.

The Sontarans are the other new innovation. A perfect marriage of costumes and visual effects, the Sontarans are an immediate hit with the fans, paving the way for a rematch sometime the following season. For actor Kevin Lindsay, who plays Linx, wearing the Sontaran costume and mask for recording sessions is an act of pure endurance. The heavy quilted uniform heats up rapidly under the studio lights, amplifying the discomfort of the actor already sealed under the thick rubber head-mask. With the helmet on as well, both vision and hearing are severely impaired, making it hard both to see where to move and to follow cues. And on top of all this, as is later reported in the newspapers, Kevin Lindsay has a weak heart severely strained by the many hours needed to record 'The Time Warrior'.

The Doctor also gets a new companion in Sarah Jane-Smith, played by Elisabeth Sladen, who tells the press: 'I am a complete newcomer, so I've very little idea what I'm letting myself in for. But I do know that because Sarah has been given the profession of journalism she can be a lot more independent than the old-style heroines.' These words are to prove very prophetic as she ultimately chalks up the record of being the longest-serving companion and gets the unique opportunity of returning to TV in a spin-off series.

GARY McKEEVER

1974

February 2

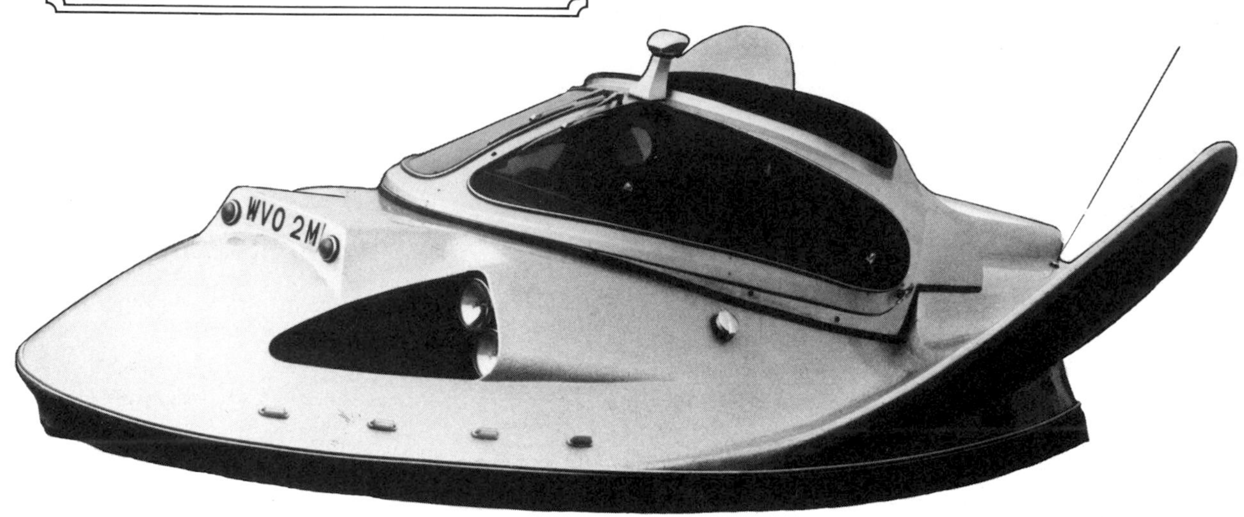

The Whomobile makes its entrance. This remarkable, flying-saucer-shaped car, known officially as Alien, makes its debut in the fourth episode of 'Invasion of the Dinosaurs' and has been made specially for Jon Pertwee by custom-car specialist Peter Farries of Nottingham. The two men first meet in January 1973 in the Midlands, when Jon opens a new Ford Main Dealers. Peter is there with his own astonishing green-and-black custom car Black Widow. So impressed is gadget-loving Jon that he commissions Peter to build a 'special' for the Doctor – but, he says it has to be legal for driving on public roads (which, of course, Bessie isn't) and it has to look like something from outer space.

The result is Alien – a fourteen-foot fibre-glass-hulled vehicle sitting on an anchor-shaped chassis with three wheels (which are hidden from view by an eight-inch rubber skirt to give the Whomobile the illusion of being a hovercraft). The Chrysler Imp 975 cc engine can propel the 14 cwt car to a top speed of 105 mph, and its special electronics system of 44 flashing lights plus mock-up computer, telephone, television and stereo give it a truly futuristic look. When Jon first presents the Whomobile at the studios there is amazement and consternation among all the other actors and crew! Amusingly, the Road Licensing Department classify Alien as an 'Invalid Tricycle' when handing out its registration plates, WVO 2M! They have no other designation, apparently, for a vehicle that is part car, part hovercraft and part spaceship! As Jon Pertwee's property, the Whomobile leaves when he departs the series, but it has since been seen at fêtes and special openings. As a matter of interest, the Whomobile replaces a motorbike in Malcolm Hulke's original script, and despite being generally known by this title, is never once referred to by name during the series!

February 8

Jon Pertwee announces he is to quit as the Doctor – and the story becomes front-page news. After appearing for five years in around 150 episodes, he says he has decided he wants to return to the stage when the present season finishes filming in April. With typical humour, Jon, aged fifty-three announces his next part is to be that of a housewife. 'It is a comedy play called *The Breadwinner* about a husband and wife, and I play the husband who decides to stay home as the housewife while his wife goes out to work.' Jon also talks about his years as the Doctor. 'I aimed at something for everybody,' he says. 'I was also keen to put more emphasis on the scientific James Bond type of adventure while retaining a typical *Doctor Who* eccentricity.' He also believes he has brought the more way-out monsters down to earth. 'I always feel that there's nothing more alarming than coming home to find a Yeti in your bathroom. OK, you might expect that in the Himalayas, but not in the average suburb. In other words, if you saw Daleks "exterminating" on Westminster Bridge it is so much more frightening than seeing them in outer space.'

Jon also reveals to Tony Pratt of the *Daily Mirror* that he can't actually stand Daleks. 'I'm not scared of them,' he says, 'just bored. They have been around too long. I prefer monsters with some life in them, like the Draconians or the Ogrons.' He elaborates on this theme to Ian Lang of *The People's Journal*: 'I think the most frightening monster we had was competely invisible – in fact, more a matter for the imagination. It was in "The Daemons". Somehow the devil had been summoned up from a churchyard. But the villian of the piece was a violent, roaring wind. A burial barrow was re-opened on a Wiltshire hillside and this great wind, with all its implications, would rush in and out with a tremendous roar. Another time we had an invisible barrier and anything which went past it immediately disintegrated into smoke. There was one scene, I recall, when the Brigadier stuck his swagger cane into this forbidden area and spontaneously it burst into flames. I found that terribly effective. I thoroughly enjoyed working up these special effect ideas with the production team – to me these situations were much more alarming than some rubberoid or wooden monster.' Pertwee also comments: 'I enjoyed every moment I worked on *Doctor Who,* but one of the features which impressed me was the way the public reacted. I would be out on location dressed as the Doctor in rather flamboyant dress, including frilly shirts and cloaks – and the people passing by would say quite casually, "Good Morning"!'

There is immediate speculation about Pertwee's successor as the Doctor, and Brian Wesley of the *Sun* even hints that the team behind the serial is "breaking up". But all a BBC spokesman will admit tantalisingly is: 'We have found a replacement Doctor Who, but all the details have to be completed, and we cannot yet name him.' In fact, within a week the secret is out . . .

February 16

Producer Barry Letts breaks the news that he has found a new Doctor – forty-year-old Tom Baker, whom he saw playing an evil magician in a feature film called *The*

COLIN-JOHN P. RODGERS

Golden Voyage of Sinbad. At the time he is offered the role, however, the former National Theatre Company actor, who has also appeared as the mad monk Rasputin in the film *Nicholas and Alexandra,* is out of work and doing casual labour on a London building site! Tom is beseiged by the press with questions. 'I was surprised when they asked me to play the Doctor,' he admits to the *Guardian.* 'But I want to play him in an individual way, but with the suggestion that although he has a human body he comes from somewhere else.' And to the *Daily Mirror* he confides, 'I'm a great fan of *Doctor Who* and the role appeals to me very much. It's also going to mean a great deal of security for me. I have signed a contract for one year with options to do more programmes. At the moment I live in a one-room flat in Pimlico and I've only got one suit and one good overcoat to my name!' He is equally enthusiastic to the *Daily Mail*: 'It's a fascinating part. Probably as interesting to an actor as Macbeth, which I have also played. You have to suggest somebody who is from another world but who has human characteristics. I'm really quite fascinated by science fiction and I'm working on ways of bringing my own interpretation and identity to the part.'

Later, Barry Letts is to admit having had a short list of possibles for the role of the Doctor – the most surprising of these being Richard Hearne. 'Richard is one of those actors who has the magic touch,' Barry says. 'Indeed for years after his *Mister Pastry* series he was still opening fêtes and carnivals in the role. I actually invited him along for discussions about his possibly being the new Doctor, but we established quite early on that this was impractical as his interpretation of the part would be to play it like Mister Pastry: a doddery old man.'

February 23

Never long out of the headlines, the Daleks are back in prominence as Terry Nation's new story, 'Death to the Daleks' is screened. Terry takes the opportunity to reveal some of the extraordinary questions he gets asked about his creations whom he describes as 'ruthless monsters without one redeeming feature'. One small boy, he says, wrote to ask: 'There aren't any lady Daleks, so how do they reproduce themselves?' Another wanted to know why the Doctor wasn't interested in his girl assistants even when he was locked in a room with them. And a third wondered why no one ever heard anything about Mrs Who. Terry says, 'When the *Doctor Who* office passed them on to me I just had to sort it out. So I told the first youngster that the Daleks did reproduce, but it was a very ugly sight and he wouldn't like watching it. As for Mrs Who, well, of course, she existed and he was very fond of her. And his girl assistants are just good chums.' Terry also tells a joke he has heard about himself and the origin of the word Dalek. The question is: What do President Tito and Terry Nation have in common? 'The answer is nothing, of course,' he says. 'However, I don't know the meaning of the word Dalek and President Tito *does.* Because in Serbo-Croat the word Dalek means "far and distant things". Isn't that incredible? I found it very, very strange and bizarre.' Equally strange was a definition he once read about the reason for the success of the programme as a whole. Terry says with a grin: 'I remember that one of the posh Sunday newspapers had a psychiatrist or someone say that children saw Doctor Who as a father figure, and it was the innate wish of every child to destroy his father!'

Yet again, though, there are calls to the BBC by certain of the TV critics to do away with the Daleks, led by Chris Kenworthy of the *Sun,* who thinks they are 'boring'. He says: 'They also seem pretty stupid. Which makes Doctor Who sound pretty silly when he goes on about their "diabolical intelligence". In the present adventure, they are obviously going to be wiped out again. As far as I'm concerned, this time it ought to be for keeps.'

March 2

Not all the visual effects and costumes work according to plan in *Doctor Who* stories, and while the series does achieve a very high rate of hitting the target, instances of failure – such is the case with the Exxilons in 'Death to the Daleks' – are not unknown. As conceived by writer Terry Nation, the Exxilons are a once proud race who have sunk back into savagery as a result of baleful radiation from the 'living' city they themselves have created. These powerful emanations have, over the centuries, saturated the bodies of the Exxilon leaving them almost a race of animated, glowing cadavers. Faced with this brief the designers devise a costume they intend will give the Exxilons a glowing appearance; the idea being to inlay the latex rubber costumes and masks with 'scotch-lite' material similar to that used on road signs and fire extinguishers to make the surfaces highly reflective whenever a light is shone on them. Once in the studio, forward projected lights will be trained on the Exxilon costumes to give them a powerful iridescence.

Tests on the material prove positive, but only when the costumes are brought in and tried on in the studio during full dress rehearsals does it become apparent that the overhead lighting, needed for any programme, will blank out the effect of the projected lights. Thus, in the three episodes of 'Death to the Daleks', when unrobed Exxilons are seen, only the barest glimmer of a reflected glow is detectable by the viewer.

March 30

One of the few sequel stories ever done for *Doctor Who,* 'The Monster of Peladon' re-introduces seasoned viewers to a host of familiar faces: the Ice Warriors, the Pels, Alpha Centauri, and Aggedor . . . 'You won't have any difficulty noticing Nick Hobbs in his latest role – he's the one with the tusks, the horns and the hide like a doormat,' reports the *Daily Express* in a preview. 'He steps out in that outfit again tonight to play the monster Aggedor, in the *Doctor Who* adventure "The Monster of Peladon". When not crouching in a monster suit Nick, twenty-eight, is a good-looking, fresh-faced stuntman who specialises in falling off horses. "I had worked for the BBC before as a stuntman, so I suppose they knew I was used to doing awkward things," he explains. The awkward things he has been doing recently include doubling for Barbara Windsor on a motorbike, and jumping through flames for – of all things – a wool advertisement. "I have played Aggedor in a previous *Doctor Who* adventure, so I know how to move in the suit," he says. "But it really is hot in there. You can't see anything except when you roar. Everytime I do roar, I take a quick look round through the mouth!"'

April 5

As one of his last official duties as the Doctor, Jon Pertwee goes to Blackpool to open the first permanent Doctor Who Exhibition on the Golden Mile opposite Central Pier. Huge crowds greet the star, and later swarm through the TARDIS-shaped gateway entrance to find models and props from various stories including 'Invasion of the Dinosaurs', 'The Green Death' and 'Planet of the Spiders'. Design of the exhibition is handled by Tom Carter and extensive coverage in newspapers and on TV (a special spot on *Nationwide*) generate tremendous public interest. The annual attendance figures soon remain stable at just over a quarter of a million people for each season lasting from Easter to the end of October, with fresh exhibits introduced each year.

This same year, the Marquis of Bath, who visited the BBC Special Effects Department Exhibition at the Science Museum in 1973, opens a similar show at his home, Longleat House in Wiltshire, which again contains a range of displays featuring the Doctor's activities and adversaries.

May 4

Opening episode of Robert Sloman's 'The Planet of Spiders', which is to be Jon Pertwee's final adventure as the Doctor – and soon the story is the subject of intense controversy over the appearance of some giant spiders. Leading the protests are Mary Whitehouse and the members of her self-appointed watchdog committee, the National Viewers and Listeners Association. They argue that since fear of spiders is such a common dread it is irresponsible of the BBC to 'allow transmission of a story that so graphically displays a race of very large spiders with the frequent habit of leaping onto the backs of their unfortunate victims'. Individual sufferers from arachnaphobia also complain to the programme – all of them unaware that the spiders seen are actually a far less realistic model than had been originally planned. Defending the use of the spiders, producer Barry Letts, who also directed the story explains that they have been created by the Visual Effects Department and he has actually turned down the original prototype made by Ian Scoones and Mat Irvine on the grounds that it was 'too realistic for comfort'! He also adds in support of the whole series: 'The dramas are just frightening enough to be interesting, completely fantastical and also very powerful. Children like identifying with someone powerful. We take great pains to have no blood or nastiness – no explicit cruelty. Doctor Who fights only if forced to, and he always spares his enemy.'

June 8

There is a genuine sense of sadness as Jon Pertwee leaves the series, expressed by Donald Gomery who writes in the *Daily Mirror*: 'Over the weekend I bit my nails as Jon Pertwee played his last role as Doctor Who. How was he going to "die" and yet allow the Doc to live on? Baffling stuff. But thanks, Jon, for all you've done for us kids.'

After the final transmission, Jon reveals another reason for leaving the role – and also confirms the earlier suggestion that he is not the only one to be going. 'For one thing,' he says, 'Roger Delgado, who played the Master, was a very dear friend of mine. When he died, I was terribly upset. Then the producer, Barry Letts, decided to leave. And so did the script editor, Terrance Dicks. And while Liz Sladen, who took over as my leading lady, is a lovely and very talented girl, it just seemed that the old team was falling apart. It was the end of an era.' He also jokes that his first break 'from my cloak and TARDIS' will be in a whodunnit. Before going onto the stage, he is to host a TV panel game, *Whodunnit.* 'I think it is a good idea to appear as myself so that people will stop thinking of me as Doctor Who,' he says. 'It won't be easy, though, because playing the Doctor takes some living down. The following for the programme is so enormous that it's difficult to get people to accept you as anyone else.'

Ten years on, Jon Pertwee is, of course, still remembered with great affection by fans of the programme . . .

November 14

The quality of the scripts written for *Doctor Who* is recognised at the annual gathering of the Society for Film and Television Awards (SAFTA) when the award for the best scriptwriting team of the year is given to the five men who created the stories for the eleventh season – Robert Holmes, Malcolm Hulke, Terry Nation, Brian Hayles and Robert Sloman. Producer Barry Letts speaks for the whole production team when he says: 'I think we did change the face of *Doctor Who* quite dramatically over the period when Jon Pertwee was the Doctor. Certainly we attracted a much older age group to the show, as was proved in the year when I had an audience survey conducted. The results showed that out of our total audience figure of nine million, 58 per cent were over the age of fifteen. We also pushed the technology of the BBC to its limits, using every new process we could lay our hands on, and, I think, introduced quite a few new elements into the stories. I enjoyed working with Terrance Dicks immensely and since leaving *Doctor Who* he and I have worked together on other projects. But nothing we do can be more rewarding than the time we spent on *Doctor Who.*'

December 16

A new Doctor appears in London – but not the expected Tom Baker. Terrance Dicks has written a stage play, *Doctor Who and the Daleks in the Seven Keys to Doomsday* which opens at the Adelphi Theatre for a four-week run. Originally, Jon Pertwee was to have taken the lead role, but instead mainstream actor Trevor Martin fills the part with a clever use of backstage film projection to show the transformation of Pertwee's face into that of Martin. One of the Doctor's earlier companions, Zoe (Wendy Padbury), plays a similar role as Jenny, with James Matthew as the Time Lord's other helper, Jimmy. The trio manage to defeat another fiendish plot of the Daleks, who are endeavouring to take over the universe with the aid of their crab-like slaves, the Clawrentulars. The play is generally unenthusiastically received – 'Will those tiresome Daleks never go away,' the *Daily Telegraph* moans – but Terrance Dicks later utilises elements of the play for his very successful story 'The Brain of Morbius' in 1976.

ANTHONY JAMES

December 28

Tom Baker makes his debut as the Doctor in part one of 'Robot' written and produced by Dicks and Letts as their swansong. But not before some very clever editing creates the moment of transformation from his previous self. To have brought back Jon Pertwee just for this one sequence would have cost the production too much. However, to have simply reprised the last minute or so from 'Planet of the Spiders' and then have it followed by the scenes immediately after the regeneration would also have been difficult since, during the couple of months between the recordings of 'Planet of the Spiders' and 'Robot', Elisabeth Sladen's hair had grown noticeably longer. In the end director Christopher Barry elects to re-record the scenes with Sarah and the Brigadier before and after the regeneration, using from the previous serial only the one camera shot of the Doctor's face changing. Maintaining a link of continuity with the Doctor's old body, Tom Baker's hair is rigorously permed for this opening scene to tidy his unruly mop of curls into the tousled, but more styled shock of hair favoured by Jon Pertwee.

Also introduced in this story is a new companion Harry Sullivan, played by Ian Marter.

Tom Baker reveals himself to be a little haunted by the performances of his three predecessors when he talks to Mary Duffy of the *Daily Express.* 'In a way playing the Doctor is not so different from the life I led for six years when I was in a monastery' he says. 'There I was trying to save my soul. Here, I save the world – and sometimes the universe – in four episodes. I'm rather tense about it because no one has seen the series yet. Going by the law of averages, someone must flop in the part. And it might be me.' Pointing out that he is the youngest man to have played the part, Tom says, 'But as friends have told me, the BBC scoured London to come up with the only middle-aged ten-year-old in the business. If it doesn't sound too solemn, what I like is the way the children respond to the Doctor. They know that though they go through terror with him, they will always be safe in the end.' Baker has, however, little cause to worry as the New Year's reviews soon prove . . .

1975

January 4

A new production team takes over – Philip Hinchcliffe as producer and Robert Holmes as script editor. Philip Hinchliffe sees where the challenge to *Doctor Who* lies, as he tells the press: 'We are now facing much stiffer competition. Since the last series there's been a tremendous shift in public taste towards science fantasy – in particular with American shows like *Planet of the Apes* and *The Six Million Dollar Man.* This means we need even bigger and better monsters – everything the special effects department can throw at us.' There is also a problem getting the right type of story, he says. 'Most television writing doesn't require the sort of rollicking good yarn we need. And many writers find it hard to adjust to our pace of escapist entertainment because what we need is old-fashioned adventure with scientific wizardry on top.'

January 18

Tom Baker has a stunning impact as the new Doctor and the final episode of 'Robot' receives widespread press review. 'With a turn of speed that even the super-human Time Lords would appreciate, Tom Baker has established himself well and truly as Doctor Who IV,' writes Patrick Stoddart in the London *Evening News.* 'Despite the nervous mumbles of one or two conservatives at the BBC and a handful of viewers who think the new Doctor's a bit silly, the tall, shock-haired and wide-eyed Tom has given the old fellow a brave new image. With his ten-foot scarf, floppy hippy hat and crumpled clothes, he's less

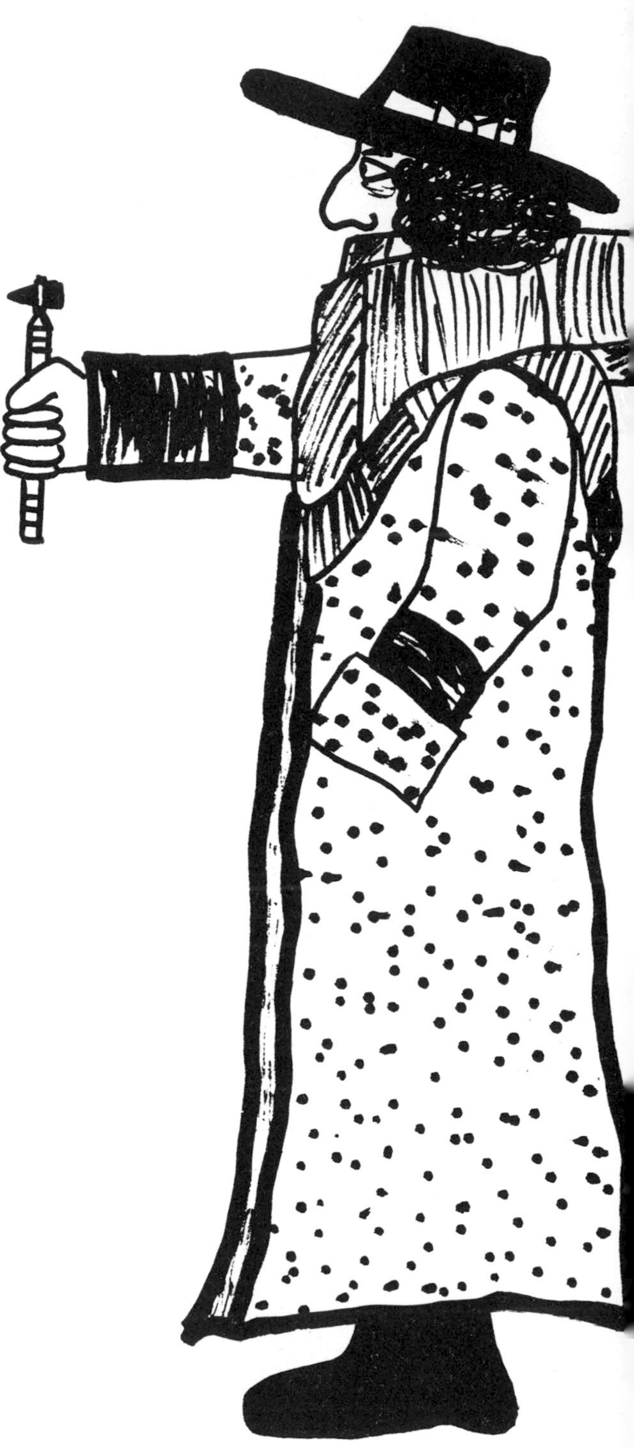

MARTIN WILLIAMS

dandified than Jon Pertwee, slightly more up to-date than Patrick Troughton and a whole generation away from William Hartnell, the original marque.' And Stephen Briscoe, of the *Yorkshire Post,* in a remarkably prophetic review, particularly likes his sense of humour. 'His appearance is decidedly eccentric, but with one adventure behind him already he seems quite the most endearing Doctor Who the Time Lords within the BBC have so far supplied us with. In fact, I should not be at all surprised if Tom Baker did not find himself becoming something of a cult figure.'

Inevitably, not everyone is happy. Martin Jackson of the *Daily Mail* feels the Doctor is 'in danger of becoming some childish prank'. This, he believes, will not do. 'For though the indestructible Doctor has had other face-lifts over the years, no one has ever played him with anything other than due reverence . . . But Mr Baker makes Doctor Who look like Harpo Marx let loose from *Horse-Feathers.'* Tom Baker answers this criticism himself. 'We are *not* playing *Doctor Who* for laughs,' he says emphatically. 'I am trying to stress his strangeness, that he is not of this world, not human, therefore his reactions will be different from ours. I take it all very seriously. He has to be genuinely lovable, not pleased by violence, and he must be honest. Humorous, but never comical.'

January 21

Doctor Who is attacked for a second time by Mrs Mary Whitehouse of the Viewers and Listeners Association after a lecture delivered by Mr Shaun Sutton, Head of BBC TV Drama, at a symposium at Manchester University. Talking on the theme of the dangers of allowing children to watch too much television, he says: 'We hear an awful lot about what children should and should not see on TV. But there is less controversy about the amount they see and this is the most important point of all.' Mr Sutton believes viewing should be rationed 'like cream cakes' and adds: 'Are we in danger of losing the complete man or woman by reducing our children's chances of developing into complete children?' Using clips from several *Doctor Who* stories to illustrate his talk, Mr Sutton says the series is an example of a quality show that teaches children about courage, morality, humour, photographic tricks and fantasy, and adds: 'Courage must be a basic ingredient of *Doctor Who.* It is expected that the hero will be brave and this is right. Doctor Who is the only science fiction hero who has a sense of humour.'

Immediately afterwards, Mrs Whitehouse disputes Mr Sutton's claim. She says that *Doctor Who* is a threat to little children. 'It can cause nightmares and bed-wetting among the under-sevens, doctors have told me,' she says. 'The programme is screened too early in the evening. Although it is technically brilliant, it is more suitable for adults. Young children often remember vividly the horrific pictures of creatures and go to bed in a tense state.' Mrs Whitehouse also tells journalists that her Association is conducting a survey into the amount of viewing by children, and they have found a 'hair-raising' number are watching between eleven and twelve hours at weekends.

January 22

There are numerous replies to Mrs Mary Whitehouse's charges against *Doctor Who* – from members of the production team, a GP and children themselves. Tom Baker is, though, first to the defence. 'I don't know how anyone can associate bed-wetting and nightmares with any specific incident or TV experience early in the day. We are not frivolous. My fan mail has proved just how much trust and confidence the children have in Doctor Who. I would never do anything which might upset that trust.' Script editor Robert Holmes adds to this: 'Children know the monsters are not real. They get pleasure from a little healthy horror. The people who make the programme mean it to be entertaining.' And Terrance Dicks, author of 'Robot', also goes on the record: 'If you don't go too far, children enjoy being frightened. Every kids' show has to have a monster or a villain. Without them, it is like a Western without a gunfight.'

In a feature entitled 'So Who's Afraid of Doctor Who?', the *Daily Mirror* asks child expert Dr Hugh Jolly for his views. 'I don't think a happy, well-adjusted child is thrown by TV programmes like *Doctor Who,'* he says. 'It is fallacious to think a normal child is thrown to the extent of wetting the bed. Bed-wetting relates to deeper problems there for some time and not by suddenly looking at TV. I wouldn't be so dogmatic about nightmares. A child with a vivid

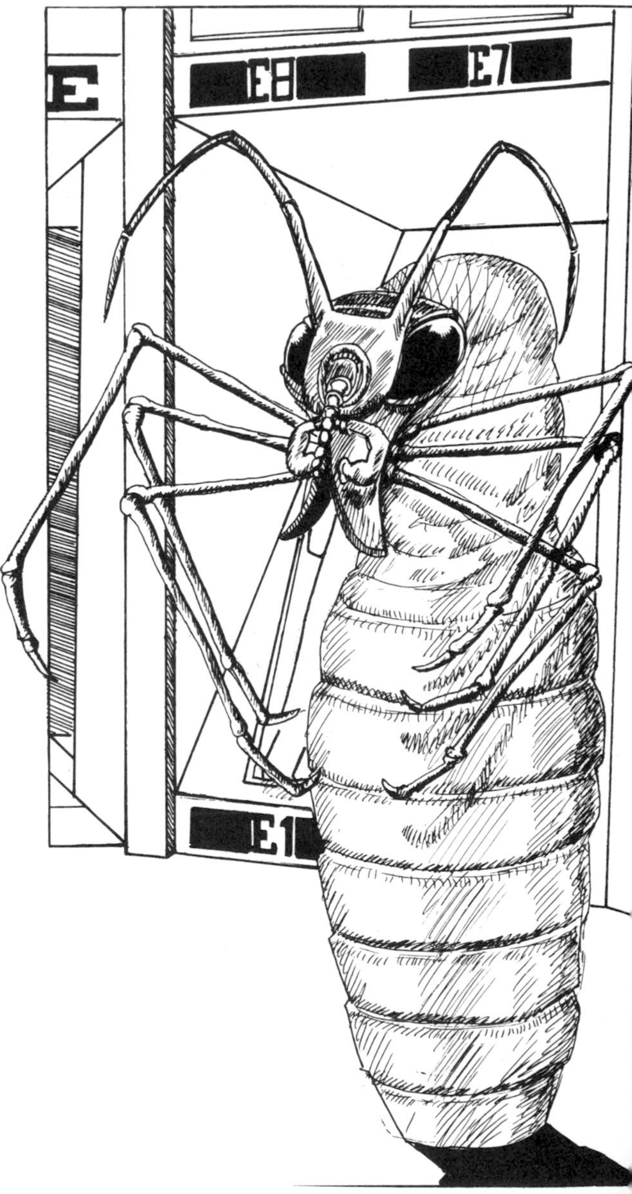

ALAN ROW

imagination might have a nightmare after seeing a programme like *Doctor Who,* but I don't think this is terribly harmful if mother is there to reassure and to talk anything out. The child then gains by this whole experience and can see it is all make-believe.' The newspaper also talks to the two sons of Bernard Wilkie, Head of BBC Special Effects, who creates the monsters. Eleven-year-old Martin says: 'I used to dream about the Daleks when I was very young. I was never terrified by them. I quite liked the Yetis, the Ice Warriors, and the Cybermen.' His older brother, Simon who is fourteen, admits he found the Yetis a bit frightening. 'But they were exciting – less humanoid than most of the robots. They certainly didn't give me nightmares.'

The London *Evening News* which carries a similar survey, reports: *'Doctor Who* is top of the TV charts with little children – despite the strictures of Mrs Mary Whitehouse', and quotes several under-sevens, including Danny Kirton, aged six, who says: 'It's the best programme on television. I watch it all the time. I've never been scared. I'm tough!' And school teacher Carole Cooles says: 'None of my children seem at all frightened by the adventures. They are always writing stories about Doctor Who.'

January 25

Controversial or not, the first episode of Robert Holmes's 'The Ark in Space' gives the new-look *Doctor Who* programme and its makers a record audience figure of

COLIN HOWARD

fourteen million. This achievement puts the series firmly in the top twenty children's programmes with figures well above those for rival show, *Space 1999*. In the years which follow, the programme is to feature regularly in the lists of most popular shows.

February 22

The two-episode story 'The Sontaran Experiment' by Bob Baker and Dave Martin begins with viewers unaware that Tom Baker fell and broke a collar bone as the crew neared completion of filming – all of which was done on location on Dartmoor. Work was completed with Baker either standing immobile or with his place taken in long shot by Terry Walsh.

March 1

The *Sun* newspaper asks its young readers what they think of Tom Baker as the new Doctor and gets some surprising answers. 'He's too weak,' says Nicholas Franklin, aged twelve. 'He doesn't fight the robots and monsters. He runs away or tries to trick them. I can't believe in him because he looks and acts like a student.' And thirteen-year-old Eve Kenworthy, adds: 'It takes time to get used to a new Doctor Who. But I don't think this one is as good as Jon Pertwee was. He is supposed to have a lot more humour, and his clothes suggest that he's going to be funny as well. But somehow he never actually is. Just a bit – well – wet.' Both children admit they may like the new Doctor when they have seen more of him.

Tom Baker is asked for his reaction. 'I get around two hundred letters a week, most of them in favour,' he says. 'But I suppose the kids who saw Jon Pertwee as a father figure will be a bit against me.' Philip Hinchcliffe also comments: 'I would say that 95 per cent of the reactions we get are in favour of Tom. In later episodes in this series he is just as athletic as previous Doctors and has stand-up fights with aliens.'

March 7

Tom Baker becomes the first Doctor to have his own weekly newspaper column, 'Doctor Who writes for You' in *Reveille.* Revealing that both he and the Doctor are rebels with an insatiable curiosity about life and living, he talks about his relationship with his fans. 'My weird and wonderful time-and-space travellings entertain millions,' he says, 'from the wise men at Pembroke College, Oxford, who record my scientific goings-on, to young people like the girls who've written to me from Sidcup and South Wales. You see, in our world, Doctor Who is really universal. With no age barriers to restrict his fans, either. I get letters from mums and dads as well as schoolgirls and boys, and that's really super.'

March 8

The new Doctor meets his oldest enemies, the Daleks, in 'Genesis of the Daleks', and creator Terry Nation and Tom Baker are jointly featured in the *Radio Times.* The writer Anthony Haden-Guest remarks 'If the

Doctor seems eternal, the Daleks seem no less so. Terry Nation killed them off once, but like Sherlock Holmes and the Frankestein monster they wouldn't stay down. Indeed, he feels, the Daleks may have gotten too big for their tin boots – a manufacturer approached him the other day to talk about Dalek-shaped *ice-cream*!' Both Nation and Baker have their own comments to make on them. 'The Daleks depend on your reaction to them,' says Terry Nation. 'If the Doctor ever treated them with disrespect they'd be dead. They're Indians, Sidney Greenstreets, income-tax men – it's good versus evil. Do you know what we have here? A new style morality play!' Tom Baker takes up the theme: 'My response to the Daleks has got to be totally real. Or else they don't exist. But they're still terrible! No humour, no jokes. And without jokes there's no optimism.' Baker says he is now really loving playing the Doctor. 'The thing about Doctor Who is that he must be eternally in the present. Like when you fall in love. You know, that wonderful sense of . . . surprise.' He is also enjoying the spin-offs, in particular being recognised. 'I was out one evening when I walked between two policemen and one says, absolutely on cue, "Good evening, Doctor!" I was delighted. And then *they* were delighted that I was delighted.' But nothing has changed his bohemian existence, says Anthony Haden-Guest. 'Right now he is living in a lorry drivers' pull-up in Shepherd's Bush. His belongings are in a couple of cardboard crates in a BBC production office. It's a lifestyle that reminds one of – well – Doctor Who.'

'Genesis of the Daleks' subsequently proves to be one of Terry Nation's favourite stories. He has said recently. 'My favourite character in a *Doctor Who* series was Davros: the man in the wheelchair who was actually perpetuating his image in his machines. He was a creator. You are made in your creator's image. That's what I wanted to do. I think it was a smashing set of episodes. I loved them. David Maloney directed it and he found production values they hadn't had there for ages. It seems to me if you have to say, "What's the best *Doctor Who* series that ever happened?", from my point of view that would be it.'

March 23

A Cambridge astrophysicist, Dr Vincent Icke, declares that the idea of a time- and space-machine like the Doctor's TARDIS *is* feasible. In a special report entitled 'Doctor Who's Time-Machine Is Not Just Kid's Stuff', the *News of the World* reports on the progress that is being made into turning science fiction dreams like those of the Doctor into reality. Dr Icke has been researching the theory that if a space-machine can maintain a constant acceleration, a speed will eventually be reached at which Earth-time no longer applies to those on board – just as happens on the TARDIS. He explains: 'This curious effect of time dilation means a spaceman could travel to the centre of the galaxy and back, while only ageing forty years. Assuming you could find a volunteer to spend forty years of his life in space, there's still one nightmarish problem. For Earth-time will have passed normally in his absence. And when the spaceman gets back he'll find himself 70,000 years in the future! By that time the planet may have become uninhabitable. Or worse, the people on it may have evolved into a different race.' (Shades of the Daleks!)

March 27

'Doctor Who has turned into tea-time brutality for tots,' Mary Whitehouse declares in yet another swingeing attack on the programme, revealing to the national press that she has written to Lord Annan and his committee investigating the future of broadcasting, suggesting that they ask for a special screening of certain stories. 'This series has moved from fantasy to real-life violence,' she continues, 'with cruelty, corpses, poison-gas and Nazi-type stormtroopers, not to mention revolting experiments in human genetics.' Mrs Whitehouse says she has received a number of complaints about the last two episodes of the 'Genesis of the Daleks'. 'It is now questionable whether it should be shown any time before nine in the evening,' she adds, accusing the BBC of trying to attract adult viewers to the series by screening the programme early in the evening.

Philip Hinchcliffe is quick to respond to these complaints. 'Though I am sure that most of our audience realises they are watching fiction not fact,' he says, 'of course, ultimately, we have to rely upon parents in the home to decide whether a programme is suitable for their child. We do take great pains to ensure that we never depict any act of violence which could be dangerously copied by children.'

Mrs Whitehouse's view is not shared by the TV critics, and indeed Shaun Usher of the *Daily Mail* takes quite a different attitude, declaring: 'Terry Nation may be hurt by the reaction, but Daleks are positively reassuring to those of us who knew Doctor Who when he was William Hartnell and we were a lot younger. The whole series is cosy, of course. As predictable and settled as the tale of the Three Bears. *Who* is pure tradition: tatty, repetitive, and in its own modest way, as hypnotic as the Ancient Mariner.' Despite the fact that this story describes the creation of the Dalek race, director David Maloney has only three actual Daleks available because of their high cost, yet with clever camera work and the use of dummy models in crowd scenes, he manages to show an awesome army of them on screen.

April 24

The second tragedy for the twelve-year-old series with the death in hospital of William Hartnell at the age of sixty-seven. The first Doctor's health has declined steadily in recent months, though he did his best to reply to the many fans who still wrote to him at his home in Marden, Kent where he lived quietly with his wife, Heather. The national press gives great prominence to his passing. 'Doctor Who, the first Dalek fighter, dies,' writes the *Daily Mirror*, recording the life of Hartnell who 'became a hero to millions of children' as the 'man the Daleks could not kill'. The newspaper quotes – appropriately – Terry Nation, who says: 'The biggest tribute to William Hartnell is that he started a show which is still going on with huge audiences. He set the high standard for all his successors to follow.' The *Daily Mail* notes how delighted Hartnell was to get the role of the Doctor at the age of fifty-five after a lifetime of playing 'what he called bastards'. The paper also quotes one of his most frequently reported statements: 'I was so pleased to be offered *Doctor Who*. To me,

RONALD BINNIE

kids are the greatest audience – and the greatest critics – in the world.' Hartnell is also accorded a lengthy obituary in *The Times* which declares: *'Doctor Who* was originally expected to run for about six weeks, but Hartnell went on to play the part for three years, becoming a national celebrity and attracting a huge personal fan mail from grown-ups as well as children.' The BBC pays its tribute to Hartnell by screening a sequence of him inside the TARDIS from 'The Gunfighters' when announcing his death on the *Nine O'Clock News.*

April 28

Doctor Who is blamed for having created an epidemic of spider phobia among young children. The origin of this fear, says Dr Michael Hession, consultant psychiatrist to the Church of England's Children's Society, was 'Planet of the Spiders', shown a year ago and, of course, the subject of complaints at the time. Writing in the *General Practitioner*, he says that fears and phobias are almost universal among young children. 'Phobias, such as those of spiders, may have cultural or family origins,' he says. 'A recent *Doctor Who* series was probably responsible for an epidemic of spider phobia among young children.'

Mrs Mary Whitehouse promptly issues a statement: 'This psychiatrist precisely underlines the warnings we have been giving of the effect of *Doctor Who* on the very small child. The BBC admits that it has done no research into the effects of TV programmes on children under five and that this programme is really meant for the intelligent ten-year-old and over. We intend to ask the BBC as a matter of urgency to finance independent research into the effect of *Doctor Who* on the under-fives, and, in the meantime, ask it to switch the programme to 6.30.'

A BBC spokesman reports that the spiders in the particular programme 'were not like ordinary spiders' and says this is the first the Corporation has heard about the claimed effects.

July 15

Issue 7 of the science fiction/horror magazine *World of Horror* is published, bringing with it the first public advertisement for a *Doctor Who* fan club. In the wake of mounting interest, the editors on *World of Horror* have for some time found their *Doctor Who* photo features to be exceptionally popular with readers, even more so with the advent of Tom Baker's Doctor.

Although the Doctor Who Fan Club has been running for some time, it is not until now that it gains sufficient public recognition to start drawing together the large number of uncoordinated fans eager for some body to represent and express their interests. Response to the advertisement is good – so good that the office running the club is quickly snowed under by requests for information, membership and collectables. Nevertheless, from the nucleus drawn to this early organisation will eventually spring the Doctor Who Appreciation Society (DWAS) and, subsequently, many of the related overseas bodies that would lead to the vast network of international fandom currently in existence in the United States, Canada, Australia, New Zealand, Italy and elsewhere.

August 30

The start of the thirteenth season and Tom Baker's second as the Doctor in Robert Banks Stewart's 'Terror of the Zygons,' a story that sees the first major use of techniques soon to be known as video effects. A development of the inlay operator's skills, video effects cover the area of special effects that are not mechanically built for the programme – i.e. a prop ray-gun is a visual effect, but the beam it emits is a video, or electronic, effect.

'Terror of the Zygons' uses an electronic effect generator for the intermediate stage in the spectacular transformations of Zygons into humans, and vice versa. The effects generator is used to create a series of rippling patterns which are switched through to a flat TV screen being seen by a camera. On another screen is a live picture of an actor waiting to be transformed. The electronic effects operator traces the outline of the actor from this second screen and makes from the tracing a man-shaped hole in a piece of card. This card is then placed over the effects screen such that the only image visible to the camera is a man-shaped swirl of rippling colour. These two camera shots are then recorded with the operator on the mixing desk fading from the live actor to the swirling image. The same technique is then used for the Zygon standing in the same spot as the human actor – a matte mask similarly being made for the Zygon's shape against the colour swirl. When these four shots are mixed and later blended together in the editing suite, the resulting effect is of an actor gradually changing into an amorphous riot of human-shaped colours, then into a riot of Zygon-shaped colour, and finally into the Zygon itself. Used several times in 'Terror of the Zygons' similar variations on this process will be the key to many of *Doctor Who*'s electronic effects over the next five years.

Two further points of interest from 'Terror of the Zygons': although offering an explanation to the mystery of the Loch Ness Monster, it was actually filmed for cost reasons in Sussex! And during the course of the story, Brigadier Lethbridge-Stewart comes up with a clear piece of prophecy for the future when he takes a telephone call from the Prime Minister and replies, 'Absolutely understood, *Madam!*'

September 3

Reviewing the new season, Sean Day Lewis of the *Daily Telegraph* says that no one need doubt that Tom Baker has been fully accepted as the new Doctor. 'My children have come to like Baker's version of Doctor Who,' he writes, 'considering him quite as clever as his predecessors and much funnier. And he further enhanced his reputation this time, by appearing in the insignia of a Bay City Rollers' supporter!'

September 6

The Doctor and his companions Sarah Jane and Harry switch on the Blackpool Illuminations at a ceremony attended by huge crowds. Several Daleks and Cybermen also attend the big switch-on in Talbot Square, along with the 'Queen of Blackpool Lights', the Fylde Coast Jazzmen,

CHRISTOPHER DENYER

the Dolly Set dancers, and a singing group, The Loving Couple. The only hitch is the delayed arrival of the Mayor of Blackpool, Councillor Harold Hoyle, who tells the delighted crowds: 'Someone locked me in one of the telephone boxes. It was a blue one – with another fellow in it . . .'

Interviewed by reporters again about Mary Whitehouse and her complaints concerning the programme, Tom Baker says: 'I think she was being rather foolish. Some children do get a bit frightened, but the series have to be exciting or no one would watch. The violence is always very fictional so as not to influence children. I invited Mrs Whitehouse out to lunch to explain all this, but she never came. Anyway, I was a compulsive bed-wetter until I was eleven and that wasn't caused by *Doctor Who!'* Tom also reveals that his style has brought a whole new female following to the series. 'I get quite a few offers of marriage from young girls,' he says, 'but I don't know whether it's me they are after or a chance to travel through space!'

October 11

'Planet of Evil' becomes unique among *Doctor Who* stories as the adventure in which the monster was invented *before* the story. Philip Hinchcliffe explains: 'We wanted to get away from the usual monster which is an actor inside a monster suit. So I asked our special effects department what we could do, and they came up with this shapeless creature idea which is all done by electronic wizardry. It was when we knew we could do this sort of creature that we asked Louis Marks to write a story incorporating it.' The story also provides a remarkable performance from actor Frederick Jaeger as a scientist who becomes an 'outer-space version of Jekyll and Hyde' to quote one report. Jaeger himself says later: 'It is eleven years since I was in *Doctor Who,* and it will probably be as long again before viewers get over what happened to me. It took eight hours in the make-up chair to transform me into that mixture of Piltdown man and Guy the gorilla!'

October 25

A curious coincidence occurs while Peter Grimwade, currently production assistant on *Doctor Who,* later to become a director, is searching for a location for the much-acclaimed Egyptian story, 'Pyramids of Mars' by Stephen Harris. He recalls: 'We were driving around districts looking for a suitable location when we stopped at a pub for lunch. By chatting to the landlord and the locals we were eventually led to Mick Jagger's house, Stargroves. And funnily enough, we later discovered the house was built by the same person who had worked on Lord Caernarvon's home, Highclere. Lord Caernarvon was, of course, the man who unearthed the tomb of Tutankhamen!'

December 13

The final episode of 'The Android Invasion' by Terry Nation, with Barry Letts directing, is to be the last UNIT story with the popular characters Harry Sullivan and John Benton (Ian Marter and John Levene) departing from the series. Philip Hinchcliffe says that UNIT has now 'had its day'.

1976

January 3

A major feature on *Doctor Who* written by Philippa Toomey appears in *The Times*. She talks to Tom Baker first. 'Everyone who has played the Doctor seems to have enjoyed it,' he says. 'I find that my face is associated with something very nice and very charming and great fun. It is certainly delightful to see the effect it has on children. I have enjoyed my life much more since I became the Doctor – I used to get terribly tired of Tom Baker.' He says he gets lots of letters from children. 'They always ask if I want any help – if I need them they'll be glad to join me. They send me St Christopher medals and things like that.' Baker adds that he does a lot of work publicising the programme and was recently absolutely amazed when 5,000 people turned out to see him in Glasgow. His biggest hazard seems to be his now familiar long scarf. 'I am constantly tripping over it,' he says. 'It's about sixteen or seventeen feet long and in damp weather it's practically twenty feet. I had a letter from a girl who had knitted one and the first morning she wore it to school she fell downstairs and broke her ankle.'

Philippa Toomey also learns of the exhausting six-day-week schedule the programme has and comments: 'Anyone who thinks it is a glamorous life should opt for a regular job in the salt mines.' Her opinion is shared by Douglas Camfield, the director of more than fifty episodes, who says *Doctor Who* is 'the most difficult show to direct in the BBC'. Script editor Robert Holmes confesses to another quite different problem. 'I dread,' he says, 'the thirteen-year-old pedant who knows more physics than I do.' Both he and Philip Hinchliffe see the Doctor as an epic hero – allowing for the eccentric image – but one who must be taken extremely seriously.

And, finally, in discussing all the controversy that has surrounded recent episodes, Miss Toomey concludes: 'Coming as it now does, immediately after the News, where baddies of every race, creed and colour (not to mention the odd monster) are clearly winning hands down, *Doctor Who* is an intensely moral and entertaining tale of the triumph of virtue and superior technology. Should we ask for anything more?'

January 24

Mary Whitehouse once more complains about the 'manic atmosphere' and 'fearsome appearance' of the central character in 'The Brain of Morbius' a story written by Terrance Dicks, from which he has withdrawn his name because of what he sees as interference with his parody of the Frankenstein legend. The letters page of the *Guardian* is taken up with furious replies to Mrs Whitehouse's charges from children, parents and even a university lecturer, Barbara Mauthe of County College, Lancaster, who feels that Morbius is no more fearsome than any other monster that has appeared in the series. And no *Doctor Who* adventure, she says, would be complete without either the Doctor or his companions having their lives threatened. 'Mrs Whitehouse should be more guarded in her attacks on *Doctor Who*,' she adds. 'It is practically an institution and any attempts to dislodge it will meet with great opposition at least from my family and me.'
Five-and-three-quarter-year-old Daniel

Fryer is just as emphatic! 'I don't think *Doctor Who* should be moved up to a higher time. It is a beautiful programme because it doesn't scare me. If it was at a later time I would stamp in anger. Sarah and Doctor Who are the best people on it. I like the pictures of the monsters and every nasty animal. It doesn't give me nightmares.' And parent Mrs Fiona Crosby sums up: 'When is Mrs Whitehouse going to realise that in most cases we parents are the best judges of what is suitable viewing for our children?'

In a rather more light-hearted vein, 'The Brain of Morbius' contains a little in-joke between members of the production team. During the mind battle between the Doctor and the Morbius monster a succession of faces are seen on the view screen – supposedly one or other of these two. In fact they are the faces of producer Philip Hinchcliffe, script editor Robert Holmes, directors Christopher Barry and Douglas Camfield, production assistant Christopher Baker, scriptwriter Robert Banks Stewart, and George Gallacio, the production unit manager!

January 31

The drama that goes on in the making of Robert Banks Stewart's 'The Seeds of Doom' far surpasses the actual story of a mad botanist who brings an alien species to Earth. First a flu epidemic sweeps through the cast as they are rehearsing, then an actor is injured in a car crash. Thirdly, a key member catches chicken pox and filming has to go on without him – with the ever-present threat that spots may well break out on any of the others! Just when Philip Hinchcliffe thinks his troubles are

WILLIAM WEBSTER

over there is one of the biggest scares in BBC history: the tape of the first episode goes missing.

Hinchcliffe remembers those nerve-wracking events vividly. 'Every year the BBC makes millions of tapes and they are all stored in a special library,' he says. 'Our tapes for the entire serial were tucked safely away – we thought – the actors had all gone away and the sets had been dismantled. We rang the library asking for our first episode and, after a check, the answer came back that they couldn't find it. It had just vanished. Panic? It was more like a mass rave. They started checking – through 32,000 tapes – and I started making plans to re-edit the serial – a mammoth job with very little time to spare. Finally, after two days they found it – it had been wrongly numbered – but in that time I aged about twenty years. It seemed as if the whole production was doomed!'

February 12

A group of London primary school children, afraid that Mrs Mary Whitehouse has the power to ban their favourite programme, *Doctor Who*, carry out a survey of the series among their friends, according to a report in the London *Evening News*. For two days the eleven-year-olds at Smallwood Junior School in Tooting interview 385 fellow pupils about their reactions to *Doctor Who*. Their teacher, Mr Graham Welch, tells the paper: 'They went to each class and found that 80 per cent of the children watched the programme and that nearly all of them enjoyed it. We found that only about 10 per cent – mostly the much younger children – were frightened by it. We also bore in mind the fact that some children are frightened by a programme but enjoyed being frightened. The children who had heard of Mrs Whitehouse thought she was a government official with the power to drop the programme. I had to explain that she only represents a pressure group.'

March 7

The day after the final episode of 'The Seeds of Doom', *Doctor Who* is rigorously defended by Alan Thompson, Professor of the Economics of Government at Heriot-Watt University in an article for the *Sunday Times* entitled 'Doctor Who's Value: Morality and Integrity'. 'As someone who writes children's fiction as a hobby,' says Professor Thompson, 'I would like to defend *Doctor Who* as a highly moral programme. It is very difficult to inject a strong moral content into children's entertainment without becoming rather boring and pedantic. Yet *Doctor Who* introduces morality in a creative and exciting manner. In every series, right always, in the end, triumphs over wrong. At a deeper moral level, good always triumphs over evil.' Professor Thompson believes the choice of a scientist as the hero encourages interest in the subject at school, and the Doctor's commitment to individual freedom against the single-minded brutality of totalitarianism is equally significant. He adds: 'In Tom Baker the BBC has the almost perfect Doctor Who: witty and humane, self-controlled, but with flashes of righteous anger when confronted with evil. Yet lurking under the surface of his assurance is a capacity for self-criticism and an ability to laugh at himself. All these qualities are invaluable to children as they grow up to face the problems of the world.'

July 6

Tom Baker's undoubted success as the Doctor leads to a wide range of Tom Baker merchandise appearing in shops during the summer months. Despite the programme being off the air, these toys, games and various promotional gimmicks are very popular. Interest is also growing in what goes on behind the scenes during the making of *Doctor Who* and the magazine *TV Sci-Fi Monthly* is the first to feature regular and serious-minded stories on this aspect.

Another little piece of *Who* history is also made when Tom Baker and Elisabeth Sladen play the Doctor and Sarah Jane in a special half-hour Schools Radio production in which they conduct listeners, with the help of the TARDIS, to various periods of the Earth's evolution. There is even an alien villain called Megron – played by John Westbrook – who opposes order and naturally requires putting in his place by the Doctor. David Little produced and Bernard Venables wrote this semi-documentary *Doctor Who* adventure for the radio – the only one of its kind.

September 4

The start of the fourteenth season with 'The Masque of Mandragora' by Louis Marks sees another major feature on the programme, and Tom Baker in particular, which appears in the *Guardian*, written by Nancy Mills. She says unequivocally: 'Baker was an inspired choice. He has turned the character into a cult figure, replete with fan clubs and Doctor Who societies all over Britain. It is rumoured that a university administrator recently broke up a student demonstration by announcing that *Doctor Who* was on the television. By the time they realised it was only Tuesday, it was too late.'

Baker is quoted at length in the article, first talking about his role: '*Doctor Who* is really an acting part,' he says. 'It's a matter of being inventive enough to project credibility to scenes which aren't credible. The programme is like a hovercraft – on a fine line all the time. You don't dare touch the ground.' Baker speaks of his success as 'preposterously out of proportion' and recalls what happened when a friend took him to dinner recently at Brook's Club. 'While my friend was telling me how people at the club leave you alone, a distinguished gentleman across the room raised his glass of port and said, "Good evening, Doctor".' Baker says he feels a great sense of responsibility to his audience. 'I wouldn't be seen dead in a pantomime. I'm not going to rip off our *Doctor Who* audience. Anyway, Aladdin's lamp is nothing compared to my sonic screwdriver!' He loves making charity appearances and recently earned £1,000 for one charity. 'I can do about a hundred autographs an hour,' he smiles, 'but I like to talk to the children as well. They like little gags – like signing "To Paul, who on earth is Tom Baker?" I'm not interested in the jaded reactions of parents to *Doctor Who*. I've never heard a really revelationary remark from adults. But little children – their imaginative reactions mesmerise me.'

Interestingly, location shooting for 'The Masque of Mandragora' has been filmed at Portmeiron, the strangely styled village in North Wales, where Patrick McGoohan had made his later-to-become-a-cult television series *The Prisoner* in the 1960s.

BARB ARMATA

October 23

The departure from the series of a companion now makes front page news – where previously it has only been the Doctors themselves accorded such prominence. After almost three years, Elisabeth Sladen is to leave the show. 'The best thing I ever did was joining *Doctor Who*; leaving it was the next best thing. I loved it, but I couldn't stay for ever. I liked playing Sarah Jane because I was working with people I liked and was recognised in public. I don't believe the actress who says she doesn't enjoy that. And I got some lovely letters from viewers. Little girls wrote to say that they dreamed they were Sarah and older people wrote telling her to be careful.' And talking of her parting in the final episode of 'The Hand of Fear', she says: 'Having got back to Earth I just decided to stay home. I wanted to go out with a big bang, blown up in a nuclear explosion, but the BBC wouldn't have it. I refused to get married off or anything sloppy like that. Unless, of course, it was to a monster. It might have been quite fun being Mrs Dalek!'

It is as well that such drastic ideas are not taken too seriously, for this is to prove far from the last appearance of the resourceful Sarah Jane, the strength of her character earning this praise from the *Guardian's* Peter Fiddick: 'I have a certain sympathy with the argument that the female side-kicks have served successive Doctors as stereotyped Little Women boosting the Great Male Ego, but Sarah, in both Elisabeth Sladen's perky performance and the scripts she progressively earned, got a sight nearer to subverting the omnipotence than Robin ever did for Batman.'

October 30

Alone for only the second time in the entire series, the Doctor travels in the TARDIS to Gallifrey and many facts about his background and the life of the Time Lords is revealed in 'The Deadly Assassin', written by script editor, Robert Holmes. That this story is destined to become something of a classic is sensed by the *Guardian*. 'You can't help being impressed by its freewheeling inventiveness,' says the paper. 'It mostly shuns the fake moralising of more pretentious space operas like *Star Trek*, and quite right too, and offers instead two key qualities: the best special effects of any television programme, bionic or invisible, tossed out week after week with astonishing nonchalance; and a sense of humour that keeps the whole exercise well in its place.' Before the end of the story, however, the programme is to be embroiled once again in controversy . . .

November 21

Tom Baker declines to become Rector of St Andrew's University in Scotland. He tells the press: 'Being nominated for Rector is a big honour and a great sign of popularity. But it would take up too much of the time I wish to dedicate to making *Doctor Who* one of the most popular characters in the world. Not only St Andrew's has a fan following for the show. There's also a Doctor Who Appreciation Society at St John's College, Oxford. It's also a winner in twenty-two other countries, including Holland, where it has just won me the award as the best actor in TV science fiction.'

COLIN-JOHN P. RODGERS

November 25

Rumours that plans have been underway for some time to make a full-length *Doctor Who* feature film are confirmed by Tom Baker. He tells Martin Jackson of the *Daily Mail* that he wants to star in the film, to be called *Doctor Who Meets Scratchman*, and see it released in time for Christmas 1977. He has a script by former companion, Ian Marter, and an agreement with leading Hollywood horror film star Vincent Price to play the villain Scratchman – an old mediaeval word for the devil. The only problem is raising the money to make the picture, even though he and director James Hill will take no pay, only a percentage.

'It has been a saddening and frustrating experience' Baker says. 'The British film industry seems to be closing down, yet here is a film which entails absolutely no risk. With millions of viewers on TV each week, we have a guaranteed cinema box-office, and you would have thought the British film industry would have snapped it up. But I couldn't get a single studio interested. We did have an approach from Hollywood, but I wanted this to be a British film. We should have opened our production office a month ago. We have even all offered to work for nothing in an effort to cut costs. But still there have been no takers!'

CHARLOTTE BRETT

Later, talking to another journalist, Keith Fisher of the *Sunday Mirror*, Baker says, 'I'm determined to make the film somehow. So maybe *Doctor Who* fans might like to invest a few quid and become shareholders? The budget is around £500,000 which means fans gambling a fiver each.' This off-the-cuff remark is to have far-reaching consequences . . .

December 29

The year ends with another complaint from Mrs Mary Whitehouse – but this time there is a reply from the BBC Director-General, Sir Charles Curran. Her complaint is about violence in the third part of 'The Deadly Assassin' – an episode which attracts the largest-ever audience for the programme. Mrs Whitehouse called the scene in which the Doctor is being throttled and his head held under water until he appears to drown 'sadistic' and 'too horrific' for a children's show. In his reply Sir Charles says the BBC is 'not particularly satisfied' with the episode, but he defends the programme as a whole as 'reasonably acceptable'. He claims that several scenes had already been edited out of the episode because they were felt to be 'a little too realistic', and he adds: 'The result was what you saw on the screen and which I myself think was reasonably acceptable although, as I say – with hindsight – the head of the department responsible would have liked to cut out just a few more frames of the action than he did.' As a result of this complaint some stricter guidelines are made about the use of horror and violence in the series.

The story also attracts great interest among long-time *Doctor Who* fans because of the reappearance in a terribly decrepit form of the Master, long thought to have disappeared from the series since the death of Roger Delgado. Although Peter Pratt makes just a single appearance as the Master, he apparently escapes from the Doctor and seems to have regenerated. Is the character *The Times* once called 'irreplaceable' going to be seen again, fans wonder?

1977

January 1

Enter a new-look companion in the shapely form of Leela, a Sevateem warrior in plunging leather costume and high boots who storms into the Doctor's life in 'The Face of Evil' by Chris Boucher. She is quickly to become a favourite with viewers – men in particular! This role as a kind of female Tarzan is a complete change for Louise Jameson, who has previously appeared with the Royal Shakespeare Company and nearly landed the role of Purdey in *The New Avengers*. Says Louise, 'I have to do a lot more action sequences than the other girls. Luckily, I am fairly sporty and I go regularly to keep-fit classes.' And of Tom Baker she comments: 'Working with him is just great. Ideas pour out of him. He lives, breathes and sleeps *Doctor Who.*' Philip Hinchcliffe also tells the press, 'Leela is tough, independent-minded and thigh-revealing. Someone in her own right and a bit primitive. We chose Louise deliberately to change the part.'

January 10

Terry Nation delivers a surprise attack on *Doctor Who* in an interview with David Wigg of the *Daily Express.* 'The Dalek Man', as Terry has become nicknamed in Faversham, Kent, where he lives in a mansion with thirty-five acres of land, is said to have become one of Britain's highest paid freelance writers as a result of the success of his creations. But, he says, his enthusiasm for the programme has waned. 'I think it's lost a great deal of the excitement and adventure with which it started out,' Nation says. 'It's taking itself a little too seriously. I think it should be more fun.' Despite this criticism, Terry Nation still talks affectionately of the Daleks, 'and why shouldn't he,' asks David Wiggs, 'because they have already survived fifteen years and are still one of the four top TV toys!'

February 11

The doyen of Fleet Street columnists, Jean Rook of the *Daily Express* also takes the production team to task over what she sees as *Doctor Who*'s transformation into a show 'no longer suitable for children'. She

SIMON FORWARD

TIM PIERACCINI

writes that after three years enjoying the programme, her six-year-old son will no longer watch. 'I blame myself', she says, 'for not noticing the extremely nasty turn which this cult, fourteen-million-viewer TV programme has taken since, I gauge, last year's Sutekh episode ("Pyramids of

G. WALES

Mars"). In which, your scalp may stir to remember, Doctor Who's girl assistant was stalked through a snapping, crackling autumn wood by two seven-foot grey-bandaged Egyptian mummies. Twin Frankensteins who would have put the wind of heaven up Peter Cushing. At the time I thought them strong, if not fetid, for a "children's programme". With wiser hindsight, I shudder to think that, while I was frying his fish fingers, my child was alone in a room with a programme which could have screwed up and permanently crunched his nerve with one mummified hand. What has gone wrong with the innocent tea-time thrill of watching *Doctor Who*?' With the year's average ratings up two million on 1975–6, she says, 60 per cent of the viewers being adults, and 'the Doctor's new thigh-flashing assistant Leela switching on the sixteen-year-olds in hordes', the answer is not immediately obvious.

Miss Rook turns to Robert Holmes who provides it. 'Of course it's no longer a children's programme,' he says. 'Parents would be terribly irresponsible to leave a six-year-old to watch it alone. It's geared to the intelligent fourteen-year-old and I wouldn't let any child under ten see it. If a little one really enjoys peeping at it from behind the sofa, until Dad says, "It's all right now – it's all over", that's fine. A certain amount of fear is healthy, under strict parental supervision. Even then I'd advise half an hour to play with Dad and forget it before a child goes to bed. That's why we switched the time from 5.15 until after 6.00, when most young kids are in the bath.'

Jean Rook also accuses *Doctor Who* of having grown out of 'a rubber monster show into a full-scale unknown horror programme', to which Robert Holmes replies: 'When it started as a true children's programme the monsters were rubber and specific and you saw them almost at once. What horrifies far more is the occasional flash of monster – bits and pieces of one. People are frightened by what *might* come round the corner or in at the window.' He adds that the show takes a high moral tone about killing. 'They're strictly fantasy deaths,' he says. "No blood, no petrol bombs, nothing a child could copy. We're not in business to harm children. We learned our lesson years ago with some plastic daffodils which killed just by spitting at people. We didn't consider that people actually have plastic daffodils in their homes. They caused screaming nightmares, so we scrapped them. You must never attack the security of a child in its home. If you make something nasty, you don't stick it in a nursery.'

The Express columnist concludes her report: 'I accept that *Doctor Who* is nerve-wrenching, spine-gripping and now

WILLIAM MERRIN

totally grown-up. Checking, I find I have forty-year-old friends who can't watch it. It's a great TV achievement. But I wonder if this inflated, ex-children's programme is over-stretching itself and worshipping its own, uninhibited cult?'

February 28

'Doctor Who is too terrifying for Europe', the *Daily Mail* headlines a report. 'Doctor Who, the science fiction hero of thousands of British children, will not be seen by European youngsters,' the newspaper states. 'He is too terrifying. "Our television is regarded as being too violent by the rest of Europe," Mr Brian Keyser, assistant head of sales for BBC Enterprises said yesterday. "We have found it impossible to sell *Doctor Who* and the series has been running for fourteen years." Mr Keyser was speaking in Brighton where the BBC presented a showcase of TV programmes for European buyers in the hope of raising £500,000. Nevertheless, *Doctor Who* will be shown to the delegates from thirty countries. It has been sold in Canada and Australia, but there it is classified as adult-only viewing.'

March 5

By a strange twist of fate, the current serial, 'The Talons of Weng-Chiang' by Robert Holmes, is not screened as scheduled in Canada by TV Ontario. According to fans it has been banned; according to TV Ontario it has been decided not to show this particular story because it is felt it might offend the country's Chinese community.

An interesting feature of TV Ontario's presentation of *Doctor Who* is the five-minute discussion spot held immediately after each episode in which a group of guest speakers, under the chairmanship of the well-known science fiction expert Judith Merrill, talk about the various issues raised in the story.

April 3

The day after the conclusion of the last story of the season, 'The Talons of Weng-Chiang', BBC 2's Sunday night hour-long magazine programme, *The Lively Arts*, devotes its entire transmission to an examination of the *Doctor Who* phenomenon under the title, 'Whose Doctor Who?' Using clips from episodes involving all four Doctors, the programme explores the ideas and attitudes which have characterised the series from the beginning and made it 'one of the most popular family shows ever devised for British television'. Presenter Melvyn Bragg also talks to Tom Baker, Philip Hinchcliffe, Dick Mills and viewers, both young and old, about what the series means to them.

Producer of the programme Tony Cash receives general praise for his work, though Stewart Lane of the *Morning Star* has some reservations: 'He provided us with some absorbing behind-the-scenes views of the creation of the giant rat in the just concluded adventure as well as Weng's own horrifying visage, and cheerful youngsters from Smallwood Junior School, Tooting, clearly enjoyed telling the camera why it was all so scary and entertaining. Unfortunately, Mr Cash got us mixed up with education psychologist John Miller, who really went a bit over the edge in trying to relate *Doctor Who* to his own work. Even worse, we had the head of an intensive care unit, Dr Sherwood Jones, with his team, making flattering noises about the "similarities" between the manner in which Doctor Who tackled his problems and the unit theirs! Really, Mr Cash, Doctor Who's hocus-pocus is quite engaging in its own right, without trying to embellish it with some mumbo-jumbo relationship with the real world.'

May 22

Doctor Who goes to the BBC's Pebble Mill Studios in Birmingham for the first time to record a substantial amount of material for the forthcoming fifteenth season. A new young producer, Graham Williams, aged thirty-three, takes over and has to make substantial changes in the content of the programmes as a result of the recent complaints. He later says: 'When I was offered the job it was made absolutely clear that the violence level had to come down, and the horror element with it. The moment I protested that this was what the audience adored, I was shouted down. Needless to say this caused Robert Holmes more than a few headaches. We had to go back over all the stories we'd been commissioning and take all the horror out, which left us with a rather nasty hole. So all we had left to fill it with was, predictably, humour – which we did.'

Graham Williams is also told to gear the show less to children, as audience research shows it should aim for 'intelligent fifteen-year-olds'. He comments, 'That was where we felt we should aim our programmes and thankfully, when we became more aware of the Doctor Who Appreciation Society and met all their intelligent fifteen-year-olds, we were gratified to find we were right.' Despite the problems that confront him, a month later Graham is telling the press: 'This is the one show that really gives me satisfaction from the job. I often have sleepless nights thinking about it and trying to make things work. But I like to see it well done.'

June 10

The Doctor is to get an entirely new kind of companion, a computerised dog named K9. The *Evening Mail*'s TV writer, Stafford Hildren, declares prophetically that this 'battery-operated barker should prove a hit with the fans who keep demanding the return of those other mechanical favourites, the Daleks'. He also quotes Robert Holmes as saying: 'K9 really is a funny little thing. The Doctor finds him with a professor in a laboratory in space. He is really well made and has an antenna which wags depending on how he is feeling. He's got a print-out of information where his tongue should be. He will be a real hit.'

June 30

Tom Baker defends *Doctor Who* against the charges of violence and horror in an interview on BBC's *Pebble Mill at One.* Talking to the presenter, Donny MacLeod, a self-confessed fan of the series, Tom says: 'I believe children enjoy being scared a little, it is a delicious sensation. The Brothers Grimm understood that, but it all depends on where it is presented. When it is in the living-room, the youngster can be swept up in the action as some awesome monster eats the world, or whatever, but he, or she, only has to turn a little bit and there is familiarity. There is Mum and Dad and fish-fingers and normality.'

Donny, who reveals his own son is also a great fan of the Doctor, says of Tom Baker: 'He has a very rare gift – and certainly one given to very few actors. He relates to children, finds it easy to communicate with them. Indeed, he told me, "I prefer their company to that of most adults. The very young ones bring me jelly babies as presents. We communicate!"'

July 18

Tom Baker's chance remark last November suggesting fans might like to contribute to the projected feature-length movie, *Doctor Who Meets Scratchman,* has had a remarkable sequel, the London *Evening Standard* reports. 'Doctor Who has received sacks of mail from his fans,' says the newspaper, 'and all the letters contained money. But sadly for Tom Baker he has had to send all the money back. This extension of his superior powers from merely travelling through time to magnetically drawing pound notes towards him arose through a misquote in a newspaper.' The *Standard* describes Tom Baker's attempt to set up the film and the offer of half of what he needed from the British Board of Film Finance. 'Baker mentioned this in an interview, but the remark came across as an appeal to his fans for funds. They quickly proved what a loyal bunch they are and he received eight thousand letters containing varying amounts. They have come from children, from parents, from grandparents. Baker was amazed, but when he inquired into the

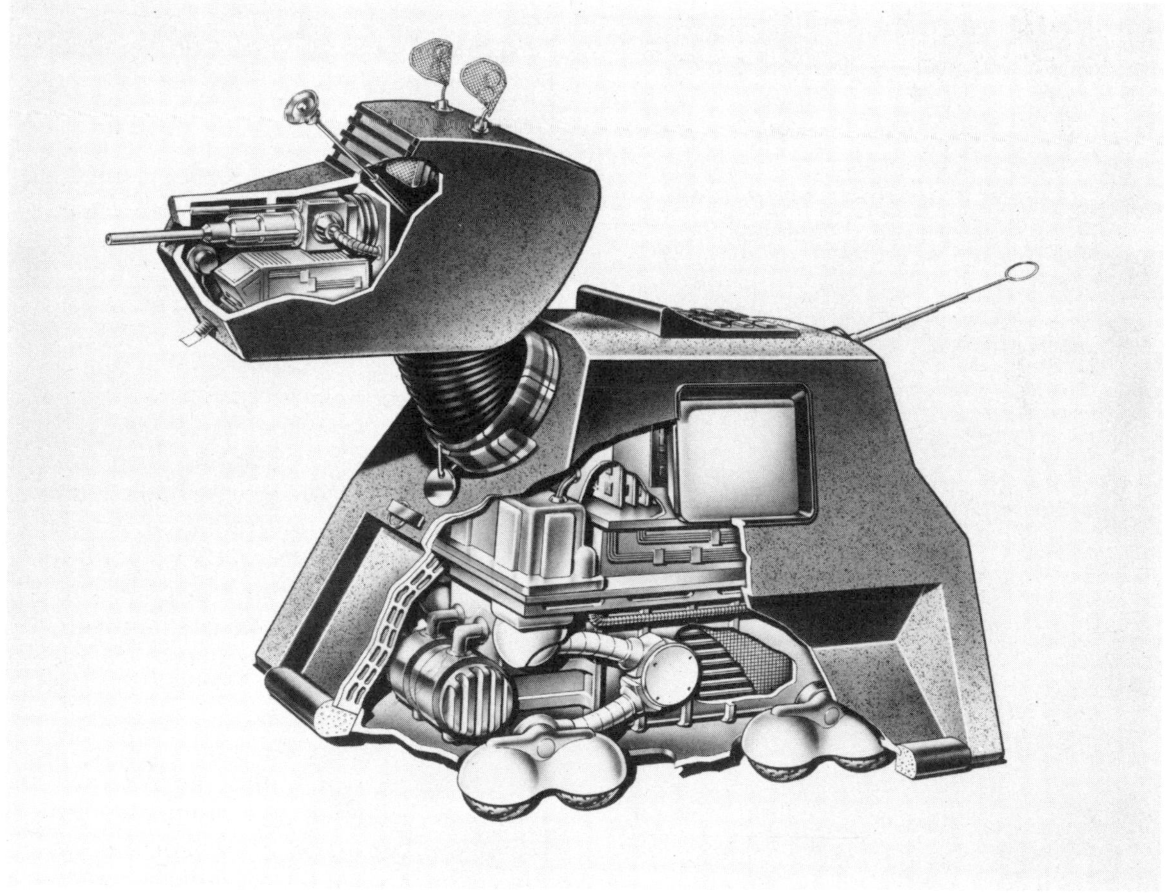

legitimacy of raising money, even inadvertently in this way, he was told he would have to send the lot back. He was advised that he should have started a company, advertised shares, and promised a dividend.' The *Standard* adds that the eight-thousand contributions are now going back, and although Baker has received an approach from a City bank, they are only interested in backing a package of three films rather than just one.

August 6

The world's first Doctor Who Convention is held in the modest surroundings of a church hall in Battersea, London, run by the Doctor Who Appreciation Society. This one-day affair is attended by Jon Pertwee, Tom Baker and Louise Jameson, and several hundred fans. From this humble beginning, conventions have developed world-wide and the British Panopticon is now held annually spanning three days of discussions, screenings, star appearances and souvenir sales.

September 3

Graham Williams opens his first season as producer – the fifteenth for the programme – with the declaration that viewers have seen the last of the Daleks. He tells the press: 'There is no doubt the Daleks have become a TV legend. They're hard to repeat. The odd times they have been brought back they've made tremendous impact the first night – all the little brothers, who haven't seen them, watching with the teenage kids who remember them. But after that curiosity show, the ratings soon drop off. So unless we can find a terrific plot to support them, they won't be back.' This view is shared by Tom Baker who calls them 'dreary, blundering things moving on one level and talking on one note', and by Robert Holmes, who says that from his point of view, 'They're no great conversationalists.' But since even their creator Terry Nation has tried and failed to kill off the Daleks in the past, is this *really* to be the end of them . . .

The first story of the season, 'Horror of Fang Rock' by Terrance Dicks sees the return of the original TARDIS control room to replace the secondary one of the previous group of stories – a wood-panelled interior with control boards hidden behind flaps. The deterioration of this set while in storage has necessitated the change.

October 10

Midway through 'The Invisible Enemy' Stanley Reynolds of *The Times* writes that *Doctor Who* appears to be losing viewers to ITV's *The Man from Atlantis* which, he says, 'has captured the imagination of children'. He feels the upgrading of the appeal to an older audience is partly to blame. 'Plots have become more complicated, the young trendy girls who previously accompanied the Doctor, have been replaced by Leela, a sex symbol. She is also a bit of a Woman's Movement sort; a militant is Leela and she kills with a knife with the ease of a Royal Marine commando.' Reynolds has spotted the introduction of a satirical note, however. 'Leela cannot be put under the influence,' he writes. 'She is too savage. "All instinct and intuition," the Doctor

1977

RONALD BINNIE

explains. Perhaps she is not a bow to the Women's Movement after all; maybe the leggy Leela is there for the dads and more earthy fourteen-year-olds, rather like those appalling rhythmic girls on *Top of the Pops.'* 'Of course, the return of the Daleks is all the programme needs; what the *Top of the Pops* dancers need is something else, but that is neither here nor there!'

October 17

Tom Baker tours hospitals in Blackpool, Blackburn, Liverpool and Preston, visiting sick and injured children. Dressed as the Doctor, his appearance delights the tiny patients and leads to him giving an emotional interview to Liz Prosser of the *Sun.* 'I saw dozens of kids, most of them terribly maimed in road accidents, often by drunken drivers. And also children dumped by cruel or inadequate parents. How can it happen that these children are *victims*? When so many men and woman with love locked away in their hearts, who yearn for children of their own, can't have them and can't adopt. *Doctor Who* has brought me so much, the least I can do is make this romantic hero useful where it really matters. With the less fortunate kids.'

October 24

'The Invisible Enemy' introduces K9, and Shaun Usher of the *Daily Mail* immediately underlines his potential, calling him a 'charming robot dog punningly named'. Graham Williams explains how K9 grew from a rough idea in Bob Baker and Dave Martin's script. 'My brief to the designers was that under no circumstances should kiddies be able to point to it and say there's a little man inside,' he says. 'First they came up with a drawing of a huge Dobermann –

PAUL PICKFORD

armour-plated and very fierce . . . I said, "It's got to be small and radio-controlled." It was agony to get it right, but we were ultimately ahead of R2-D2 in *Star Wars*.'

1978

February 12

Tom Baker takes part in a publicity stunt outside the American Embassy in Grosvenor Square, London, where he and a group of the most famous monsters from the series queue for their visas and are featured in several newspaper spreads. The *Daily Express* reports: 'Tom Baker and his unlikely band of pilgrims were setting up a special mission for their earthly masters at Television Centre. They aim to sell the programme – British audience twelve million – to American TV. And hopes are high . . . after all the Americans made the film *Star Wars* a blockbuster.'

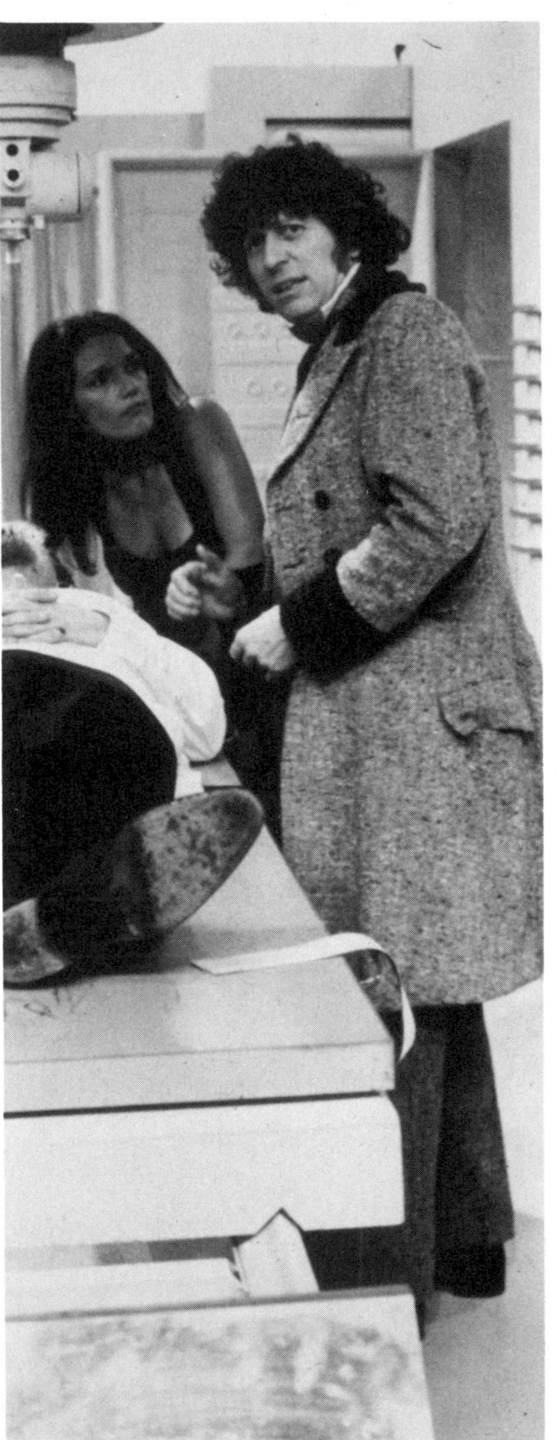

March 11

Protests greet the news of the departure of the Doctor's latest companion, Leela (Louise Jameson), who decides to stay on Gallifrey with K9 at the end of David Agnew's story 'The Invasion of Time'. (A K9 Mark II is, though, revealed before the end to forestall complaints of *his* disappearance!) Peter Dunn writes in the *Sunday Times*: 'The latest *Doctor Who* ended with the Sontarans routed, Gallifrey saved and threatening noises from the programme's producers about writing out the Doctor's mate, Leela. Fathers who have elbowed their offspring aside each Saturday evening to gaze upon the fawn-legged lady are invited to join the latest protest movement, SOL – Save Our Leela.' According to the *Sun*, Louise Jameson brought sex-appeal to the programme during her year on the screen, 'and the proportion of adults in the audience shot up to 60 per cent during her stint'. Louise herself says: 'It was an opportunity to learn the television business quickly. I enjoyed it – but I want to get back to the theatre, and away from my loin-cloth image.'

April 28

Because of the interest generated by the departure of Leela from the series, the *Daily Mirror* builds a major feature around the announcement of the Doctor's new companion, Romana, to be played by Mary Tamm.

Of her part as a Time Lord, Mary, who is aged twenty-seven, says: 'Becoming a *Doctor Who* girl is like becoming a James Bond girl. I'm looking forward to the part immensely.' The *Mirror* reports that she was picked for the role from hundreds of possibles and it is 'worth about £15,000 a year to her.' But, says reporter Tony Pratt, each of Mary's nine predecessors in the series has, at the end of their appearances, 'been faced with the ultimate horror – the Curse of Doctor Who himself.' He writes: 'For despite their unstinting devotion, the nine beautiful and intrepid actresses who decorated the good Doctor's police box during the last fifteen years have gathered little in the way of a rich reward for their devotion. Most of them have achieved national fame through the series, but regret the *Doctor Who* tag which clings to them. The majority have found TV work scarce for months – or even years – after quitting the series. But still there are always candidates.' Brief interviews with each of the nine girls reveal that not one regrets having appeared in the series, nevertheless . . .

May 5

Another former companion makes headline news. Katy Manning poses in the nude with a Dalek for a girlie magazine, and tells journalists: 'I did it for the money. I was skint. I'd had two good holidays abroad, three months out of work – and to top it all, the VAT man was after me. So why say no when an offer like that is manna from heaven?' Of the photographs, she jokes: 'I'd never pose for full frontal pictures. Anyway, why should there be a fuss about my going topless? To catch a glimpse of anything you'd pretty well have to put me under a microscope!' Jon Pertwee comments: 'Typical Katy!'

August 11

News that the BBC is to set up a merchandising operation in Australia to promote *Doctor Who* following its success in Europe and in line with forthcoming plans in America, gets a headline in the *Sydney Mirror* finance section, 'BBC Plans Dalek Invasion of Australia'. The paper says: 'Luke Skywalker and his *Star Wars* colleagues could find themselves under attack from those *Doctor Who* villains – the Daleks. Products to be launched could include *Doctor Who* scarves, toy Daleks and board games.'

At the same time, however, Clement Semmler of the *Sydney Herald* labels *Doctor Who* 'vulgar trivia' and receives a stinging reply from Antony Howe, President of the Australian Doctor Who Fan Club. 'Devotees of the invincible Doctor's

ROLAND JEFFS

stories', he writes, 'would point out that war as such is not glorified, that person-to-person violence is shown as regrettable, that high moral standards are essential in politics (intergalactic or plain mundane), and that preservation of living environments is paramount. In other words, *Doctor Who* has an interior moral effect on the viewer, which is not a mere simplicity of goodies versus baddies, for it has a much deeper level of morality, as in all true SF. This programme has survived for fifteen years and perhaps your critic might be prevailed upon to think again before dismissing it. Vulgar it is not, unless he means it appeals to a wide section of viewers?' And Anthony also adds: 'The ABC programmers are reluctant to admit the popularity of *Doctor Who* and have twice threatened to axe the show. Hundreds of signatures and letters were sent to the Programme Department in 1976, representing a cross-section of viewers from school children to university professors.'

September 2

As the sixteenth season of *Doctor Who* begins in Britain, the programme makes its debut in America, starting with the first Tom Baker story, 'Robot'. Time-Life Television are responsible for handling the series and it opens on 75 US stations. In the months which follow a number of stations drop the show because of poor ratings, but others pick it up and within a year the programme is regularly broadcast on 92 stations. These changes lead to claims in certain media magazines that the series is a flop in America and one report says that 'a bare handful of stations that began running the show in September continue to do so nine months later'. American fans of the show protest at such charges, and Time-Life respond by releasing details on the nearly one hundred stations taking the programme and an emphatic statement that, '*Doctor Who*'s success in America is undeniable!'

In the UK the new season under the new script editor Anthony Read has a central running theme for the first time in the series' history; the whole sequence is appropriately entitled 'The Key to Time'. The opening story, Robert Holmes's 'The Ribos Operation', sees the debut of Mary Tamm as Lady Romana, which provokes this comment from Richard Last of the *Daily Telegraph*: 'It was salutary to see television's more agreeable tyrant and chauvinist, Doctor Who, getting his comeuppance from a Time Lord whose superior status reduced him to a quaking schoolboy . . . I don't doubt he will reassert his infallibility before a couple of episodes are out.'

Of the 'Key to Time' season, Graham Williams says later: 'The concept itself was quite easy to get together, but I knew I needed stories which could still be self-sufficient in their own right. You can't depend on an audience's loyalty for 26 solid weeks . . . at the same time, though, each story had to lock into an overall quest and that presented quite a number of very taxing problems. I found it a very refreshing challenge to do, but I knew I didn't want to repeat it the year after!'

September 30

'The Pirate Planet' marks the writing debut in the series of an author destined for world-wide fame, Douglas Adams, who was offered the commission after completing his radio series *The Hitch-Hiker's Guide to the Galaxy,* later to become an enormously successful television series and best-selling book. Once again, though, it is Mary Tamm's playing of the redoubtable Romana that catches the critics' eyes, Keith Baker of the *Belfast Telegraph* calling her the Doctor's equal, 'with a deferential bow towards the Bionic Woman, Wonder Woman and Women's Lib all at once'.

October 28

Another milestone for *Doctor Who* – the first episode of the one hundredth story, 'The Stones of Blood' by David Fisher, is transmitted. Scheduled to run for four weeks, this landmark series finishes almost on the eve of the programme's fifteenth anniversary.

November 23

The fifteenth anniversary of the start of *Doctor Who* is again marked by a special review on the children's programme *Blue Peter.* Curiously, however, the presenters use the same script as for their previous programme in 1973 and feature almost exactly the same clips from earlier episodes!

The evening news programme *Nationwide* also marks the anniversary with presenter Frank Bough interviewing Tom Baker and Mary Tamm, with a surprise appearance of Carole Ann Ford from the very first cast.

LORI McADAMS

1979

January 20

Yet another milestone for *Doctor Who* – the first episode of the six-parter 'The Armageddon Factor' by Bob Baker and Dave Martin is the 500th episode to be screened. The story also introduces pretty Lalla Ward playing Princess Astra, who is to have quite an effect on the Doctor. Firstly, on screen, she is to return to the series later as a regenerated companion while, off screen, she is to become Mrs Tom Baker.

The *Daily Mail* marks the start of the year with a special report that the series is now being transmitted to 30 countries around the world. Reporter Patrick O'Neill also believes he's discovered the secret of Doctor Who's success. 'For fifteen years reaching 500 episodes tonight,' he writes, 'the wily old Time Lord has pretended to be a celestial boy scout. But he is really an old-fashioned cowboy in disguise. Instead of a horse, he rides into one hundred sunsets – with one hundred different suns – aboard his TARDIS. He doesn't drink, he doesn't smoke, and his only difference from the rest of humanity is that, when it comes to producing offspring, he doesn't do what a man's gotta do. Despite his escorting eleven of Britain's sexiest actresses around the universe, nobody knows where the girl in the very first series, Susan his grand-daughter, came from. "We have never quite worked that one out," said producer Graham Williams. "We can only assume that Time Lords' children are found under a cosmic gooseberry bush. The Doctor is too high-minded to get involved with girls."' Patrick O'Neill also reveals that a reappearance of the Daleks 'for the first time in five years' is being predicted for the autumn . . .

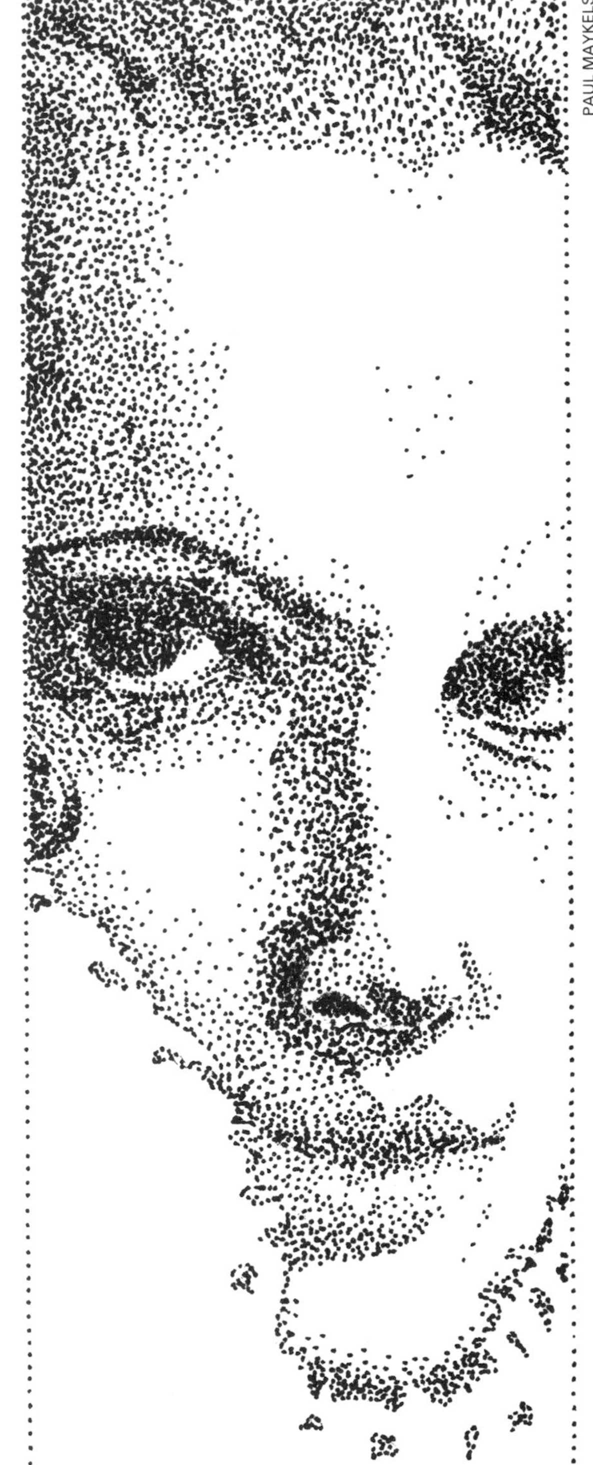

PAUL MAYKELS

February 2

Tom Baker makes a major promotional tour – arriving in Sydney, Australia, to a tumultuous reception.

Describing Baker as the most popular of the four actors to have played the Doctor and now the centre of a cult, the *Australian TV Times* reports: 'His visit to Australia provoked mob scenes that would have gratified the Beatles in their heyday. Often he had to be smuggled out through back doors. Fans, both earnest scholars and straightout sci-fi lovers, were constantly at his side. His appearance during the sixth Test match between England and Australia drew attention from the match – occasionally he was mistaken for England fast bowler Bob Willis. In Brisbane, Baker recalled cheerily: 'A great big raunchy fellow came up and asked me if I was Bob Willis. I said no. Then he said, "You're Doctor Who!" and asked me to autograph a $20 note.'

Tom Baker also reveals that numerous famous actors and actresses who have become fans of the series have intimated their willingness to appear in a story – among them Glenda Jackson and the American, Elaine Stritch. 'One hears such lovely feedback from people about the show,' he says. 'It's now so jolly and successful that it's a big thing with other actors; nearly everybody wants to be in it. It's six weeks of fun.' He also tells the magazine how he has developed the Doctor. 'The jelly babies were my idea,' he says, 'but the costume grew. I had several weeks before I took over the part, so instead of the designer laying down his college art rubbish at me, we went out to "play" for a couple of hours each day. We went to wardrobes and played around and it gradually evolved. The scarf is actually too long because we bought too much wool and the woman knitted it all up!'

February 7

Lalla Ward is announced as the Doctor's new companion following Mary Tamm's decision to leave the series and to return to the theatre. Mary tells the press: 'From the outset I had decided to appear in just one series, and being the type of show it is, one year with *Doctor Who* has been a long one. When I first started it was a big shock. It was a six-day-week job and exhausting. So much so that I lost a stone in weight within the first month!'

There is widespread press coverage for Lalla Ward, the *Daily Mirror* picking up the coincidence that the girl who is the daughter of a real Lord – Viscount Bangor – is herself to become a Time Lord in what it calls 'an amazing switch'. Lalla explains: 'Romana will dematerialise as Mary at the end of the present series and rematerialise as me in the next. It sounds complicated, but it's very simple for a Time Lord.' And she also tells the *Daily Mail*: 'I used to be terrified of the monsters in the series. When I was a child I hid behind the sofa. But now I think some of the human baddies are even more frightening.'

February 24

As Mary Tamm departs from the series, another character emerges who is to feature in future stories, the evil Black

Guardian. The part is played with splendid malevolence by Valentine Dyall, a fine character-actor fondly remembered by older viewers as the 'Man in Black' who recounted ghost and horror stories on BBC Radio in the immediate post-war years. The Black Guardian is said to be on the side of chaos and destruction, and his most implacable enemy is the White Guardian, who represents law and order. The Doctor only manages to escape from the Black Guardian on this occasion by building a randomiser into the TARDIS which makes plotting his flight impossible . . .

May 1

The Doctor travels abroad for the first time – or to be more precise the programme goes on location to Paris for the first time to film sequences for 'The City of Death', a story written jointly by Graham Williams and the newly appointed script editor, Douglas Adams. Tom Baker is in effervescent mood and is soon creating news stories for the accompanying journalists. Chris Kenworthy in the *Sun* writes: 'Doctor Who made it as a big noise in Paris this week. On his first visit there, television's top time-traveller tripped the burglar alarm in a museum of modern art and put the fear of the Time Lords up the gendarmes.' According to Kenworthy he accidently set off the alarm during a chase sequence filmed in the Boulevard St Germain. 'Baker rushed up to the art gallery and rattled the doors. But because it was a public holiday, the gallery was closed and the alarm went off. Without even the benefit of the TARDIS, the cast, crew and cameras vanished without trace before the authorities arrived,' the reporter added.

Tom Baker particularly enjoys the anonymity of working in the French capital. 'It is something of a novelty to be able to walk down the street without everybody stopping you,' he says, although he has to admit that he still caught many an eye when he was on the streets during the May Day celebrations. There was only one disappointment for him during his time in Paris, Alan Tillier of the *Daily Mail* reports: 'Doctor Who may be 750 years old,' he says, 'but he does not know about one local tradition – that the Coquilles Bar on the Left Bank, which was used as a location for the confrontation of the Doctor and the arch villain, Scaroth (Julian Glover), is closed on May Day. The sign said *Fermé* and no pleadings were going to change the patron's mind. Coincidentally, the bar next door was called Who's – but the reply was the same. However, at the Notre Dame Café, the patron failed to recognise the Doctor – France adamantly declines to buy the show – and allowed filming on his terrace.'

June 10

Another of the *Doctor Who* backroom boys, Mat Irvine, visual effects designer, is extensively featured in an article about the series in the leading American science fiction magazine, *Starlog*. Talking about the launching of the show in America, Mat says: 'It seems slightly ironic to us that it has taken fifteen years to get started there. I read a lot of American publications and there has been a great deal about Gerry Anderson. But *Doctor Who*, which is the longest-running science fiction series in the world, never gets a mention in the States because it's never been sold in a big way before. We've just made an inroad . . . fifteen years late!'

Irvine continues: 'For someone coming to it fresh, as the majority of the American market will be, it may seem very strange. It will probably seem totally British. There's no concession at all as there was with *Space 1999* which was pointedly made for the American market. The British market was secondary in that case, let's face it. I'm not knocking them for that, it's economics. But *Doctor Who* is made in the typical British stiff upper-lip fashion, and it's been made totally for the British market. I think that if the Americans can take it in that attitude, it will go down well.' Mat's words are to prove strikingly prophetic . . .

July 6

Sad death of another of the *Doctor Who* stalwarts, the ebullient Malcolm Hulke, a contributor over a dozen years of stories for all the Doctors except the first, and creator of a number of memorable monsters including the Chameleons, Silurians, Sea Devils, Ogrons and Draconians. He was also co-writer with Terrance Dicks of the second longest of all the stories, the ten-episode 'War Games' in 1969, which explained for the first time the Doctor's origin as a Time Lord.

August 8

Three weeks prior to the return of *Doctor Who* an extraordinary attack is launched on the programme in the London *Evening Standard* which links it with *Star Wars* and describes both as 'lust in space'. Writer Peter McKay declares: 'The stories are gibberish. So is the action. Little effort is made to make the thing believable; or, failing that, amusing. This is not just an adult view of a children's programme. My own children and their friends think it is gibberish too. The real fans of *Doctor Who* are not children at all. They are middle-aged men who enjoy watching half-naked young girls being chased by space monsters. No matter what time the stories are set in, or what new girl is chosen to be the Doctor's accomplice, one thing remains constant. The girls are always half-naked. And they are always being chased. The same is true of *Doctor Who*'s American rival, *Star Trek,* a superior piece of nonsense, in which the space ladies wear very short skirts. *Star Trek* is, though, far easier on the eye than *Doctor Who.* Tom Baker's interpretation of the Doctor – the first and best was that of the late William Hartnell – is simply annoying. I sometimes wish that, with his long silly scarf, he suffer an Isadora Duncan style fate in the engines of a passing space cruiser. USS *Enterprise,* perhaps.'

September 1

'Daleks Herald Attack On New Season', the *Daily Telegraph*'s Robin Stringer writes as the seventeenth season of *Doctor Who* sees the return of the Time Lord's most indestructible enemies after an absence of more than four years in 'Destiny of the Daleks' written by Terry Nation. Press attention this time focuses on Ray Cusick, the BBC designer who was given the task of making Terry Nation's basic idea a reality. 'The first thing was how to afford them,'

ALISTER PEARSON

says Ray. 'Money is always a big problem. I decided I wasn't going to do anything cheap – originally they had discussed building them with cardboard – and I was allocated £750. I worked out the original drawings in three hours, did a couple of sketches in the office on Friday afternoon, and took them home to finish on Sunday afternoon. I realised they would have to have a human operator, so the basic design was shaped round a man sitting on a tricycle. I wanted midgets inside at first, because I thought it would be good to make the Daleks smaller than humans. I was making mechanical actors really.'

The *Sun* newspaper decides to find out what it is like to be a Dalek actor and Cy Town, who has played the role for nine years, says: 'We work the Daleks with our feet and have to wear rubber shoes. It's particularly nice on location in the winter when the other actors have to hang around and freeze. I sit comfortably inside the Dalek, cosy and warm and reading. In the studios, though, it is not so good – we swelter! We're dependent on the other artists getting us out – it needs two people to pull the tops off. Sometimes they forget and I get a little panicky until I hear someone shout, "My God, we've forgotten the Daleks!" and they rush to get us out.' Cy Town also admits his job can have amusing moments. 'Sometimes people stand talking beside a Dalek in the studio and forget that there is someone inside,' he says. 'The things I've heard! I know who's living with whom, what they think of different directors and the BBC bosses and all sorts of scandal!'

Reviewers are delighted at the return of the Daleks and the arrival of the Doctor's new companion. Robin Stringer writes: 'Poor Romana, newly incarnated by Lalla Ward, now also equipped with a long scarf that's always getting in the way, was not at all taken by some of her experiences. By the end, she found herself in a time-honoured role, horror-struck and backed against the wall by who else but the Daleks. It bodes well.'

September 29

Start of the Paris-filmed story 'City of Death', which confirms Tom Baker's claim that famous actors like to appear in the series – when John Cleese and Eleanor Bron make unheralded appearances as a couple of art-lovers. Because the close encounter of Doctor Who with Basil Fawlty in the final scenes of the story comes as such a surprise to viewers, it is repeated the following August with, as Patrick Stoddart describes, 'the BBC trumpeting their coup'. On this re-showing, the new producer, John Nathan-Turner says: 'I don't think John took much persuading to do the show. *Doctor Who* is a bit like *The Muppets* – everybody likes the idea of popping up in it, if only to impress their children.'

October 10

The Doctor gets a magazine wholly devoted to his adventures after years of being just the star of comic strips. *Doctor Who Weekly*, the brain-child of Dez Skinn, one of the most innovative comic men in Britain, is launched by Marvel Comics and offers a mixture of feature articles and comic strips. The publication is to run for 43 issues as a weekly and then become the *Doctor Who Monthly* in September 1980. The magazine has appeared in a constantly developing format to this day, and the continuation of the *Doctor Who* comic strip gives it the world record for being the longest-running strip adaptation of a film/TV concept.

October 13

Tom Baker makes a nostalgic return visit to his home-town of Liverpool which he left 'as a skinny fifteen-year-old with bulging eyes' and now comes back to a huge welcome as 'the idol of millions of kids'. Jenny Knight of the *Daily Star*, who accompanies him, headlines her report 'Traveller Tom Returns To Find His Roots' and notes: 'The fans weren't all children in Liverpool's new city-centre shopping precinct. He was mobbed by housewives and workmen as well. Ironically, one of the few places he wasn't bothered by cries of 'Exterminate' and 'Look out there's a Dalek' was in the once notorious Scotland Road area, where he lived. For the street where he was born no longer exists – another victim of time and social upheaval.' Tom makes no secret of how much he is enjoying his fame. 'With a TV programme like *Doctor Who*, which has entered the national consciousness,' he says, 'you become a part of everybody's life. Even the Prime Minister, Mr Callaghan, recognises me.'

December 22

'The Horns of Nimon' by Anthony Read catches the mood of Christmas with some sparkling comedy and in-jokes which delight the critics and viewers alike. It is with this seemingly appropriate story that Graham Williams takes his leave of the series, for quirky humour has been a hallmark of his time in the producer's seat. 'Tom Baker also had a lot to do with that,' he says. 'He would take every opportunity he could get to inject his own quirkiness and I didn't discourage it until it reached the point at which I felt it was going over the top. Like a scene I cut out at rehearsal for 'The Stones of Blood', with Romana and K9 presenting the Doctor with a fifteenth-anniversary birthday cake. That I felt was a case of suspension of disbelief being turned on its head!'

Taking over from Graham Williams is John Nathan-Turner, aged thirty-two, a man who has been associated with the series in one capacity or another on and off for ten years and brings a really comprehensive knowledge to his task. 'I can remember watching the first episode as a lad,' he says, 'but it didn't really catch my imagination until I joined the BBC in 1968 and worked on the programme the following year as a call boy when Patrick Troughton was the Doctor. I worked on two John Pertwee stories and then spent the last three years as production unit manager. I think they asked me to be producer because there was no-one else as familiar with the programme as I was and, of course, they knew I desperately wanted to do it!' John has a number of changes he wants to make to the programme, but before any of this can happen he has to handle a production crisis that has remained unresolved since October . . .

The fifth Doctor, Peter Davison, in 'Enlightenment' (1984)

Above: The Brig, played by Nicholas Courtney, the only actor to have appeared with all the Doctors

Right: The Doctor in 'Snakedance' (1983)

Above: The Doctor's famous foe, the Master, now played by Anthony Ainley, in a still from 'Planet of Fire' (1984)

Left: The Time Lords of Gallifrey, from whose august ranks the Doctor originates, in a still from 'Arc of Infinity' (1983)

Overleaf: A remarkable gathering for 'The Five Doctors', Terrance Dicks's story to mark the twentieth anniversary of the programme in November 1983

1980

The sixth Doctor, Colin Baker, and his latest companion, Perpugilliam Brown – Peri for short – played by Nicola Bryant, in 'The Twin Dilemma' (1984)

CHRIS SENIOR

January 12

The Eighties – the third decade of *Doctor Who* – begin with the Doctor defeated for the very first time. Not on the screen, where he triumphs against the evil Nimons in the final episode of 'The Horns of Nimon', but figuratively speaking, with the BBC's decision to cancel the trouble-torn production of a six-part story, 'Shada', which was to have been Graham Williams' and Douglas Adams's last contribution as producer and script editor. The trouble which leads to this premature end to the season began last October – although there was little hint of any such thing when filming began of Douglas Adams's story at Cambridge University – even if Tom Baker did have some trouble learning to manoeuvre a punt on the river Cam! A hazardous bicycle chase through the town was also completed before the actors and crew moved back to Television Centre to film the rest of the story about the struggle between the Doctor and an evil scientist called Skagra for possession of a rare book called *The Ancient Law of Gallifrey*.

Before work could be completed, however, industrial action at the BBC brought everything to a standstill and when this was resolved, *Doctor Who* was one of several productions that had to be cancelled. (The completed film is stored in the BBC vaults where it remains to this day: an extract being used later in 'The Five Doctors'.)

As his first task, John Nathan-Turner attempts to have the story reduced to 100 minutes but it requires just one further filming session to complete it for presentation as a Christmas special. John remains optimistic for this project until June when, because of the unavailability of a suitable spot, the final cancellation instruction is given. Of his never-to-be-seen adventure, Graham Williams says by way of an epitaph that it was 'an epic story that had something for everyone'.

February 4

Another sad event for *Doctor Who* – the death of David Whitaker, the programme's first script editor and the man who played a major part in the shaping and development of the series with Verity Lambert. The author of several scripts during the first decade of the show, David also wrote the first novelisation, *Doctor Who and the Daleks*, and helped script the two Peter Cushing feature films based on the Doctor's adventures.

February 26

First hint of the changes John Nathan-Turner is planning for the programme come in a short piece by Patrick Stoddart in the London *Evening News*. 'Doctor Who appears to be growing tired of women,' he writes. 'After a succession of cave-girls, Time Princesses and other curvacious cohorts, it seems that the good Doctor will be sharing the TARDIS with a teenager boy in the future. The BBC is looking for a lad to play a kind of cosmic Artful Dodger to join the Doctor when the new series begins in the autumn. If the new character works out, the BBC plans to plunge him into further misadventures for a long time to come.'

April 12

The successful launching of *Doctor Who* in America is demonstrated by the first two-day Doctor Who Convention, which is held in Los Angeles and attracts 1,000 people paying £8 per head. Reporting on what it sees as 'the spectacular arrival of the TARDIS in Hollywood', the *Daily Mail* reports: '*Doctor Who* is now on most nights of the week here and although not aired by a major network has built up a vast following. The programme, mostly taken for granted in Britain (*sic*), is seen here in the early evening and is becoming as popular as the late-night antics of Benny Hill.' Reporting on the convention which takes place on an unusually wet weekend, the newspaper says: 'There were Tom Baker look-alikes, Daleks, a specially constructed TARDIS, and the appearance of two of the stars of past shows, Elisabeth Sladen and Ian Marter. Their emergence from the TARDIS and chat with a Dalek on Sunset Strip quite bemused the uninitiated locals!'

May 9

The hinted-at changes in the programme are confirmed with the news that Lalla Ward is leaving the show, and the Doctor is to have a new boy-companion in eighteen-year-old Matthew Waterhouse who will play Adric. Of his incredible rise from unknown to star, Matthew says: 'Less than a year ago I was sitting three A-levels at school and taking time off from revision to watch *Doctor Who*. Now I'm rehearsing with Tom Baker, Lalla Ward and K9 and joining the series.' Prior to landing the role, Matthew has been in the BBC News Information Department where he heard 'on the grapevine' that a new male assistant was required for the Doctor. Despite having no formal acting training, he auditions and gets the part. Of her departure, Lalla Ward says: 'I shall be sorry to leave the series, but John Nathan-Turner and I decided it was time for a change. Doctor Who has never been without a girl alongside, so it really is something different.' The way in which she is to leave, she says, is still a secret . . .

June 7

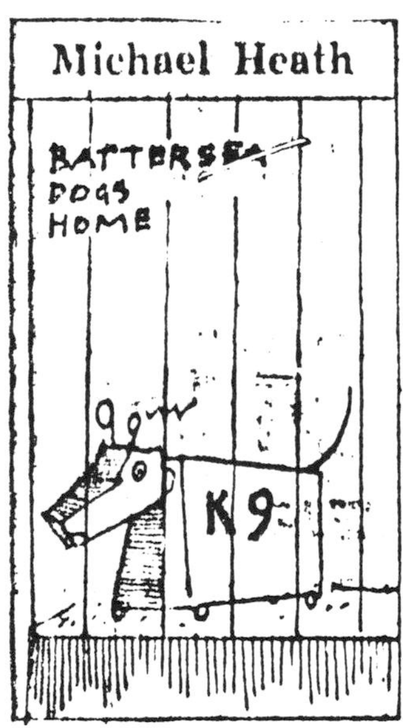

A front-page story in the *Sun* newspaper asks: 'Will the cruel Beeb really kill off K9?' According to reporter Hilary Bonner the Doctor's mechanical mongrel is facing the axe from the series and has been left out of certain key episodes in the next series.

Producer John Nathan-Turner is asked if the 'heroic hound who has become a great favourite since he was collared three years ago' is to leave the show. 'It is true that K9 will be rested from some episodes,' John says. 'But the scripts for the final programmes have yet to be written.' The *Sun* immediately launches a Save K9 Campaign. 'Help the superdog who has seen off the Cybermen and Ice Warriors win his toughest-ever battle,' demands the paper. 'Send us your protest today!' Dog expert Mrs Barbara Woodhouse, who met K9 on Terry Wogan's chat show, *What's On Wogan?* adds her voice to the protest. 'I thought he was extremely well behaved', she says.

June 15

Jon Pertwee becomes the first of the former Doctors to appear at a gathering of non-UK *Doctor Who* fans when he attends a party laid on by Australian enthusiasts in Sydney. Since this date, all the Doctors with the exception of William Hartnell have been increasingly in evidence at conventions and special festivities.

July 2

From *Doctor Who* to *Star Wars*: following the success of Dave Prowse in *Star Wars*, a number of other actors from the BBC series are recruited for the second film, *The Empire Strikes Back* when it is shot primarily in Britain. Dave, of course, returns as the evil Darth Vader, and among others appearing are regulars such as Julian Glover, playing the Commander of the AT-AT Walking Tanks, and Michael Sheard as an Empire Cruiser Admiral. Jeremy Bulloch who featured with William Hartnell in 'The Space Museum' plays bounty-hunter Boba Fett, while Milton Johns, a traitorous Time Lord, is an Empire Officer, and John Hollis from 'The Mutants' appears as Lobot, who helps rescue Princess Leia from the Imperial Storm-Troopers. When it goes on general release, the picture becomes something of a 'Spot the *Doctor Who* actor' for fans of the series!

July 12

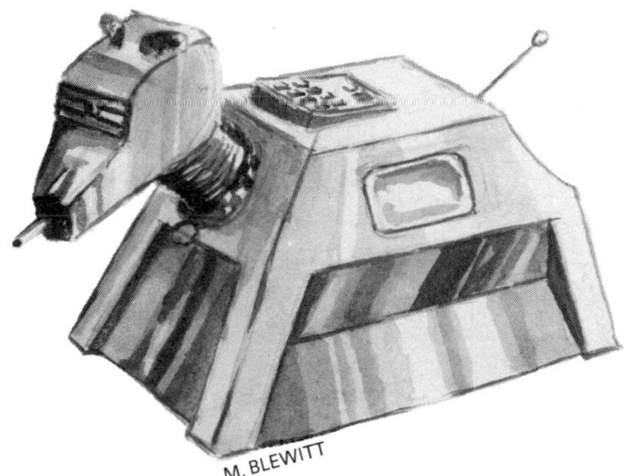

'Doctor Who's dog will still have his day' the *Sun* reports, revealing that K9 is not to leave *Doctor Who* following letters from thousands of young viewers who write to the newspaper in protest at the very idea. John Nathan-Turner says: 'K9 will appear in 20 of the next 28 episodes. Originally it was difficult to use him on bumpy terrain. But we now have a tracking system he runs on so that he can appear in many more scenes.' Among the many young readers who respond to the *Sun*'s appeal is Roseanne Serrelli, aged nine, who says; 'I wrote to the Queen to ask her to save K9 because she is a dog-lover herself. And I got a very nice letter back.' There are also petitions from schools, and twelve-year-old Gary Milton sums up what the newspaper believes are the feelings of thousands of children when he writes: 'If the producer decides to exterminate K9, I hope K9 exterminates him first.' The tremendous publicity which John Nathan-Turner has generated for *Doctor Who* even before his first production creates a wave of interest in the autumn season after all the disappointment of the New Year . . .

August 1

Prior to the screening of the first story in the eighteenth season, John Nathan-Turner gives an in-depth interview to *Starlog* magazine. He reveals another major change he has instituted of dropping six-part stories in favour of four-parters. 'I found that many of the six-parters in recent years have really been two four-part stories condensed,' he says, 'unmasking one villain at the end of episode four and then having another villain. I just think four is the ideal length for the programme in its current form.' He is also reducing the comedy element of his predecessor. 'We're trying to approach it much more seriously as an adventure/science fiction in which there is humour, rather than something which is dominantly humorous.'

John says he and his new script editor, Christopher H. Bidmead, are planning to use new writers for future stories 'to come up with fresh ideas and fresh outlook for the programme' and that he is particularly keen on continuity. 'You might as well get the history right and then change it if you absolutely have to because it doesn't quite work within the framework of your particular four-parter.' John also tells the press that he is planning to give the entire

MICHAEL PEARCE

programme a glossier and more expensive look. 'I want to take the show very firmly into the Eighties,' he says. 'With the success of *Star Wars* and *Star Trek* we have to attempt more imaginative effects and I am also bringing in the idea of having a guest star in every story. I think the reason the show has succeeded for so long is because of the constant change of actors. Each of them has been able to bring new approaches and new ideas to their parts.'

August 29

The status of *Doctor Who* as a public favourite and Tom Baker as a cult figure is underlined when 'The Doctor Who Experience' is unveiled in the Hall of Fame at Madame Tussauds in London. In the ensuing months and years, millions of visitors are to file past the lifelike waxwork of Tom Baker dressed as the Doctor. Keeping him company are a Dalek, Davros, Foamasi, Meglos, Nimon and a Sontaran. For a time, too, K9 is also present . . .

August 30

'Quantel' gets its first outing on *Doctor Who*, ushering in a new era of electronic effects for the series. Developed, in part, by British Telecom (then The Post Office) Quantel is a TV image-processing device that takes television picture signals and converts them into digital form. This digital information is then treated in exactly the same way as a computer program treats data – i.e. it can break it down, re-sort it, move it into different locations, and even output it in a modified format. To the viewer the reassembled television picture can appear as normal, the only difference being that, on cue, the image can be made to flip over, page-turn to a new image, expand forward, diminish away and even fragment into arrays of multiple images.

Many of these techniques are to be used on *Doctor Who* in the forthcoming years, but for part one of 'The Leisure Hive' by David Fisher – the first story to be made under the auspices of technically orientated producer John Nathan-Turner – only its zoom-out capabilities are used: in the first instance to show the picture of the Doctor and Romana on Brighton beach diminishing away to a star field, and in the second, and more important, example to show the hitherto impossible shot of the TARDIS materialising while the camera itself appears to be tracking back on a scene. In this latter instance the camera itself does not track – the materialisation sequence is shot as normal and the Quantel unit is used to zoom away from the action in the middle of the picture.

September 27

Another new special effects process is tried out on *Doctor Who*, this time the scene-sync equipment which will later be used to even grander effect in the major BBC production of *The Borgias*. Developed by an outside company, Scene-Sync is a control system allowing a slave camera to follow exactly the movements of a master camera. In the case of 'Meglos,' the master camera is a studio camera trained on a group of actors walking about on a totally blue set. The slave camera is set up to shoot a much smaller model stage where the set of the Zolpha-Thura screens has been built. Up in the gallery the two scenes are merged together using CSO. The scene-sync process is thus employed to match the movements of the actors on the big set that have been captured by the master camera, with corresponding camera angles on the model stage shot by the slave camera. Due to the expense of hiring the scene-sync equipment, 'Meglos' is the only *Doctor Who* story to date to make use of this technique.

Star guest in this story is Bill Fraser who generates considerable publicity because of his attitude towards K9. The *Daily Mirror*, for instance, quotes Fraser as saying that he believes he will soon be 'the vilest villain since the Daleks'. And for why? Bill explains: 'I play something horrible that comes from behind a tree. I only took the part on the condition that they would let me kick K9! I expect all *Doctor Who* fans will hate me – but I have never been too keen on that tin dog!' Bill Fraser's part in 'Meglos'? Grugger!

October 8

K9 is definitely to leave the series next year, John Nathan-Turner announces.' He is restricting our writers because he never gets anything wrong.' The *Daily Mirror* headlines its report 'K9 Gets The Boot' and says the time-travelling dog is to go because he is too bright 'and makes it too easy for the Doctor to get out of trouble'. In a major feature in the *Daily Express*, Douglas Orgill reports that 'not since the death of Dickens's Little Nell has the nation faced such a trauma', and talks about the horrified reaction to the news among children. To prevent K9's disappearance, one child suggests, 'Couldn't they make him a bit less clever?', while another recommends giving him some companions: 'I'd like a lot of them, a pack of them – they could hunt Daleks!' Out of a class of 23 children at Wimbledon Chase Middle School in London, Orgill finds that 18 of the youngsters would rather see the Doctor and his companions leave the series than K9! He does, though, extract a promise from John Nathan-Turner: 'There could, one day, be a Mark III K9 . . .'

JAMES ADAMSON

ANDREW MARTIN

October 23

A new companion for the Doctor, Australian actress Janet Fielding, aged twenty-three, who is to replace Lalla Ward and play an air-hostess named Tegan. Janet, the first foreigner to be cast as an assistant, is headlined in the London *Evening Standard:* 'Tough Aussie For Doctor Who'. She has been picked for the role from over one hundred girls despite only one previous TV appearance in a bit-part in a Hammer horror series. Janet says: 'I was delighted to get the role because I was weaned on *Doctor Who* at home in Brisbane. I grew up respecting the Doctor.' And of her part, she adds: 'Tegan is young, bright, brash and assertive and she's not at all afraid of putting the Doctor in his place. She tends to charge in without thinking at times, but deep down she's a very caring person.' Tegan will be the Doctor's sixteenth female assistant, and the *Standard* remarks: 'He's been surrounded by more girls than *Playboy* boss, Hugh Hefner!'

October 24

Doctor Who is back on the front pages again with the news that Tom Baker is to give up playing the Doctor after seven years. And what captures the imagination of reporters at the news conference to announce his departure is the suggestion the new Doctor could be a *woman*! Tom says: 'I'm quitting while I'm at the top. I've been seen by 100 million viewers in 37 countries and get recognised all over the world. There's nothing more I can do but repetition.' And his successor? 'It could even be a woman,' David Wigg of the *Daily Express* quotes him. 'After all, there is no reason why the Doctor should always be a man.' John Nathan-Turner will not be drawn on this, however. 'We know who we want to replace him,' he says. 'But I cannot give you any clue to the identity of this person as negotiations are still continuing.'

Tom's decision results in several in-depth interviews, and he talks to William Marshall of the *Daily Mirror* with his usual candour. 'Finishing with *Doctor Who* is a great emotional jolt after playing it so long,' he says, 'but we need these emotional jolts in our lives, they are good for us. The Doctor has made me quite well off and believe me there was no row with the BBC. It was strictly my decision. I enjoyed every single minute of it. It was never hard work, simply because it was such fun.' And his future? 'Who knows? Maybe I'll end up digging ditches or working behind a bar, even heaving coal. I wouldn't mind a bit. I need to work. Any work. I am looking forward to the unknown, the wonderful idea that anything or nothing could happen to me.' Spoken like a true Time Lord!

October 25

The first appearance of Adric in 'Full Circle' also marks the debut of another teenager, Andrew Smith, a fan who actually scripted the story. The boy's big break into television warrants a special feature by John Craven in *Radio Times* and he also talks to John Nathan-Turner. 'Andrew has been sending in scripts and storylines to the *Doctor Who* office for some years,' says John. 'Christopher Bidmead and I read through them, liked his ideas and commissioned him. He's by far the youngest writer we've had – he must have been a baby when the Doctor began his travels!' And Andrew, from Glasgow, tells John Craven: 'It's not easy for a new young writer to take over such a well-established series. But you have to forget everything and tell yourself there's never been another *Doctor Who* story.' After seeing the transmission of his four-part story, Andrew comments: 'It has come out even better than I visualised it.'

November 1

Such is the interest in who is to be the new Doctor that the *News of the World* asks its readers for suggestions. How about Larry Grayson, offers A. Reynolds of Brentwood, Essex. 'He's a riot in *The Generation Game:* can you imagine him saying "Shut that door!" as he enters the TARDIS?' Stephen Orris of Ipswich suggests John Cleese. 'No Dalek in his right mind would stand an intergalactic incident with Basil Fawlty, especially if Sybil played his assistant!' Ron Moody is put forward again, this time by Mrs M. Benham of Southampton. 'He is a good character-actor, and has just the right amount of madness for the part.'

Taking up the hint by Tom Baker that a woman might play the part, Mrs Annette Gibbs of Somerset offers Frances de la Tour who 'has a twinkly sort of humour and slight pathos which make her a must for the first woman Doctor Who', while Mrs M. Marsh of Bristol recommends Prime Minister Margaret Thatcher. 'She's great at sorting out the baddies down here on earth, so I am sure she would sort out the Daleks. An Iron Lady Doctor Who!' There is even a touch of prophecy about Andy Montague's letter from Sussex: 'Would it be possible for me to play the part? I know it's only a fantasy, but I think I'm the right age. I'm fourteen and after every regeneration, the Doctor *does* become younger . . .'

COLIN-JOHN P. RODGERS

November 4

All the speculation about the next Doctor is ended with the announcement on BBC's *Nine O'Clock News* that Peter Davison, already well known for his role as the vet Tristan in the series *All Creatures Great and Small* is to be the new – and youngest – Time Lord. In announcing the casting, John

Nathan-Turner reveals he has known Peter, aged twenty-nine, since they both worked together on *All Creatures Great and Small,* and he tells the *Daily Mirror*: 'Peter is an ideal actor for the role. He has the right combination of light humour, drama and realism, is very popular with children and has a large following with women viewers.'

Peter himself admits to having been completely taken aback when offered the part, feeling that he might be too young to play the Doctor. He tells the press: 'I was only twelve years old when *Doctor Who* started and I used to be terrified. But I've been a fan ever since. It's a dream part and I've been on cloud nine since I was offered it.' Talking about his ideas for the role, he says: 'Tom Baker played the part as a total eccentric. I would like to be more down-to-earth. We thought we needed something English and more youthful. I'm going to be a more heroic Doctor Who!' Asked whether the arrival of a vet in the series might save the much-lamented K9, Peter jokes: 'No, I'm afraid he will have to be put down. He's getting too old.' Peter is also amazed when his name and photograph are shown on the main news programme of the evening. 'I really had no idea *Doctor Who* was so important. Some of my friends thought I'd died when they saw my picture!' he says.

November 21

Yet another change for *Doctor Who* – a second female companion for the Doctor is announced, and under a heading 'Who's Crowd', the *Daily Mail* comments: 'It's getting rather crowded in Doctor Who's time-machine these days!' This third new assistant of the year is nineteen-year-old Sarah Sutton, who is to play Nyssa, daughter of an alien Consul: she joins the Doctor after tragedy overcomes her father. Sarah, an actress since the age of ten and star of BBC's major production of *Alice through the Looking Glass,* says of her new part: 'I used to be scared stiff by the programme, but I still switch on every Saturday. I am over the moon at being chosen.'

November 22

Veteran *Doctor Who* writer Terrance Dicks achieves his ambition to write a vampire story for the series with 'State of Decay' – an earlier version of this adventure having been dropped in 1977 when the BBC decided upon a major production of Bram Stoker's classic novel, *Dracula. The Scotsman*'s critic Stanley Eveling is one of several writers who praise the current season. 'The new episodes of *Doctor Who* are full of childlike imagination,' he says, 'the best for a long time. Here they have kings and queens like cardboard people always walking hand in hand, and an old spaceship they live in and, below, the thump of a giant vampire's heart. Good ghoulish entertainment for all ages.' This was to prove a view not shared by certain other people . . .

December 12

No sooner has the last episode of 'State of Decay' been transmitted than John Nathan-Turner finds himself on the receiving end of several complaints about the vampire content of the story. He comments: 'Yes, we did get into a bit of trouble from the RSPCA and the Institute for Terrestrial Ecology over our showing of vampire bats. They've apparently spent years trying to educate the public to the idea that bats are just mice with wings, and then along we come and rekindle the old phobias. I believe there was even a question asked in the House of Lords about it.'

December 13

Tom Baker and Lalla Ward decide to continue their on-screen travels off screen, and are married at Chelsea Register Office. Talking about his feelings when Lalla completed her filming for the series two weeks earlier, Tom tells Brian Wesley of the *Daily Star*: 'I couldn't bear to see her go. You see I felt something right from day one – the very day Lalla started work on the show two years ago. It was only when Lalla finished, leaving me to carry on with my last series, alone, that we both realised we had to make the fateful decision to get married. We suddenly discovered we were appalled to face the prospect of being apart.' And Lalla adds: 'We've always got on terribly well, but it is a lot easier to know one's true feelings now we are not working together.' The wedding of 'Doctor Woo' – as reporters call Baker – and his faithful assistant attracts widespread newspaper coverage and even cartoon comment.

'. . . And whosoever knoweth just cause or impediment'

DAVID J. HOWS

1981

January 16

A week prior to the departure of Romana and K9 in 'Warriors' Gate' it is announced that although the mechanical dog will not reappear in the series, his creators have been asked to write a new story about him for a completely separate production. The *Sun,* trumpeting its campaign to 'Save K9' reports under a headline 'New Leash of Life For K9' that this 'dogged persistence' has paid off, and quotes a BBC spokesman: 'We got a huge number of protests when it appeared K9 would be axed for good. So we have asked his creators for a story featuring the dog, but he will not be a permanent character again.' A delighted Dave Martin tells the paper: 'We are pleased the BBC has decided he won't be blasted into oblivion after all. We have already drafted out the new storyline and K9 should be back on the screen in the autumn. My own family are great K9 fans – if he had been exterminated, I would have been in the dog house!'

The *Daily Mail* also talks to John Leeson, the actor who provides K9's voice. 'I became K9 physically,' he recalls. 'At rehearsals I played the dog crawling around on my hands and knees. I found to my alarm that I had rather grown into the character!' Would he miss playing the electronic dog on a regular basis? 'The trouble was he was being used as a sort of tin-opener for getting the Doctor out of scrapes,' he says. 'Theoretically, he is such a brilliant computer that if he were allowed to work properly he would have got the Doctor out of trouble on page 7 of episode one. That's why his batteries had to keep going flat!'

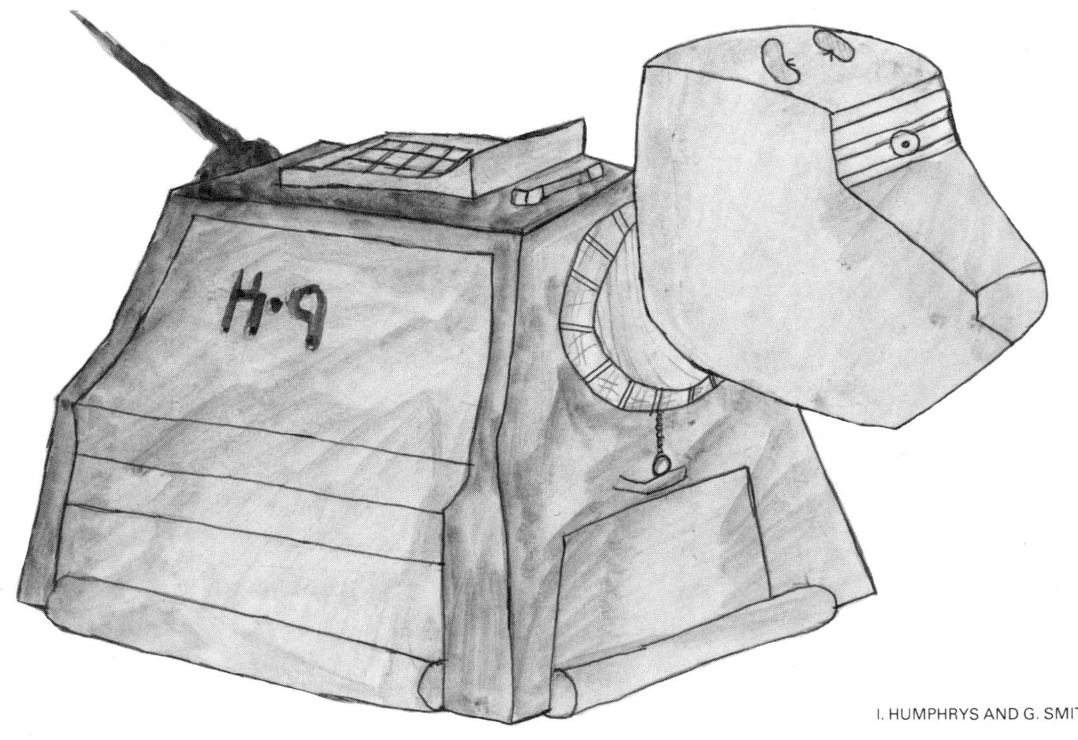

I. HUMPHRYS AND G. SMITH

February 21

ALISTER PEARSON

A dramatic reappearance in 'The Keeper of Traken' of the Doctor's most fearsome humanoid foe, the Master, last seen in a terribly decrepit form in 'The Deadly Assassin'. Disguised as the evil Melkur, and here played by Geoffrey Beevers, the renegade Time Lord is seeking a new body and finally insinuates himself into the form of Consul Tremas, played by Anthony Ainley. At a stroke, this gentle, peace-loving man is turned into the fiendish, hellbent Master so beloved of viewers in the Jon Pertwee era. John Nathan-Turner explains this sensational return. 'I believe every continuing and popular hero should have his Moriarty,' says John, 'the arch foe who knows the hero every bit as well as the hero knows him. We were lucky once we had decided to bring him back to be able to find the Master's 'Deadly Assassin' costume which we had been given to understand had been junked. We also wanted to give the impression he had decayed even further before making the transfer of his 'soul' into Anthony Ainley as the new Master.'

A skilful actor in his own right, Anthony is still only too well aware of the problems that face him in the role. 'There are obvious hazards in doing a part someone has made successful before,' he says, 'but I was never in any real doubt about taking it on. Certainly, at the back of my mind there is the thought that everyone enjoyed Roger Delgado's portrayal – but that means I've got to try and be just as good in return.' When the Doctor sets off in pursuit of the Master he is joined by Tremas's daughter, Nyssa, the newest companion.

MARK TRY

February 28

The start of the fateful story 'Logopolis', which is to introduce the brash young air-hostess Tegan Jovanka to the Doctor, Adric and Nyssa, is overhung by the grim presence of the Master. The plot progresses inevitably towards the terrible conflict which necessitates the Doctor's regeneration into his new, youthful body. After seven years in the role, the departure of Tom Baker is viewed with apprehension by many viewers.

March 21

The badly injured body of Tom Baker's Doctor slowly regenerates into that of Peter Davison, who is briefly glimpsed before the end of 'Logopolis'. After this the programme goes off the air for what is to prove the longest-ever inter-season break – almost a whole year – before Davison can establish his Victorian-style, reckless but innocent new Doctor.

This finale to the series receives a host of congratulatory letters in the *Radio Times.* '"Logopolis" outclasses any *Doctor Who* story made since Jon Pertwee left in 1974,' writes Stephen Poppitt of Huntingdon. 'How ironic Tom Baker's last story should be the best he's ever made.' Nigel Broomhead of Nottingham is delighted to see the Master back: 'Here we all were, eagerly awaiting the Doctor's fifth incarnation and we're given an extra one, the third incarnation of the Master. Anthony Ainley looked remarkably like the late Roger Delgado, and now the Master is humanoid again, we look forward to him being as evil as ever.'

The only complaint, curiously, has to do with the timing of the programme. T. Mullany from Swansea writes: 'On behalf of football fans I would like to protest against the earlier timing of *Doctor Who.* The 5.10 start meant it was impossible for me to return home from the match in time to see a whole episode. Two generations of viewers were being lost to the programme: the father and son who go to watch football together. Please return *Doctor Who* to its traditional slot after six o'clock . . .'

April 5

First major feature on Peter Davison preparing for his role as the Doctor appears in the *Sunday Times.* Describing the series as a 'British institution loved by millions of young-at-hearts the world over', writer Alan Corbett asks Peter where he thinks the appeal of *Doctor Who* lies. 'It has to be frightening,' he says. 'That's what attracted me when I was young, that's what everyone remembers about it. It's a surrealistic fear anyway, not people being mugged on their way home, or anything like that.' As a child his favourite Doctor was Patrick Troughton. 'He had just the right blend of desperation and dealing with the situation seriously while at the same time bringing out the humour of it. In recent years it's got rather too jokey for my liking. I guess I'll have trouble winning over viewers used to Tom Baker's performance, as well as viewers who have seen me in other parts, but it's been done before.'

Peter also reveals he has had a little experience of television science fiction having played a cameo role in *The Hitch-Hiker's Guide to the Galaxy* earlier in

BYRON C. WOODS

the year. 'But,' he says, 'I can't view *Doctor Who* in terms of science fiction because it's such a unique show – it's so difficult to categorise. One thing I don't really like about it so much are the stories where the Doctor lands on a planet where there are two nations at war and he sorts everything out. I don't like him being all-powerful and saying, "These are the goodies and these are the baddies, live in peace ever after", and flying off into the sunset. He shouldn't be infallible. People like him because he's a bit crazy and he's not quite so boring as the standard good-guy.' One determination he has is not to play the part for a long time like Tom Baker. 'That doesn't mean I'll only do it for a year or something like that,' he adds, 'but I don't want to outstay my welcome.'

M. BLEWITT

May 27

Kit Pedler, co-creator with Gerry Davis of the Cybermen, and scientific adviser to the series, dies aged fifty-three. His knowledge of technology and his uncannily prophetic view of the future were strikingly revealed in several *Doctor Who* stories such as 'The War Machines' and 'The Moonbase'.

June 27

One of the most striking of all changes for *Doctor Who* is announced – the programme is to be moved from the traditional Saturday evening spot it has occupied for eighteen years to a twice-weekly early-evening slot. When the new season begins in January 1982 the show will be seen on Tuesdays and Thursdays at around 7.00 p.m., says BBC Head of Drama, Shaun Sutton. He adds: 'The feeling is that we have stuck in a particular pattern for a very long time and that the show might do better if we change to this new format. We will try it as an experiment and, if it does not work, we will probably revert to the old Saturday-night idea.'

It is intended that each episode will end on a cliff-hanger, but instead of the season running for six months this new twice-weekly spot will reduce it to three. Peter Davison also tells the press he has a clearer idea of how he will play the Doctor. 'I think he will look a bit like Tristan in *All Creatures* – only brave,' he says. 'That's the way one child wrote and said I should play it, and I rather agree with him.'

OLIVER MURRAY

August 14

Although still to be seen as the new Doctor, Peter Davison demonstrates the determination of a Time Lord to get to his first major Doctor Who Convention, Panoptican West, staged by the North American Doctor Who Appreciation Society (NADWAS) in Tulsa, Oklahoma. Because of a strike by American air-traffic controllers it is feared that he will have to disappoint the thousand fans gathered to honour him. But Peter recalls later: 'I didn't want to let all those fans down, and after all I'm supposed to be an intrepid time-traveller. They were amazed when I turned up, because they thought it was much too dangerous to fly. Some of them had driven for twenty hours to get there. It was a very brief visit – twenty-four hours in Tulsa you might say – but very enjoyable. They really do love Doctor Who. He has a cult following all over the world.'

November 2

To bridge the large gap between the eighteenth and nineteenth seasons of *Doctor Who,* producer John Nathan-Turner sets up a special season of earlier stories showing the various Doctors which carries the series title 'The Five Faces of Doctor Who'. He explains: 'I thought it was essential to keep the show on the boil with the public. In addition, after seven years, there was a whole barrage of viewers who only knew Tom Baker as the Doctor. So inevitably it was going to be the hardest job yet moving over into a new Doctor. So my main reason for wanting to do a "Five Faces" season was to re-educate the public and to educate initially the younger viewers that there had been other actors who had played the part.'

WILLIAM MERRIN

The five stories selected for the season, to run through weekly until early December, are: 'An Unearthly Child' with William Hartnell, 1963; 'The Krotons' with Patrick Troughton, 1968; 'Carnival of Monsters' and 'The Three Doctors' with Jon Pertwee, 1973; and 'Logopolis' with Tom Baker and just a glimpse of Peter Davison, 1981. Heralding the series, Patricia Smylie of the *Daily Mirror* calls *Doctor Who* 'one of the biggest money-spinners in show business' and says all addicts of the show 'will enjoy being given a nostaligic TARDIS trip back over its eighteen years' run.'

Geoffrey Hobbs of the *Daily Mail* takes the opportunity to ask Peter Davison for his comments on his predecessors. Of William Hartnell the new Doctor says: 'There was something very mysterious about him. He was almost evil in a way, and certainly the most bad-tempered of all the Doctors. He was also the most forgetful, more like an absent-minded professor than the others.' Of Patrick Troughton: 'Patrick was the muddler. He was always getting into a mess. Although he always won through in the end, a lot of the time it was more by accident than design.' Of Jon Pertwee: 'Funnily enough, being a comedian, he played the Doctor straighter than any of the other actors. The way he did it was almost like melodrama a lot of the time.' And Tom Baker: 'He was the most eccentric. And he was certainly the most bizarre. But the great thing about Tom was his unpredictability. He kept you guessing because you never knew what he was going to do next.'

November 14

Peter Davison makes his first public appearance in the new Doctor's Victorian cricketer costume on a float in the Lord Mayor's Show in London. Thousands of fans on the streets and millions more watching television see the youthful new Doctor on the British Insurance Association float in company with the TARDIS and an impressive array of monsters and aliens including Daleks, a Cyberman, a Sontaran, an Axon, Scaroth, a Robot of Death, an Ogron, a Draconian and a Sea Devil. Probably the warmest members on the exhibit – which has been organised and created by Toby Chamberlain – are Peter Davison's wife, Sandra, who rides in the driver's cab, and a Yeti covered from head to foot in its own 'fur coat'!

NICK HARRIS

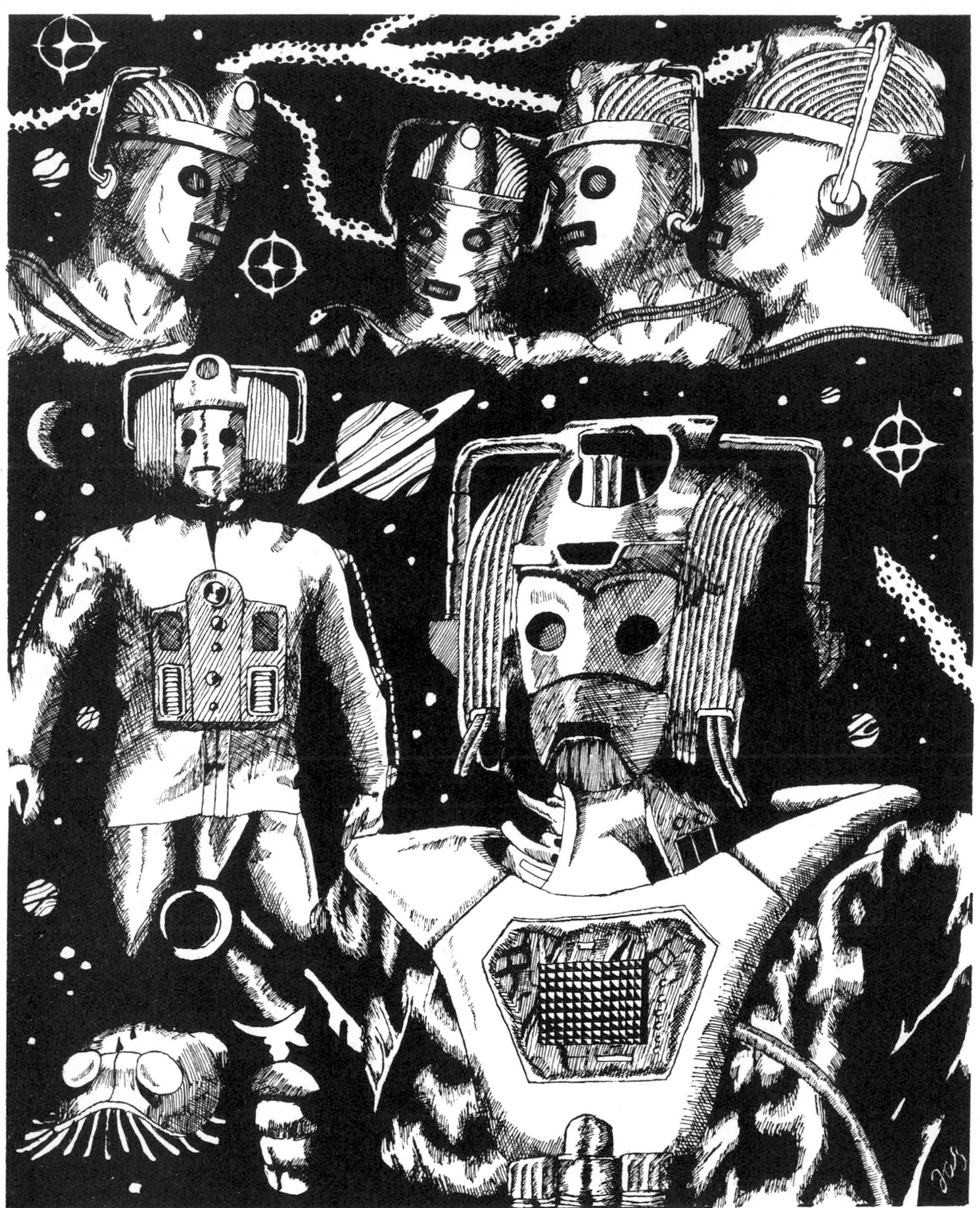

I. A. STUBBINGS

December 3

The end of the 'Five Faces of Doctor Who' season brings in widespread praise from the critics who almost to a man dwell nostalgically on their own memories of the series. Richard Boston in the *Observer* writes: '1963 was the year in which, according to Philip Larkin, sexual intercourse began – "Between the end of the Chatterley ban and the Beatles' first LP". Nor was that the only important thing that started in 1963, as I soon discovered on returning to these shores after missing the *annus mirabilis* by spending it in, of all places, Sweden. It was also the year in which *Doctor Who* began. I made up for lost time as soon as possible, immediately succumbed and have hardly missed an episode since. It has rankled for years that I missed the beginnings of the series. Now the omission has been repaired by the BBC's very own TARDIS . . . and over a period of five weeks we have been richly treated to a selection of the temporal and spatial adventures of the intrepid and resourceful Doctor.' Richard Boston has special praise for Ron Grainer's theme music and warns, 'if they ever do change it, then that's the last television licence I'll be buying!' Philip Purser of the *Sunday Telegraph* finds himself most impressed with the very first story. 'I found,' he writes, 'I remembered the establishing sequence almost shot for shot, with the TARDIS's humble phone-box exterior gratifyingly revealing spacious quarters within. It must be odd for Verity Lambert still in her young womanhood, to be reminded that she founded an institution.'

The success of the season convinces the BBC that it is possible to show the various Doctors in close proximity to one another, and gives John Nathan-Turner a special idea. 'At the back of my mind,' he says later, 'I was already thinking about a Five Doctors special to mark the twentieth anniversary of the show. The 'Five Faces' season therefore proved a double-edged weapon; firstly, it enabled us to bridge satisfactorily the very long gap between Tom and Peter and, secondly, it set up the concept of five Doctors with the public, giving impetus to the special.'

December 28

The promised return of K9 in a 50-minute special *K9 and Company* in which the mechanical dog is reunited not with the Doctor but a former companion, the journalist Sarah Jane Smith (Elisabeth Sladen) to help root out a case of witchcraft in the Cotswolds area of England. Producer John Nathan-Turner hopes this pilot story will prove the forerunner of a series, but the public response is not strong enough. There is, though, a re-run of the special in 1982, and it retains to this day the distinction of being the only *Doctor Who* spin-off actually made and shown.

POLICE PUBLIC CALL BOX
ANDREW KERR

1982

January 4

On the Monday morning of Peter Davison's arrival as the fifth Doctor in 'Castrovalva', the *Guardian* newspaper takes the unique step of devoting a leader column to the change of time-slot for the programme headlined 'Tardis Lands On The Wrong Day'. Calling the change a bad blunder, it says that the decision is one which 'displays an extraordinary failure somewhere in the BBC hierarchy to understand the essential Saturday-ishness of the whole operation'. Saying that the change will deny many regular viewers still on their way home from work the chance to see the programme, it fears *Doctor Who* will be destroyed by this violent wrenching from its natural context. The *Guardian*

STEPHEN WALLIS

demands: 'If Mr Alastair Milne is not to forfeit the hope that has been riding on him since his recent appointment to the Director-Generalship, he must intervene now and order that this sacrilege be stopped.'

With 'Castrovalva', *Doctor Who* gets another change of script editor, former radio writer Eric Saward taking over from Christopher H. Bidmead. Eric admits: 'I like fast-moving adventure stories and I'm pleased to be working with a young and very active Doctor, rather than one who stands back, with his companions, and cogitates, comments and assists from afar.' And of the overall impact of the series, he adds: 'I don't think we should aim necessarily towards being frightening. Exciting, yes. Interesting, yes. Hopefully, stimulating, and if we can be a little frightening along the way, then I shall be happy.'

January 5

Following the second episode of 'Castrovalva', protests about the time-change arrive by phone and mail in the *Doctor Who* production office. John Nathan-Turner defends the move. 'Times and viewing tastes have changed these last few years,' he says. 'BBC 1 no longer has the absolute hold it once had on the Saturday evening ratings. In those days you started with *Grandstand* and went right through to *Parkinson* at the end of the day. People do a lot more channel-switching on Saturdays and I earnestly believe that if we had stayed on Saturday we would have lost a lot of viewers.' (By the end of this season, John is able to substantiate his claim by pointing to an average viewing figure of ten million.) He is, though, not completely happy with the twice-weekly episodes being on following days – 'this means you really only get one cliffhanger per four-part story' – and hopes in the future to get a day or two's gap between the episodes.

January 8

Radio Times runs a full-page feature on Peter Davison, and writer Renate Kohler reports that the Doctor has, over the years, become a 'kind of national monument'. Now, she says, 'the tension and speculation that surround the election of each new actor to the part is not unlike that surrounding the election of an American president!' Peter Davison is quick to admit that he is aware of the 'instant charisma' that surrounds the part. He says that he wants his Doctor to have a 'sort of reckless innocence' and while he doesn't plan to copy his forerunners, 'I do bear in mind a particular aspect of each one.' He also reveals that before starting work he went to talk to Tom Baker. 'We met in a bar one evening to discuss the part,' Peter recalls, 'and he was all set to give me advice. But it was *Top of the Pops* that night and the noise was so furious all I heard was "Good Luck!"'

January 12

Doctor Who uses the most expensive prop ever seen on television – a British Airways Concorde, valued at £30 million! The supersonic aircraft is filmed during location work at Heathrow Airport for a future story entitled 'Time-Flight', written by director turned author Peter Grimwade, and the juxtaposition of the Doctor and his TARDIS with the Concorde which disappears in the story provides ideal picture material for the national newspapers, *The Times* in particular.

The making of the programme at Heathrow is also the first time cameras working on a fictional story have been allowed at the airport: by special permission of the British Airports Authority and British Airways. To set up the location work took a year, according to John Nathan-Turner, who also explains a bit of luck they enjoyed while at Heathrow. 'The day we were due to film, one of the two Concordes at the airport developed trouble, so British Airways had to use the one they'd put aside for us. That meant filming three days later instead. On the day we filmed there was just a bit of snow on the ground which we can accommodate in the script, but on the day we *were* to have filmed there were raging blizzards which would have ruined it for us.' The weather in fact provides the actors with their only problem: the two girls, Sarah and Janet in particular. 'It was so cold they got themselves togged up in thermal pants between takes,' recalls John, 'then took them off again ready for filming!'

TANYA THOMAS

March 13

The Cybermen, dramatically re-styled, return for the first time since 1975 in script editor Eric Saward's own story 'Earthshock', a costly, inventive and fast-paced story which pushes *Doctor Who* straight into the BBC's top ten programmes

MARK TRY

PAUL VYSE

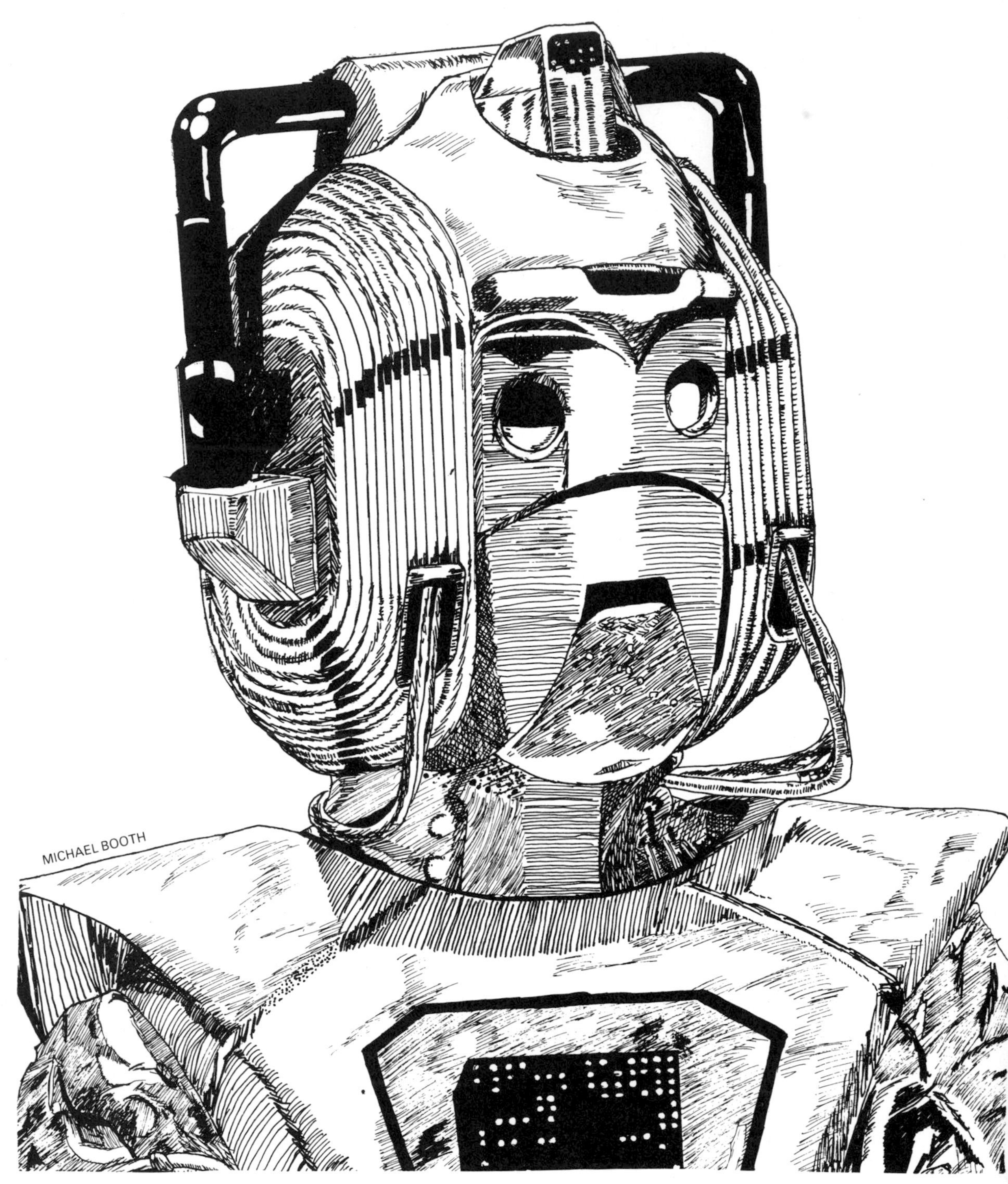
MICHAEL BOOTH

of the week. Commenting on the story, Eric says, '*Doctor Who* has been going for so long now that it has its own myths which are an integral part of it, and I think it is nice to dip back into the past and resurrect things like the Cybermen – although to maintain the show's viability they must also develop.' Eric admits that the Cybermen were his favourites among the old monsters, and he has watched all the old stories featuring them, before incorporating several elements into the new image. 'They are very menacing as a concept,' he adds, 'being physically so large, so militaristic and so ruthlessly dedicated that I found it challenging to try and bring them back with all the old impact.'

The reappearance of the Cybermen prompts Gavin Scott to review 'Who's Monsters' in *Did You See?* 'On the sci-fi horror scale I'd give the Cybermen 8 out of 10,' he says. 'And I remember being enthralled as a child when a Dalek was opened up and something slithery fell out! That must have been one of the best moments of television science fiction.' Gavin believes that successful monsters have to be both revolting and attractive. 'Some of those in the science fiction films of the 1950s were really pathetic. They looked as though they were made from old cereal packets!' Gavin also tells his viewers that he thinks the modern monsters are more realistic 'because our shock threshold has gone up – in other words we don't get scared as easily.' But as a word of comfort for younger viewers he confesses: 'I admit that, like a lot of other *Doctor Who* fans, when I was young, I watched some of those creatures with my fingers over my eyes – and there is nothing really wrong with that!'

March 16

The sudden death of the Doctor's companion Adric in the final episode of 'Earthshock' draws widespread press coverage and a host of telephone calls and letters to the programme. 'Doctor Who's Lad Is Dead Unlucky,' the *Daily Mail* headlines its report, declaring: 'Doctor Who's crewmate Adric died trying to save

the world – and he wasn't too happy about it. Actor Matthew Waterhouse said, 'I was a bit disappointed and upset. I wanted to be written out of the script but instead I had to die. The Doctor's companions normally leave by falling in love or going off to help some underdeveloped planet – there's never been one of them killed before."' In fact, two previous companions, Katarina and Sara Kingdom both gave their lives for the Doctor, but this does not prevent letters of complaint to the *Radio Times.* 'It is positively infamous,' writes Richard Sturch of Buckinghamshire, 'for the first time since the foolish new times began, I manage to see the last episode of *Doctor Who* only to see one of his companions killed, which surely has never happened before? I wish to protest.' So does Simon Culhane of Middlesex: 'Poor Adric, blown up by a Cyberman's home-made bomb while attempting to save the dinosaurs from extinction. It was only fitting that the credits were rolled in silence and I, like many other fans, mourn his passing.' A Sussex reader, Mrs K. F. Hartshorn, raises a point no one else seems to have considered: 'What does not seem to have been grasped about the "sad death" of Adric is that the Doctor and his associates went *back* in time and witnessed the explosion which is supposed to have disposed of dinosaurs, etc; and Adric was apparently killed in the explosion. Then how could he have been alive in the future to go back in time?'

There is an even more pointed note of controversy struck by the scene showing some of the Cybermen with 'plastic bags' on their heads, thereby generating the fear that children might copy this dangerous practice. John Nathan-Turner apologises: 'I accept this complaint. Children should not play with plastic bags – or even unsealed plastic sheeting as was used in "Earthshock".'

GARY McKEEVER

March 25

Peter Davison becomes the first of the Doctors to be featured in Eamonn Andrew's show *This Is Your Life* whilst still playing the role. Peter is confronted by Eamonn in the somewhat unlikely surroundings of Trafalgar Square, but it is in the studio that people from far back in his childhood, and others right up to his days with *Doctor Who,* are conjured up. Several members of the production team have had to live with the secret of this programme for several months, before the moment Peter finds himself presented with the celebrated red book of his life . . .

CHRIS SENIOR

March 30

The dramatic confrontation of Peter Davison's Doctor with his old adversary the Master completes a successful first season for the new Time Lord. BBC 1 Controller Alan Hart is also able to announce that the programme has picked up three million more viewers, and he expresses general satisfaction with the changes which have been made. Not so the critics. Margaret Forwood of the *Sun* is unhappy about the time-spot, the stories and even the Doctor himself. 'Let us hope', she writes, 'that *Doctor Who* goes through a time-warp and winds up back in his old Saturday-night spot. The switch to a twice-weekly format has been the show's biggest disappointment since I discovered that you could render a Dalek harmless simply by pushing it over. *Doctor Who* used to be a tradition. Now it is a non-event.' Miss Forwood feels Peter Davison 'has somehow failed to make any impact at all' and that the stories 'seem even sillier than ever'. Christopher Evans in the *New Scientist* is no more encouraging. 'When we add to this a degeneration in the standards of acting and direction, an almost total loss of wit and an increasing tendency to blind the viewer with pseudo-science, I think we are justified in claiming a decline in standards.' These views are to be quickly disputed, however, by the fans . . .

April 24

The media attacks on the programme bring a flood of letters to *Radio Times* and the editor gives over a page to 'the new Doctor Who and the old fans'. Elizabeth and

Rodney Holt of Tameside write on behalf of 'one grateful family' for the new series. 'Monday and Tuesday evenings have become quite sacred meeting-times, to be missed only under extreme circumstances,' they say. 'The time of the programme is just right for our six- and seven-year-old children and has brightened up the winter weeks at school. Completing each story in two weeks holds their attention and keeps us all from the pangs of impatience!' Mrs Sarah Bell from Rotherham rises to defend the new Doctor. 'I am tired of reading comments in the press disparaging Peter Davison,' she says. 'I like him very much and hope he has a long and happy time

VICTOR C. WRIGHT

playing the part.' Miss A. Bradbury of Enfield is also 'now accepting Peter Davison as the Doctor though I thought I never would' and approves of Adric's departure, 'which was very well performed and much better than the usual departures – assistants going off with secondary characters or electing to remain on certain planets'. There is a suspicion among several readers that Tegan is about to leave the series, one reader declaring that none of Peter Davisons's predecessors would have left a girl-companion apparently abandoned at Heathrow Airport. 'I do hope this is not for long,' writes Nigel Cooper of Dorset, 'and that we shall see her back in the TARDIS for the next serial. Tegan is a first-class character, too good to lose; and if she can't come back, could we perhaps see her in her own series?' The letters editor is able to assure all readers that she *will* be back in 1983 . . .

May 8

Doctor Who goes on location to Europe again – this time to Holland where sexy new outfits for Janet Fielding and Sarah Sutton make good stories for the accompanying journalists, and get the two girls labelled 'the Doctor's Harem'. While filming of Johnny Byrne's 'Arc of Infinity' takes place, the *Daily Mail* reports: 'Doctor Who's girl-assistants are getting a new look, following viewers' complaints that they were covered up too much. The letters, thought to be mostly from fathers, rolled in when actress Sarah Sutton switched from a short skirt to trousers in the last series. Now they have gone, and in their place come short pantaloons and a clinging blouse. Her fellow time-traveller,

Janet Fielding, will get a shoulder-revealing "boob tube" and short culottes.' John Nathan-Turner tells the press: 'We are granting viewers their wish – and showing lots of leg.'

According to the *Daily Star* 'the new outfits certainly caused a sensation in the streets of Amsterdam' – and indeed Janet Fielding confesses: 'My frillies are so tight I can't wear the usual thermal underwear!' Sarah Sutton reveals that she is making the change because of a flood of letters asking why she usually wears trousers. 'I wore a skirt just once in the last series,' she says, 'and got a lot of compliments.' Peter Davison tells reporters that he has received suggestions that there should be a relationship of some kind between him and one of the girls. 'But,' he says, 'the golden rule is no hanky-panky. Originally the Doctor was a grandfather figure. Then a sort of father. Then a favourite uncle. Now he is just a good friend to the girls. Even though I'm the youngest Doctor, I honestly don't think the kids would like to see kissing in the series. One youngster wrote asking me if I was married to Tegan because she moaned at me all the time!' Peter says that the Doctor has strict morals and each actor that plays him has a responsibility to maintain the tradition. 'The audience – especially the children – has to believe that men and women can be close friends sharing a home without sex. It is also my responsibility to see this healthy image continues off the screen – it wouldn't do for me to be involved in any scandal.' Peter in fact gave up a lucrative TV commercial for beer when becoming the Doctor. Curiously he finds himself better known in Holland for his part in *All Creatures Great and Small* and during filming is frequently greeted with a 'Good Morning, Dr Herriot'. The *Daily Mirror* explains: 'The Dutch are currently enjoying this series which is re-titled *Dr Herriot. Doctor Who,* once popular here, is seen no more. Two years ago, before Davison took over the role from Tom Baker, the series was banned for being too frightening for the children. Nobody asked the children, of course, who are still upset about the decision!'

July 12

As a result of the success of last year's re-runs of five of the Doctor's adventures in his various regenerations, the BBC puts on a short season, 'Doctor Who and the Monsters' re-showing Jon Pertwee's 'The Curse of Peladon' (1972), Tom Baker's 'Genesis of the Daleks' (1975) and Peter Davison's recent 'Earthshock', which again help bridge the gap until the start of the new series.

July 15

DIANNE C. LERNER

As Sarah Sutton flies from Heathrow to a Doctor Who convention in America, she reveals that she is leaving the series. 'I've been in the show for almost two years,' she says, 'and I think that is long enough. I want to move on, possibly to the theatre, and I know the writers like to change the Doctor's assistants quite regularly to keep the show interesting. I would like a happy ending, though – I certainly don't want to be bumped off!' And speaking about the convention in Chicago to which she is going, she adds: 'For a lot of people Doctor Who is real and actually exists.'

July 16

What is to prove the world's largest Doctor Who convention opens at the Americana Congress Hotel in Chicago attracting over 10,000 US fans for the two-day event. Another 3,000 without tickets have to be turned away. Attending the gathering are Sarah Sutton, Anthony Ainley, Terry Nation and John Nathan-Turner, who says later: 'The hotel was absolutely besieged. There were Doctor Who look-alikes everywhere, and people had travelled from all over America. Some were very upset at being turned away.'

Such is the media interest in the convention that two television documentaries are made, as well as innumerable radio interviews and major feature articles in many papers. The *Chicago Tribune* writes that *Doctor Who* has become 'the focus of a cult known as Who-ites' who are devoted to watching and promoting the programme in America as well as collecting the ever-growing mountain of memorabilia. The *Doctor Who* theme tune, it reports, has become a disco and jukebox hit, and has already given rise to a New Wave band called the Daleks. Diane Mermigas of the *Chicago Daily Herald* adds that such is the appeal of the show 'it has turned several million American adults into fanatic followers'. It is just what Yankee sci-fi enthusiasts who have been searching for a new fixation since *Star Trek* was cancelled by NBC in 1969 have been wanting, she says. Predictably, an American professor of sociology, Bernard Beck of North-Western University, is on hand to explain this phenomenon. 'It is just another example of the way things are going,' he says. 'Social life is no longer conventionally or institutionally organised by neighbourhoods or large families. The height of modernism is to make a life around interests shared in common with other people. Science fiction is the sort of thing that literate people are not ashamed of anymore to claim as lightweight entertainment, and conventions are a major alternative to singles bars.'

Peter Davison does not attend this convention, as the Tom Baker stories are still being shown in America, but he does make his first convention appearance in England at the Birmingham gathering staged by the Doctor Who Appreciation Society.

September 15

The replacement for departing Sarah Sutton is announced – Mark Strickson, aged twenty-three, who is to play the initially hostile and ever-unpredictable Turlough. Mark, something of a traveller himself, having just spent two years touring Britain's canals as a member of a

VITALY SABSAY

theatre company, is the twenty-fourth companion, and yet another actor who can recall the series from his childhood. 'I remember watching *Doctor Who* as a kid,' he tells the press at a photocall, 'and it's strange to find myself now taking part in it. But it's an amazingly different world and great fun.'

October 11

Verity Lambert, the young producer who brought the idea of *Doctor Who* from basic concept to televised success story, takes another step up the ladder of success when she is appointed Head of Film Production at EMI and becomes Britain's first woman movie-mogul. Her appointment is widely publicised in the national press, as is her hand in the creation of *Doctor Who* – a period of her life she has never ceased to look back on with gratitude and affection. 'I can honestly say that *Doctor Who* has always had a corner of my heart,' she says.

November 4

Doctor Who is declared a 'syndication goldmine' in America, by Bob Greenstein, marketing director of Lionheart Television International, who are distributing the series. The show is now on its way to earning millions of dollars a year, and Mr Greenstein believes it got off to a comparatively slow start in America because 'it was ten years too early. There was no viewer acceptance and there were only 72 episodes of the series then.' It was the '172 high-camp half-hour episodes starring Tom Baker' which caused the explosion in the show's popularity, he tells *Electronic Media*, although he admits 'we didn't know what the hell we had.' Within a year, the TV stations broadcasting *Doctor Who* had an estimated weekly audience of 98 million viewers, Greenstein says. '*Doctor Who* is only beginning to scratch the surface here,' he adds. 'The most surprising thing is that they don't make shows like it in this country because no one thinks they will sell. Can you believe it?'

November 21

A member of Prime Minister Margaret Thatcher's Cabinet, Lord Cockfield, the Trade Secretary, is known to his colleagues as 'Lord Dalek', according to *Mail on Sunday* writer Peter Simmons. 'His nickname comes from his clipped way of speaking,' says Simmons, 'and he has been chosen by Mrs Thatcher to exterminate the flood of Japanese imports into Britain and bring down barriers stopping Britain selling more abroad.'

December 6

Hollywood correspondent Randy Lofficier, calls *Doctor Who* 'one of the most entertaining science-fiction series in the world' in a major feature headlined *'Doctor Who* Captures American Imagination'. She writes: 'On the eve of its twentieth year, the key of *Doctor Who* success deserves to be studied. If the realisation was not always impeccable, especially in its early days, the characterisations and the sheer imagination contained in its stories, have made the series an institution. The eager fan reception in this country has shown that this appreciation has been carried across the Atlantic. *Doctor Who,* like Tarzan or Sherlock Holmes, appeals to all of those who truly love epic adventure in the grand ol' classic tradition.' Randy Lofficier's husband, Jean-Marc, is of course the man who has provided an excellent study-aid to the show with his two-volume *Programme Guide* . . .

December 23

Three leading members of the *Doctor Who* team combine in a light-hearted break from the series when they stage a Christmas pantomime, *Cinderella,* at the Assembly Hall Theatre, Tunbridge Wells, which runs until 15 January. Written and directed by John Nathan-Turner, the production stars Peter Davison as Buttons and Anthony Ainley as Baron Hard-up. Peter's wife, Sandra Dickinson, also appears as Mirazel, the fairy godmother.

TONY SMART

December 30

A front-page exclusive story in the *Sun* breaks the news that the twentieth anniversary of *Doctor Who* next year is to be marked by a special programme on 23 November. 'The clock is being turned back on Britain's favourite time-traveller, Doctor Who, next year,' writes Nick Ferrari, 'for a remarkable "Who's Who" parade of the show's stars. All the Doctors will be featured in a special edition to celebrate the Time Lord's twentieth anniversary.' He says the BBC has been secretly working to bring all the actors back together, with a "similar-style" actor taking the late William Hartnell's place. Jon Pertwee tells Nick Ferrari: 'I know the BBC have approached all the Doctors and I was delighted to say "yes". My days as Doctor Who were great fun.' Full details of this special are to remain closely guarded for two more months – and provide a number of surprises . . .

ERGON

PAUL PICKFORD

1983

N. PARKS

January 3

The twentieth season begins with 'Arc of Infinity', the Johnny Byrne story shot partly on location in Amsterdam the previous year, which provides viewers with a first look at the sexy new outfits for Nyssa and Tegan. The story also offers further insights into the Time Lord community on Gallifrey, and introduces a somewhat suspicious character named Commander Maxil, played by an actor who is later to appear in the series in a very important role *indeed*– Colin Baker.

February 1

'Who is Turlough?' asks the title of the first episode of 'Mawdryn Undead' by Peter Grimwade, which introduces Mark Strickson as the strange young schoolboy destined to become the Doctor's latest companion. The story also brings back Valentine Dyall as the evil Black Guardian, and creates a piece of Who-history with the return of Nicholas Courtney as the now-retired Brigadier Lethbridge-Stewart. This appearance by Nicholas is a unique moment for him and the series, making him the *only* actor to have appeared with the first five Doctors!

Despite not having been seen in the programme for almost seven years, the Brig has a large fan-following around the world and is often invited to conventions. Talking about his return to the show he says: 'Peter Grimwade knows the Brigadier very well and what he has written is very much in character. It is just like coming back to old times.' And reminiscing on

D. G. CARELESS

Doctor Who from his unique viewpoint he gives his verdict on each of the five Doctors: 'Hartnell I think you would describe as tetchy,' he says, 'while Pat Troughton was whimsical. Jon Pertwee had great panache and Tom Baker eccentricity. Peter Davison is vibrant and very talented.'

February 4

Peter Davison makes his first appearance in costume as the Doctor at a US convention – the weekend-long Omnicon IV held at Fort Lauderdale, Florida, and attended by over 1,000 fans. With him are his wife, Sandra, and John Nathan-Turner. There is much praise for the producer and his efforts helping to promote the series in America, and a motion is raised and passed by fans that Sandra Dickinson should become a future companion of the Doctor. Peter Davison, asked if he nurses any secret ambitions, reveals he would like to play a villain, and another proposal is made from the floor that in a future story the Doctor and the Master should switch identities!

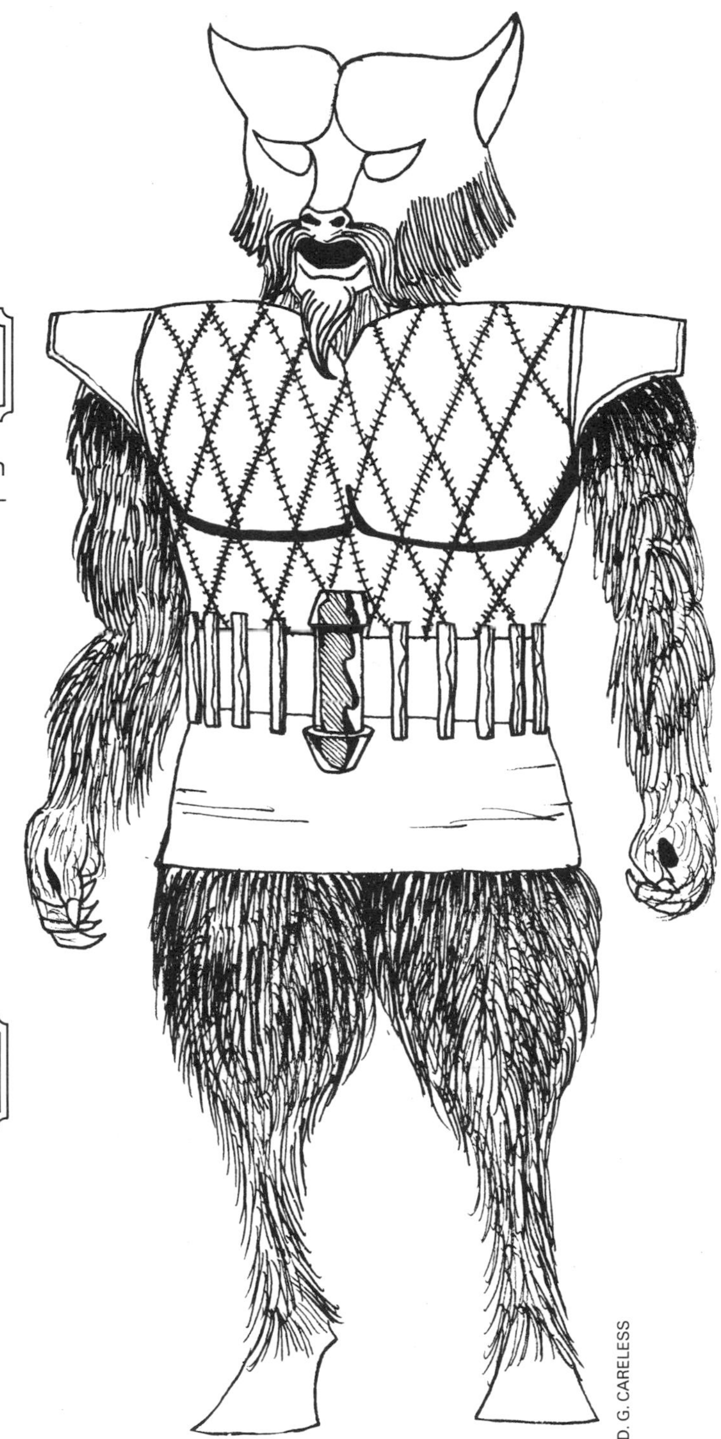
D. G. CARELESS

February 23

The delightful Nyssa takes her leave of the Doctor to stay among the pitiful Lazars that she and the Time Lord have been trying to help on board the spaceship *Terminus*. According to Steve Gallagher's story of the same name she hopes to put to use her knowledge of bio-electronics to find a cure for the Lazars' disease. Sarah Sutton reflects on her role as Nyssa: 'She was a challenge to play and it was great fun trying to get my tongue round all the long technical words I couldn't pronounce!'

March 1

The penultimate story of the season, 'Enlightenment', with the so-far unique distinction of having been written and directed by women, Barbara Clegg and Fionna Cumming, is transmitted . . . but only just. An industrial dispute at the BBC

BILL A. HOOPER

the previous December has caused a two-month shut-down at Television Centre, and 'Enlightenment' comes within a whisker of sharing the same fate as 'Shada'. But fortunately the strike is resolved and the story is filmed in mid-January allowing just enough time for post-production work to be completed in time for transmission in the allotted spot.

The last story of the season, 'The King's Demons' by Terence Dudley – a two-parter – also just makes it in time for transmission on 15 and 16 March. It is notable for the return of Anthony Ainley as the Master, though his involvement in the adventure is carefully concealed from viewers so as not to spoil their surprise by the use of a cunning anagram of his name in the *Radio Times* list of credits! (For the record, he appears disguised as the character Sir Giles played by 'James Stoker' – which rearranged makes 'Master's Joke'!)

March 4

'Peter is a tonic!' declares *Daily Star* television columnist Stafford Hildred in an assessment of the season. 'Peter Davison deserves an intergalactic acting award for adding new dimensions to *Doctor Who,*' he writes. 'Tom Baker was a hard act to follow, but with his pyjama trousers and air of

MIKE TUCKER

TIM PIERACCINI

permanent surprise, Peter has done it. The sci-fi series is as entertaining as ever, and I understand the Daleks will be returning in the special anniversary adventure being recorded for November. But a really great move for the Time Lord would be a switch back to Saturday nights . . .'

March 17

After weeks of speculation, a press conference re-uniting almost all of the Doctors is called to release details on the 90-minute anniversary special, 'The Five Doctors' written by Terrance Dicks. Peter Davison, Jon Pertwee, Patrick Troughton and Richard Hurndall, a well-known character-actor with a striking similarity to William Hartnell, assemble in a Buckinghamshire country mansion with Bessie and a waxwork model of Tom Baker to pose for cameramen. John Nathan-Turner explains the absence of the fourth Doctor: 'Tom has other commitments and is not available to play in this production.' (In 'The Five Doctors' Tom is to make a brief appearance in a scene shot in 1979 for the story 'Shada' which, of course, was never transmitted.) Evidently delighted to be part of the team, Richard Hurndall says: 'I admired William Hartnell very much and I have tried to play the part as he would have done.' And as to the future of the series after the special, John Nathan-Turner says: 'I don't see why it should not continue for another twenty years – it is too popular to stop now!'

MARGARET JONES

March 18

Two of the Doctors, Peter Davison and Patrick Troughton, appear on BBC Television's *Nationwide* programme to discuss the *Doctor Who* phenomenon. Presenter Sue Lawley again raises the idea of a female Doctor, to which Patrick Troughton mischievously replies, 'What a good idea!' More seriously he reveals: 'I would love to make a *Doctor Who* film. Perhaps a remake of "Evil of the Daleks" – it would be nice to make it with all the others.' He even nurses a small ambition to return to the series, he says, but *not* in the obvious role. 'I'd just love to play one of those monsters. I'd have to be completely concealed, of course, and there must be no credit in the *Radio Times*. It would be marvellous – and without anyone knowing!' Peter talks about his own pleasure in playing the role, and some of the problems of being instantly

JEREMY DONALD

recognisable wherever he goes. 'I can't get much privacy,' he says. 'I've tried wearing woolly hats and dark glasses, astronauts' hats with big brims and even a huge trilby pulled over my face – but someone always sees through my disguise.' How long will he continue to play the part? 'I'll know when the time is right to leave,' is all he will say.

April 1

William Hartnell to meet Peter Davison – the first Doctor and his fifth regeneration are to be reunited in a forthcoming story entitled 'The Phoenix Rises' according to the *Doctor Who Monthly.* Apparently unscreened footage of the long-ago cancelled Malcolm Hulke story 'The Hidden Planet' has been discovered, and is to be combined with new film using doubles and the present *Doctor Who* cast for a unique time-and-space adventure. This extraordinary revelation is accompanied by a photograph showing William Hartnell in conversation with William Russell and Peter Davison. Many a *Doctor Who* fan's heart beats faster on reading the news . . .

But the date of the story is the give-away. It's actually an April Fool's joke cleverly perpetrated by writer Richard Landen. So cleverly, in fact, that the BBBC production office is deluged with telephone calls and letters about when the story is to be screened. A special disclaimer has to be prepared to be read or posted to each – naturally disappointed – enquirer!

April 3

The first major event to mark the anniversary takes place at stately Longleat over the Easter bank holiday weekend – 'The Doctor Who Celebration: Twenty Years of a Time Lord'. BBC organisers estimate a total attendance of 50,000, but over 35,000 crowd into Lord Bath's grounds on the first day, and even more the second. The roll call of personalities is the finest for any *Doctor Who* gathering: Patrick Troughton, Jon Pertwee, Tom Baker (not a model this time!), Peter Davison, Heather Hartnell (the first Doctor's widow), Anthony Ainley, Nicholas Courtney, Richard Franklin, Carole Ann Ford, Valentine Dyall, John Leeson, Liz Sladen, John Levene, Sarah Sutton, Mark Strickson, Janet Fielding, and John Nathan-Turner, who is Master of Ceremonies for the various question- and-answer sessions with fans.

Other highlights include a charity auction with Tom Baker's brown coat fetching £810, a Cyberman's suit going for over £200, and even a Gallifreyan book from the untransmitted 'Shada' selling for £100.

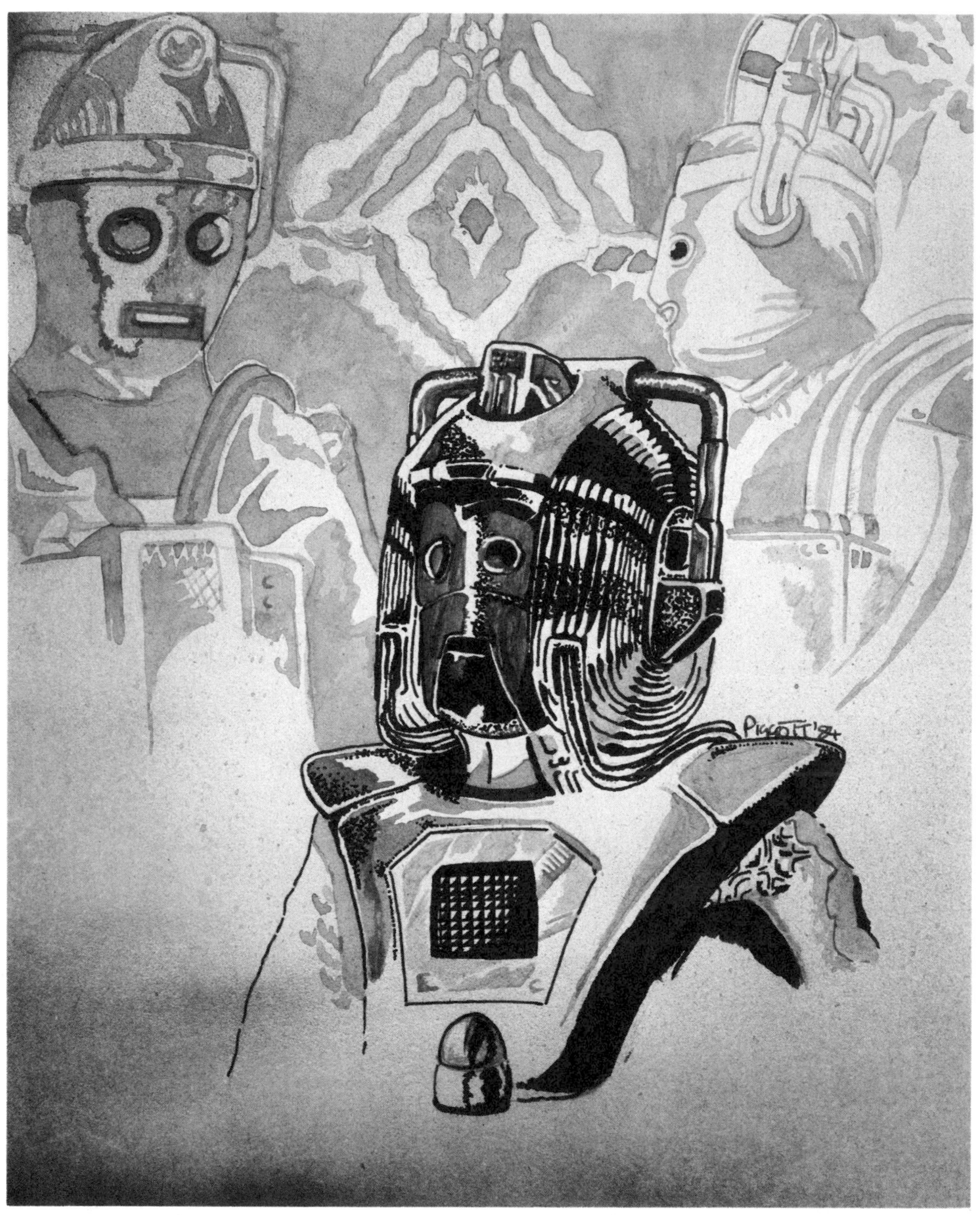

BARRY PIGGOTT

There are numerous monsters and aliens on view, sets from 'The Five Doctors' and a make-up department tent where fans can view costumes from the series and try out special make-up. The event attracts enormous publicity, most newspapers making much of the crowds: 'Doctor Who Has Waiting Room Only' the *Daily Mail* headlines its report. 'The size of the crowd took the BBC by surprise . . . but for the lucky ones who got into the various exhibition tents it was a science fiction paradise.'

Surrounded by many Doctor look-alikes, the originals have comments to make on the extraordinary gathering. 'I love attending this sort of thing,' says Jon Pertwee. 'I thrive on it. You know these people don't really want to ask me questions, they want to show off their knowledge of *Doctor Who.* And that's all right, because what they really want is to be me or me as the Doctor.' Patrick Troughton sees a reality behind the public's fascination for the series. 'It's all true, you see,' he says. 'The universe is teeming with life. Earth is just a tiny part. It's the beginning of the realisation that we are not alone. But there is a fantasy element too. I am a great fan of *Star Trek* and never missed an episode. I suppose people like *Doctor Who* for the same reason I do *Star Trek.'* Tom Baker believes it is the challenge of the programme that kept him 'young and fresh'. And he adds, 'All that fantasy is good for the mind. But I have to admit that some of the people I have met had theories about *Doctor Who* I could not understand. I asked them what they wanted and they all wanted the same thing. To travel with the Doctor in the TARDIS!' And Peter Davison contributes the latest viewpoint: 'I think part of the Doctor's appeal is that he is not stereotyped. He's not a macho figure. He solves things, but in his own way. The series takes itself quite seriously, but not too much, and it's great fun to do.' Carole Ann Ford, who appeared in the show earlier than anyone else there, has the last word. 'There is nothing else like *Doctor Who,'* she says. 'In spite of opposition from things like *Star Trek* it's still the most popular science-fiction programme. The girls who have appeared alongside the Doctor represent the people watching. They would like to be us sharing the adventure.'

June 23

The American Academy of Science, Fantasy and Horror gives its 1983 Saturn International Award to *Doctor Who* as the best foreign programme, with Tom Baker getting the best foreign actor award for his portrayal of the Doctor. *The Stage* magazine also reports that plans have been finalised in America to mark the twentieth anniversary with a coast-to-coast birthday party stretching from New York to California and involving 80 US television stations. Says Wynn Nathan, President of Lionheart Television: 'We're shooting for the *Guinness Book of Records* – with over 7,000,000 US fans singing "Happy Birthday" to our hero, Doctor Who, on 23 November, when the 90-minute special "The Five Doctors" goes out.' Mr Nathan also urges all fans to send birthday cards to the Doctor to mark this unique event.

July 5

The first 'American' joins the cast of *Doctor Who* with the announcement of a new companion for the Doctor, the delightfully named Miss Perpugilliam Brown, an American student, to be played by 21-year-old British-born Nicola Bryant. She is transformed from the obscurity of drama school to the front pages of the national papers with the news which will make her

BILL MARSH

the twenty-fifth assistant. This leap to fame is all the more amazing when Nicola tells journalists that she had predicted it to her family nine years ago. 'We were sitting watching *Doctor Who* and I said I would be in it one day. They all laughed at me then, but now they are laughing because it has come true!' And she adds: 'I'm still a little amazed. I was crawling around in my nappies when the series started. Later my sister and I used to dare each other into watching the programme as we were so scared – particularly of the Daleks.' Nicola's character, Perpugilliam, – an old English name typical of a certain sort of wealthy American family, which will be shortened to Peri – is to meet the Doctor on a Mediterranean holiday – wearing only a bikini. John Nathan-Turner tells the press: 'She'll often be wearing leotards and bikinis. A lot of Dads watch *Doctor Who* and I'm sure they will like Nicola.'

July 28

Another era in the history of *Doctor Who* comes to an end with Peter Davison's announcement that he is giving up the role of the Doctor at the end of the twenty-first season next March. The news is broken on

ALAN READ

the BBC lunchtime News and Peter says: 'I decided when I took the part it would only be for three years and that will be up next January. There is a danger, I feel, of actors becoming stereotyped if they stay in a series too long. And I've always done three years of everything else. It's a nice round figure. But it has still been a most enjoyable role.' (To date, Peter's is the shortest run as the Doctor – just 74 episodes.)

There is immediate speculation about who will be the next Doctor, the *Daily Mail* declaring that the search is on for an older actor. John Nathan-Turner says, 'We've tried a young one and now we're after someone older. What I have in mind is an actor with the magic of the early, eccentric Doctors. I think one of the strengths and successes of the programme is because of the differences between successive Doctors.'

August 1

Brian Blessed is to be the new Doctor according to a rumour picked up by newspapers as far flung as the *Yorkshire Telegraph & Argus* and the Australian *Sydney Morning Herald* and given front-page prominence. Several television reporters are convinced the hugely entertaining character-actor is destined to be the sixth Doctor, and from London the *Morning Herald*'s correspondent tells his readers on the other side of the world: 'Older men are walking a little straighter this week with the news that the prized role of Doctor Who is to go to Brian Blessed, forty-five, who has enjoyed great success on both stage and screen since he won acclaim as PC Fancy Smith in the long-running BBC series *Z-Cars.*' Listing some of his other triumphs, the paper goes on: 'But it was as the rumbustious but lovable winged man in *Flash Gordon* that Blessed showed his likely *Doctor Who* personage – noisier and more irascible than recent inhabitants of the role, but with a flashing, warming smile which will surely charm even Daleks away from extermination. Aficionados are already saying Blessed can be the best Doctor Who since the redoubtable Jon Pertwee . . .' Brian Blessed, however, is saying nothing of the sort, the rumour having apparently originated from the Doctor Who Exhibition in Blackpool! And so the speculation goes on . . .

August 17

The *Daily Star* invites its readers to nominate a new Doctor and is deluged with mail. Among the suggestions are Bernard Hill – 'He would make a desperate Doctor'; Matthew Kelly – 'What a laugh he would be'; and star-gazer Patrick Moore – 'With his baggy suits he wouldn't need the television wardrobe department'. The idea of a female Time Lord is revived yet again with the actresses put forward including Jill Gascoine, Sandra Dickinson and Beryl Reid, – 'She is the kind of woman who would take pleasure in jaunting around in a telephone box and seeking out the Daleks' writes her proposer.

The *Daily Express* columnist James Murray also takes up the theme and thinks the actress should be 'mature and a bit eccentric', listing as possibles Patricia Hayes, Maria Aitken, Anna Ford, Pamela Stephenson, Shirley Williams, Diana Dors, Esther Rantzen, Annie Walker, Jan Leeming and Angela Rippon. But, he goes on, 'my favourite for the job would be the Salvation Army's wonderful Catherine Bramwell-Booth, mature enough at one hundred to smite all Doctor Who's enemies in outer space with the charm of her tongue alone.'

But none of these suggestions – male or female – are anywhere near the final choice . . .

August 19

An actor who once had a small part in a *Doctor Who* story and actually tried to kill the Doctor, emerges as the man to fill the role of the sixth Time Lord, forty-year-old Colin Baker. Following the announcement on BBC Television, the press is quick to headline the transformation of villain into a goodie. The *Daily Record* reports: 'Actor Colin Baker, once a J.R.-type television-screen villain, is to take on the role of one of the small screen's most loved heroes, Doctor Who. Colin was a forerunner of J.R. Ewing as the man viewers loved to hate when he played Paul Merroney, the "nasty" in the BBC series *The Brothers.'* The paper also cites two other villainous appearances as Babon the Berserker in *Blake's 7* and as the Gallifreyan guard Maxil in the Doctor's adventure 'Arc of Infinity', of which he tells journalists: 'At the end of one episode I actually shot the Doctor – but not to get his job, though!'

Colin, who first started training to be a solicitor before going into acting, and thereafter enjoyed a number of hits on the stage and in television, has earned himself the role after a performance he was scarcely conscious of having given. John Nathan-Turner explains: 'I'd got to know Colin when he played a captain of the guard for us, and we met up again this summer when one of the production team got married. The *Who* crowd were sitting together on the grass, having a good time, and for the whole afternoon, Colin kept us all thoroughly entertained. Even though I wasn't actively looking for a new Doctor then, I thought, "Aha! if he can hold the attention of fifteen hard-bitten showbiz

MARGARET JONES

professionals for hours, then he can do the same with an audience.'''

Of his casting, Colin Baker tells the press: 'I allowed myself a good twelve seconds before accepting. I am stimulated and excited by the opportunity and very conscious of the responsibility. It's the most marvellous part to be offered. *Doctor Who* has been running for more than half my life and I used to be hooked on the series, certainly in the William Hartnell and Patrick Troughton days. If you'd told me then, it would have been knock me down with a feather time.' Colin adds that it is a real pleasure to be playing the good guy for a change, and plans to portray his Doctor as 'quirky, witty and unexpected'. To this John Nathan-Turner adds: 'We want to make him a little more eccentric than Peter's been. A bit more crotchety, too, with perhaps a kind of acid wit.'

September 12

The Daleks are on the rampage again – and as ever attract newspaper coverage. The evil machines are photographed on location at Tower Bridge, where Peter Davison is filming an encounter with them for next season's story 'Resurrection of the Daleks' written by script editor Eric Saward. Peter says: 'Every actor who plays the Doctor has to face his most deadly enemy sooner or later and they've got to me just before I leave.' This marks the Daleks' thirteenth appearance – they starred with William Hartnell in five stories, two with Patrick Troughton, three with Jon Pertwee and two with Tom Baker – and this fact causes the London *Evening Standard* to speculate: 'Will it be an unlucky number for Peter Davison?'

October 5

The making of a full-length *Doctor Who* film is raised again. The project, known as *Doctor Who – the Motion Picture,* has been several times discussed, John Nathan-Turner reveals. 'The possibility of a film has come up on a number of occasions in the past four years,' he says, 'but each time the idea has fallen through. The BBC were never very happy with the *Doctor Who* films made in the Sixties and would want to be very closely involved with any such new project. They would also want whoever was playing the Doctor on television to star in the film. I myself wouldn't want Robert Redford or someone like that as the Doctor! I am determined that it will happen sooner rather than later.'

October 29

The biggest-ever screening of 70 episodes of *Doctor Who* takes place over this weekend at the National Film Theatre in London as the British Film Institute's tribute to the series. Devised by Jeremy Bentham and Manuel Alvarado, the special event not only shows the development of the programme but also that of British Television itself over twenty years. Entitled 'Doctor Who – the Developing Art' the screening begins with 'An Unearthly Child' and runs through typical adventures of all five Doctors to Peter Davison's 'Earthshock'. Among those who attend the discussion sessions are Heather Hartnell, Patrick Troughton and John Nathan-Turner, who, with capacity audiences,

MICHAEL G. CLARK

discuss the personalities and techniques of making the series.

November 19

The *Radio Times* gives over its front cover to *Doctor Who* for the first time since 1974 with a special painting by Andrew Skilleter marking the twentieth anniversary and the showing of 'The Five Doctors'. Ian Levine, a well-known expert on the series, writes a lengthy profile on the actors and actresses who have made *Doctor Who* the world's longest-running science fiction show.

The national press also devote extensive features to the series: *The Times* arts correspondent, David Hewson pointing out – not altogether correctly – that 'only two characteristics of the original remain: its immense popularity and the singular ability of the scenery to move every time an actor bumps into it'; while Philip Oakes in the *Sunday Express* wishes the Doctor happy birthday now he is 720 – 'his last twenty years being counted by courtesy of the BBC in Earth-time.' John Nathan-Turner just takes quiet pleasure out of the fact that the show is now sold to 54 countries and has an international audience of one hundred million. He tells Philip Oakes: 'There is absolutely no reason why it should ever come to an end. It's like the BBC's own *Mousetrap.* Twenty years is no age at all.'

November 23

'The Five Doctors' is screened across America – and in Chicago, four of the Doctors and a host of companions gather for 'Doctor Who: The Ultimate Celebration'. The two-day event, held at the Hyatt Regency Hotel, attracts over ten thousand fans, who attend the discussion sessions, video screenings, autograph and photo sessions, and an impromptu cabaret performed by the stars themselves. New companion Nicola Bryant gets her first taste of the amazing world of *Who,* while former companion Mary Tamm is equally overwhelmed by what she sees. 'It was extraordinary,' she says later. 'All the actors who have played the Doctor and many other actors and actresses past and present were flown out and put up in a Chicago hotel for two days. The show is hugely popular there and some of the fans queued for hours to get our autographs. We were treated just like royalty, and everywhere we went we had up to six bodyguards looking after us. On one occasion I went to the loo escorted by two huge guys with walkie-talkies!'

Extensive coverage of this convention is carried on BBC Radio and Television news broadcasts, and the TV magazine programme *Did You See?* devotes twenty minutes to the anniversary. Ludovic Kennedy screens interviews with John Nathan-Turner and Terry Nation as well as clips showing each of the five Doctors. After the festivities, John says: 'I think things will get a little quieter now. I'm certainly not thinking of anything to mark the twenty-first anniversary . . . yet.'

November 25

The long-awaited 90-minute special 'The Five Doctors' is transmitted in the UK with Peter Davison and his predecessors Tom Baker, Jon Pertwee, Patrick Troughton, and

RadioTimes
Who's Who?
Doctor Who's twentieth anniversary is celebrated
by 'The Five Doctors' who again face their enemy The Master
in a special feature-length story on BBC1.
Inside: companions in space . . . a Who Who's Who

Richard Hurndall standing in for the late William Hartnell. Several companions, the Brigadier, K9, the Master, a Dalek, some Cybermen, and a number of Gallifreyans are brought together in a fiendish plot to destroy the Doctor – all five of him! 'But don't worry about the intergalactic plot,' the *Daily Mail* urges readers in its preview, 'just enjoy the reappearance of all those monsters we've grown to know and love!'

By one of those strange twists of fate that seem to have bedevilled important moments in the history of *Doctor Who,* an NGA strike of printers prevents any Saturday or Sunday newspapers and the show is unable to get a single review! Director Peter Moffat does, though, later pass a few comments on the continuing success of the show, which he attributes to a mixture of horror and naivety. 'It has a touch of *Frankenstein* and *Listen with Mother,'* he says. 'It also has a home-made quality about it, plus a touch of magic, of course.' Peter believes it is the series' simplicity that makes it distinctive – and its strict morality. 'All the young people in it are polite and sweet. There is no bad language and the morals are impeccable.'

December 10

A Golden Egg for the Doctor! In a moment of pre-Christmas fun, Noel Edmonds, host of the popular TV programme *The Late, Late Breakfast Show* presents Peter Davison with a Golden Egg Award for an unscripted moment which occurred during the filming of one of next year's stories, 'The Awakening'. The incident took place when Peter had just dismounted from a horse-drawn cart and was about to go through a specially built lych-gate leading into a churchyard. The horse should have remained where he was – but such is Peter's magnetism that the animal complete with cart decided to follow him through the gate, completely demolishing it in the process!

At the presentation, the horse and cart are brought onto the set and encouraged to repeat the award-winning performance through a similar gate – this time, though, it causes nothing like the same destruction!

ROBERT SHAW

BOX
PULL TO OPEN

1984

January 5

'Warriors of the Deep' commences the twenty-first season of *Doctor Who* with a re-match between the Doctor and two foes from his Jon Pertwee incarnation – the Sea Devils and the Silurians. The script by Johnny Byrne requires a lengthy sequence of underwater shots bridging episodes one and two. By tradition all water scenes are filmed at the big water-tank at the BBC's Ealing film studios. But, since the production team wanted to shoot the entire programme on video (to avoid the grain change between film and video footage), they cannot use Ealing, which does not permit the use of video equipment on the premises. To get around this problem the whole production moves down to Southampton for two days of video shooting at a swimming baths.

January 10

Colin Baker unveils the sixth regeneration of the Doctor as a 'more alien person with an appalling sense of dress'. His multicoloured patchwork outfit of striped trousers, waistcoat, tie and 'coat of many colours' has been arrived at as a result of

OLIVER MURRAY

direct orders from John Nathan-Turner, who told the BBC's costume department he wanted something 'in bad taste'. Baker's appearance naturally delights the press photographers at the photocall and gets widespread coverage.

January 11

The end of the Doctor's famous time-travel machine, the TARDIS? In a surprise announcement, John Nathan-Turner says the machine is now out of date and should be replaced after twenty years of interplanetary duty. 'We are considering

MIKE GOODMAN

MARTIN F. PROCTOR

the idea,' he says. 'A whole generation of young *Doctor Who* fans have never seen a genuine police box because there are none.'

Colin Baker reacts instantly to the suggestion. 'It's a crying shame,' he tells the press. 'We ought to have a campaign to save the police box!' This new battle for the Doctor receives extensive coverage, with the *Daily Mail* headlining its story: 'Save My TARDIS Plea by Doctor Who' Baker's only consolation, if this should occur, he says, is the news that he is to have a new companion in the form of a space-age cat!

January 19

An impressive cast of special actors for this season's two-part story, 'The Awakening' by Eric Pringle: Glyn Houston as Colonel Wolsey and Denis Lill as Sir George Hutchinson (both men have previous appearances in *Doctor Who* to their credit: Glyn in 'The Hand of Fear', 1976, and Denis in 'Image of the Fendahl', 1977), as well as ex-*Liver Birds* star Polly James. The story is the first for the series by Eric Pringle, while director Michael Morris is also making his debut behind the cameras.

January 26

Skilled actor William Lucas steps into the role of Mr Range in former script editor Christopher Bidmead's story 'Frontios'. This part was originally cast with Peter Arne, the actor whose tragic death in his London flat made front-page news in which his association with *Doctor Who* was stressed above all his other acting work – though he had yet to appear in the series. This adventure of the Doctor on the hostile planet which gives its name to the story also features Peter Gilmore, star of the *Onedin Line,* and a former *Angels* actress,

PAUL FISHER COCKBURN

R. L. FRANCIS

Lesley Dunlop. The apparent destruction of the TARDIS in episode one gives added credence to John Nathan-Turner's earlier announcement . . .

February 8

Because of the BBC's intensive coverage of the Winter Olympics from Sarajevo in Yugoslavia, the planned return of the Daleks in a four-part story, 'Resurrection of the Daleks', has to be dramatically re-shaped by producer John Nathan-Turner and director Matthew Robinson. The four episodes are meshed into two 50-minute episodes, the first time the series has ever occupied such a transmission period. Nevertheless, there is tremendous press and public interest in the reappearance of the Doctor's oldest enemies, and script editor Eric Saward's story also brings back the creator of the Daleks, Davros himself.

KAREN DAVIES

Highlight of the story is the explosion of a group of Daleks, executed with stunning effect by visual effects designer Peter Wragg. 'I had to build them of a soft material,' he explains, 'because they had to explode in the studio – and it's not a good idea to have solid Daleks exploding when there are actors around!' Although the Daleks cannot, as ever, see off the Doctor, the story marks the departure from the series of Tegan. Though actress Janet Fielding refers to her part as 'a mouth on legs – she's quite dreadful really', she leaves with fond memories of the rest of the cast and crew. 'In the end Tegan decided enough was enough where the Doctor was concerned, and in a way I felt the same,' she says.

Once again, though, the Daleks are the centre of controversy. Complaints are made to the *Radio Times* about 'Resurrection of the Daleks'.

Mrs Caroline M. Nicholas of Dyfed in Wales writes: 'The first episode really was the limit. The Daleks arrive, there is a battle and we are shown a close-up of a man with a horribly burned face! At 7.05 in the evening, a time when small children are not yet in bed but sitting around the television with the family. My three-year-old daughter was terrified. We had to switch off immediately.'

And Mrs L. Webster of Sidcup in Kent makes another point: 'I'm writing to complain about the smoking in the first episode of 'Resurrection of the Daleks' (a crew member of the space station and a soldier). There was no need for it in the story, and it would have been just as good without it. Surely the BBC should give a good example on a children's programme.'

KENNETH HORLOCK

February 19

An appeal for missing episodes of *Doctor Who* is made through the *Sunday Times* which reveals that 130 are missing from the BBC Archives – mostly from the William Hartnell and Patrick Troughton eras, with just a handful from the Jon Pertwee period – having been either lost or destroyed. The Head of the BBC's Film and Video Library, Anne Hanford, says: "We didn't know in 1964 that *Doctor Who* would turn into a cult programme. Nothing was ever destroyed without the knowledge of the producers, who never once said that we were destroying priceless history." Since 1976 everything has been carefully preserved, but the missing episodes are "rather like chapters missing from *Alice in Wonderland*" to quote expert Ian Levine.

STEPHEN GREENACRE

Anne Hanford says that episodes have been turning up in the interim from all sorts of strange places – including a TV station in Australia and the vaults of a Mormon church in London! – and the BBC has declared an amnesty on any copies of the series that may be in private hands, merely wishing to borrow them to make a copy. This news has started a massive hunt, the *Sunday Times* reports: 'Dedicated fans are said to have risked injury to snatch the junked films from flaming incinerators rather than see their hero vanishing in a final time-vortex. Some believe that all the lost copies are buried beneath the Chiswick flyover. Many are totally convinced there's a Dr No type collector who has hoarded all the episodes.' Any offers of help?, the paper adds.

February 23

The location work carried out last autumn at Lanzarote in the beautiful Spanish Canary Islands shows up with stunning effect in Peter Grimwade's 'Planet of Fire'. Producer John Nathan-Turner has always been a great believer in 'making locations show' and the island scenery gives added emphasis to the plot. The beauty is emphasised by the introduction of the lithesome and scantily clad Nicola Bryant as the American student, Perpugilliam Brown, destined to be the Doctor's new companion. It is a far from comfortable introduction, as Nicola later reveals. 'Although there were several dangerous scenes, I refused to have a stand-in,' she says, 'so I got cut and bruised sliding down a mountainside of sharp, volcanic ash, nearly froze to death in the Atlantic pretending I was drowning, and then spent ninety minutes in a smoke-filled cave. As if that wasn't enough, I was accidentally dropped on my back!' Nicola needed frequent treatment from the make-up girls to cover-up the cuts and bruises, and added ruefully, 'I'm so thrilled to be playing the part, but I never knew it would be so painful!' Peter Davison pays tribute to her dedication. 'She is very keen and uses every spare moment learning the business,' he says. 'And she looks more like a James Bond girl than a *Doctor Who* girl. Watching her it's as much as I can do to persuade myself that I am right to leave the series!'

With the appearance of Peri, there is also a return for the Master played with even greater sardonic intensity by Anthony Ainley. But departing the series is the enigmatic Turlough, though at last his true nature is explained . . .

Heralding his appearance, Colin Baker appears on *Blue Peter* in full regalia. During his interview, the regeneration process of each of the previous five Doctors is shown, and Colin reveals that his big ambition is to meet the Daleks in a future story!

The sixth Doctor is also featured in *The Times* and in a special colour page in the *Radio Times*. He tells interviewer Kate Griffith that he has already been well received by fans in Britain and America, where he was recently introduced as 'Peter Davison's replacement'. He is enjoying the role enormously, he says. 'It is everybody's dream to play their hero, whether it is Lancelot or Biggles or Doctor Who, because they are characters in modern mythology. I always suspected it would be good fun. I feel almost as though this part was made for me, or I was made for this part.'

March 16

In a complete break with tradition, the regeneration of the Doctor into his new persona does not begin to take place in the final story of the season in order to carry viewer-excitement about the newcomer over into the next series. Instead it occurs in the sixth story, 'The Caves of Androzani' by veteran *Doctor Who* writer and former script editor, Robert Holmes. The transformation of Peter Davison into the colourfully bizarre figure of Colin Baker is handled in a strikingly inventive way by director Graeme Harper, and another unique feature of the story are the cameo appearances of each of the old Doctor's companions, Nyssa, Tegan, Adric, Kamelion and Turlough, and of course the Master.

PAUL HOLDER

TIM PIERACCINI

JUSTIN CHUBB

March 22

The miracle has happened again – the Time Lord from Gallifrey has a new appearance and a fresh lease of life to set off on a new generation of adventures. Colin Baker makes an eagerly and thankfully short-awaited first full appearance as the sixth Doctor in the dramatic story of 'The Twin Dilemma' by Anthony Steven.

The *Daily Telegraph* welcomes the second actor named Baker to play the role as 'an unpredictable, querulous and occasionally satirical Doctor'.

It is yet another unique moment in time – almost exactly twenty-one years from the days when Sydney Newman began to realise the dream which is now a world-wide phenomenon. From the series' almost murky black-and-white beginnings, with an audience of a few million rather puzzled viewers, it has grown to become an international cult enjoyed by some 110 million people in many nations and speaking many tongues. Indeed, it has gone far beyond Newman's original ambitions, generated by a mixture of highly imaginative storytelling, inspired acting, inventive production, brilliant use of the very latest advances in television technology, and perhaps most of all the faith those on either side of the screen have in the magic inherent in those two words . . . *Doctor Who.* The question mark may still remain about the man – as it always should – but the success which envelopes him is beyond dispute, both at this time and doubtless for many years to come.

ACKNOWLEDGEMENTS

Artwork by *Doctor Who* fans from Britain, Australia, Canada and the United States of America, has been included in this book and the Publishers would like to thank the following for their contributions:

Cas Adamson
David Adamson
James Adamson
Barb Armata
Dianne Bedford
Mark Bentham
Ronald Binnie
M. A. Blewitt
Michael Booth
Charlotte Brett
Justin Bright
Ray D. Brooking
D. G. Careless
Justin Chubb
Michael G. Clark
Paul Fisher Cockburn
John F. Crichton
Karen Davies
Christopher Denyer
Jeremy Donald
Simon Forward
Andrew Fournier
R. L. Francis
Mike Goodman
Stephen Greenacre
Nick Harris
Stuart J. M. Hill
Paul Holder
Bill A. Hooper
Kenneth Horlock
Colin Howard
David J. Hows
I. Humphrys and G. Smith
M. Hyland
Anthony James
Roland Jeffs
Margaret Jones
Andrew Kerr
Dianne C. Lerner
Simon Lewis
Lori McAdams
Stephen McArthur
Jim McDade
Stephen McKay
Gary McKeever
Simon Mackie
Bill Marsh
Andrew Martin
Paul Maykels
William Merrin
Alan Morton
Dean Moston
Oliver Murray
Michael P. Paget
N. Parks
Michael Pearce
Alister Pearson
Ivan John Phillips
Paul Pickford
Tim Pieraccini
Barry Piggott
Martin F. Proctor
Alan Read
James Robson
Colin-John P. Rodgers
Alan Rowley
Vitaly Sabsay
Dan Schaefer
Chris Senior
Robert Shaw
Tony Smart
Robert Smith
I. A. Stubbings
Simon Terry
Tanya Thomas
Jeffrey Trim
Mark Try
Mike Tucker
Julian Vince
Paul Vyse
Philip Wagstaff
G. Wales
Stephen Wallis
William Webster
Andrew Weir
Andrew J. White
Martin Williams
Clive N. Williamson
Byron C. Woods
David Wright
Victor C. Wright

ANDREW WEIR

The Publishers would also like to thank the *Radio Times* and the artist Andrew Skilleter for permission to reproduce the front cover of the 19-25 November 1983 issue of the *Radio Times*. All the photographs of the *Doctor Who* programme are BBC copyright, reproduced by courtesy of the British Broadcasting Corporation.

Doctor Who, galactic anti-hero, lives on

ALAN ROAD

YEARS before astronaut Neil Armstrong took his giant leap for mankind ... made inter-planetary travel a reality, ... William Hartnell took a small step ... the BBC and created the role ... Doctor Who.

'Dr. Who' series draws

by Diane Mermigas

ed professionals in their 20s and 30s.

These diehards secretly delight in the scientific mumbo jumbo exchanged by the good doctor, his trusted K9 (a computerized dog with an IQ of more than 300) and a revolving door of unimpassioned female companions ranging from helpless ... to fiercely independent

"The reaction is always the same," owner George Breo said. "They say, 'I thought I was the only one who watched "Dr. Who."' There are a lot of people who fear others will think they are crazy if they show any genuine interest in wearing a T-shirt around the house or getting knitting instructions for making their own trademark 'Dr. Who' scarf."

Gary Colabuono, owner of Moondog Comics at 139 W. Prospect Ave., Mount Prospect, and 1402 W. Schaumburg Road, Schaumburg, also prides himself on providing "safe haven" for "Who-ites."

Goodbye K9 ... Rust in Peace

WITH his electronic tail wagging, K9 departs Dr Who in two weeks.

The BBC are being very cagey about how the computerised canine disappears. John Leeson, the 37-year-old actor who provides the staccato voice, is reassuring. 'You can't imagine that, being British, we would let the ... suffer,' he said.

'Two of our Daleks have disappeared'

BY SHAUN USHER

TWO of the BBC's Daleks are missing. And today 10 million children will be asked to help find them.

Dr. Tom? I'd rather see Dr Jon

THE Daily Express is, in my opinion, completely out of touch when it refers to Tom Baker as "the best Dr Who." Jon Pertwee was definitely the best—his performance far excelled that of Tom Baker.

A. NATTRASS (aged 16), Hinckley, Leics.

"Have you noticed how young the Doctor Whos are looking nowadays?"

Dr Who's film hits time snag

MARTIN JACKSON

TOM BAKER

'Saddening, frustrating'

Nothing scary about Dr Who say children

DANNY KIRTON

I'm not scared

STATTERSFIELD

A big fan

PERRY DEBOO

It's exciting

Baddie ... new yo...

COLIN BAKER, the TV actor we loved to hate, has landed the part ...

Dr Who gets back to his old routine

Daleks found

By HUGH WHITTON

DR. WHO is top of the TV charts with little children — despite the strictures of Mrs. Mary Whitehouse.

WHO'S WHO?—

Actor PATRICK TROUGHTON who ... role of the mysterious Dr. Who talks to ...

Who is Dr. Who? Echo answers 'Who' but gets us nowhere. In plain terms the answer is Patrick Troughton, an actor most people think they know, but one with so chameleon-like a range of character portrayals—from Alan Breck in Kidnapped to the pawnbroker in David Copperfield, from Paul of Tarsus to the schoolmaster in Dr. Finlay's Casebook —that there seems only one way to pin him down.

Will the cruel Beeb really kill off K9?

By HILARY BONNER

DR WHO'S mechanical mongrel K9—scourge of the Daleks—is facing the KO.

TUE 14th JUNE 1977

Dr Who's 'Master' dies

BY SHAUN USHER

The Daleks g... to know all th... saucy gossip

By PHILIP PHILLIPS

HERE, FOLKS, is the inside story on ...—those villainous pepperpots ... their enemies through Dr Who ... e-x-t-e-r-m-i-n-a-t-e.

SAVE HIM!

SAVE K9 from the beastly Beeb! Help the superdog who has seen off the Cybermen and Ice Warriors win his toughest-ever battle.

U.S. fans go wild for Dr Who and Nyssa

DAILY EXPRESS Monday July 19 1982

TEN thousand Dr Who fans ...

TECHNOLOGY

How the Queen met Dr Who

IN 1971, Desmond Briscoe, head of the BBC's radiophonic workshop, was presented to the Queen at a radiophonic concert in the Royal Festival Hall. "The radiophonic worshop? Ah yes, Dr Who," said the Queen, neatly expressing everything most of us know about the workshop.

The workshop, which pioneered electronic music in Britain, celebrates its 25th anniversary this month and Briscoe, who has been its head almost since its inception, is now retiring. "What people don't realise," he complains, "is that on any normal day they probably hear 15 minutes, if not more, of our music."

The radiophonic team in fact creates music for over 200 programmes a year. Suitably, it has devised its own commemorative composition for its birthday: Inferno Revisited, an electronic descent into hell, using computer synthesisers as well as traditional techniques such as a slowed-down recording of a boiling kettle to represent the wailing of souls in torment.

The composition, which can be heard on Radio 4 next Sunday, was devised in the workshop's sprawling Maida Vale studios, which today employ seven full-time composers and are overflowing with electronic and acoustic equipment. All very different from the "one room, one engineer and a mini-budget" that Briscoe recalls as a founder member in 1958. "Most people thought of electronic music as ...

Briscoe: childhood dreams

It enables a composer to sample a sound of, say, breaking glass or a foghorn and encode the characteristics of that sound in the computer, which transfers it to the keyboard.

Briscoe, who won the Gold Award for Outstanding Contributions to Radio in 1977, will not completely disappear from the workshop. He will remain on contract to pursue various schemes.

Time's up, ...